"Adultish: The Body Image Book for Life is an excellent resource on body image for people of every age! Dr. Charlotte Markey has done a remarkable job of synthesizing research and connecting her readers to experts in the field, to create a very readable, understandable and thorough discussion of all topics on body image today. I am very grateful to Charlotte for bringing this must-read book into the world."

DENISE HAMBURGER, BE REAL Founder & Executive Director

"Feeling good about your body – or even at peace with it – has never been more challenging. Dr. Markey's book combines powerful personal stories, expert voices, and the latest research on a range of topics that affect body image. Her compassionate tone and interactive self-reflection exercises will make this a supportive and useful guide for young adults navigating the world's appearance pressures."

OONA HANSON, Parent Coach and creator of Parenting Without Diet Culture

"Adultish: The Body Image Book for Life, written by distinguished researcher, educator, and multifaceted advocate Dr. Charlotte Markey, uses her characteristically kind, compassionate, clear, and authoritative style to provide a focused yet flexible set of principles and practices for escaping this debilitating trap. This book will inspire you to re-envision and respect your body."

MICHAEL P. LEVINE, PhD, FAED, co-author of The Prevention of Eating Problems and Eating Disorders

"*Adultish* is packed full of cutting-edge knowledge and evidence-based, achievable strategies that can improve how you think and feel about your body and shape how you care for, nourish, and move your body. You'll realize why working toward a more positive body image can enhance your life in other ways you may not have even considered – such as your relationships, confidence, health, well-being, body trust, self-compassion, and joy in life itself. From beginning to end, you'll learn to decipher myths from facts when it comes to eating, body image, and health. It is certainly an impactful read!"

TRACY TYLKA, PhD, FAED, Body image researcher, Editor of Body Image and coauthor of Positive Body Im Workbook: A Clinical and Self-Improvement Gui

T0191096

"Charlotte Markey has done it again! She has become the go-to resource on accessible content about body image. This book reads like a love letter to adolescents and young adults about how to care for their bodies to build and maintain body confidence. It's an incredibly thoughtful, robust guide to the connection between how we fuel ourselves, the ever-changing messages imposed by the world, and our physical and mental health."

CARA NATTERSON, MD, Pediatrician, *NY Times* best-selling author, founder of puberty positive company Order of Magnitude

"In the non-shaming voice of a knowledgeable best friend, Charlotte Markey helps us to understand that the baggage we carry about our bodies is not our fault. At the same time, she reminds us that cultivating a healthy adult relationship with our bodies is in our power. In *Adultish*, Dr. Markey emboldens us to sluff off the weight of negative body culture and embrace trust, self-love, and appreciation for different shapes and sizes. It's in these changes that we truly feed us all."

DR. ROBYN SILVERMAN, national best-selling author of *How to Talk to Kids about Anything*

"Dr. Markey does it again! It's another book that can help guide folks through confusing years of life – this time, the adult 'ish' ones. She starts by letting her readers 'in' that she had similar eating and body image confusions in her own adultish years. And as I read, I could feel that guiding her content. So, for a path to understanding what science currently says about eating, increasing body- and self-acceptance, discerning many nuances of 'healthy' habits, and outmaneuvering social media's impact, *Adultish* is an important, useful, and empowering read."

ALLI SPOTTS-DE LAZZER, author of *MeaningFULL: 23 Life-Changing Stories of Conquering Dieting, Weight, & Body Image Issues*

"In a society where so much misinformation about health is swirling around and the conversation about 'wellness' has become more and more confusing, this book is a breath of fresh air and should be a requirement for all to read. I love the way Dr. Charlotte Markey provides insight, empathy, education, and action items in this incredible book. One I will be recommending to all my clients!"

JENNA WERNER, Registered dietitian and owner of Happy Strong Healthy

ADULT*ISH*

The Body Image Book For Life

Dr. Charlotte Markey

Illustrated by Olivia Herrick

CAMBRIDGE
UNIVERSITY PRESS

CONTENTS

CHAPTER 1: What Is Body Image?   7

Chapter 1 offers some of the basics and explains why body image matters so very much.

CHAPTER 2: Love Yourself   19

Chapter 2 focuses on reasons to love your body and take good care of it and provides some techniques you may adopt to increase your positive feelings about your body.

CHAPTER 3: Nourish Your Body   37

There is a lot of confusing information available to us about nutrition and what we should and shouldn't eat. In Chapter 3, I use the latest science to provide an overview of basic nutrition information.

CHAPTER 4: Cancel Diet Culture   55

New diets designed to supposedly help us lose weight are always appearing, but instead of actually working or helping us to become healthier they tend to be quite harmful. In this chapter, I explain why dieting negatively affects our mental and physical health.

CHAPTER 5: Intuitive Eating   75

Chapter 5 focuses on intuitive eating, a psychologically healthy approach to eating that relies on physical signals from your body to guide your eating choices.

CHAPTER 6: Eating Disorders   95

Many people engage in disordered eating, and some will go on to develop eating disorders. This chapter discusses the causes, consequences, and treatments for eating disorders.

CHAPTER 7: Mental Health   117

Body image is one component of your mental health, but it is related to many other aspects of your psychological well-being. In Chapter 7, I discuss other common mental health issues that may affect you.

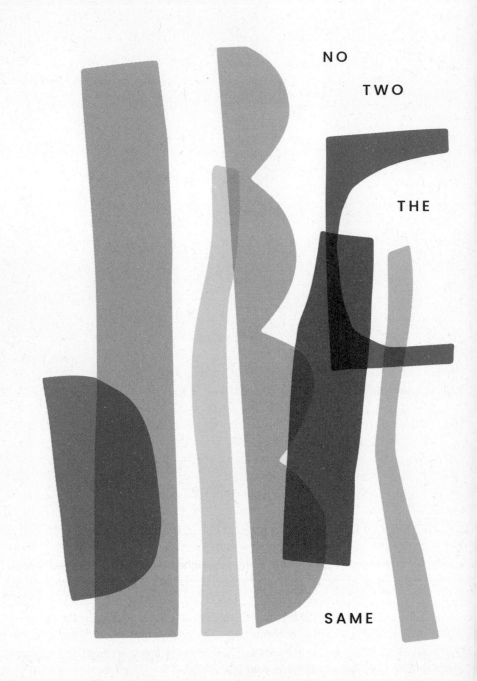

NO

TWO

THE

SAME

INTRODUCTION

There's so much I wish I'd known as a teenager and young adult. I try to answer the questions I had back then in this book.

I think that most of us go through life carrying a metaphorical backpack on our backs. In it is a large brick of insecurity. There are also sharp stones in our backpacks that add to the weight and press into our bodies; each represents a piece of ourselves that we wish we could change. What if that big brick was tossed aside? What if we could take some of the stones out of our backpacks, and not be burdened and irritated by our noses, thighs, and unruly hair but instead accepting of them? What if we could go through life feeling lighter and more comfortable with ourselves?

My metaphorical backpack was very heavy when I was young. I've spent the last 25 years of my career driven by the desire to lighten others' loads. I hope to help young people feel less weighed down by insecurity. I want this for my own teenagers, who are on the brink of adulthood; I want this for many of the college students I teach; and I want this for the readers of this book. Throughout this book, I discuss a variety of psychological and physical health issues important during the teen years and young adulthood. The thread that connects all of these topics is *body image*. **How can you become comfortable in your own skin?**

The longer I study body image the more I appreciate that many questions we have about how we think and feel about our bodies elude easy answers. Sometimes researchers refer to our efforts to adjust physically and mentally to our bodies as "body image work," but I hope you can come to appreciate it as a process of self-discovery. This book can help you understand yourself better and more fully appreciate how the forces around you often conspire to detract from your development of a positive body image. With knowledge as a foundation, we can work together to reject social norms that harm mental health and make all of us feel like we are not enough as we are.

You are enough. And you will keep getting better.

CHAPTER 1

WHAT IS BODY IMAGE?

#AppreciateYourself

"You are not a drop in the ocean.
You are an entire ocean in a drop."

– Rumi, *thirteenth-century Persian poet*

MY STORY: Alex René, 21 years old, she/her, USA

Some days, I really love and appreciate my body for what it is. I like my nose, curly hair, and stomach in particular. But some days, I don't even want to leave the house; the very features that make me feel unique and beautiful seem to change overnight into parts of myself I want to hide. I can wake up, look in the mirror, and not feel good about anything I see. I don't remember exactly when I started to feel ambivalent about my appearance – and myself in general – but it began early in life.

I was always close to my mom and we bonded over clothes from the time I was young. I loved "shopping" in my mom's closet for fancy dresses I hoped to someday wear. I knew my mom was saving them for me because she wasn't wearing them herself. My mom would claim that she was fat or needed to lose 15 pounds before she could wear whole sections of her wardrobe. My mom's negative self-talk was my introduction to the world of body hate. It didn't help that people started to tell me more and more as I became a teenager that I looked like my mom. It just wasn't clear to me if this was a compliment. My mom didn't view herself as beautiful, so how could I?

One moment that I will never forget was when I was in high school and crop tops were just becoming super trendy so I had a number of them. My mom did not like me wearing them and would make me show her what I was wearing every day before I left the house. While I was at school one day my mom put all my crop tops in a trash bag. When I got home, she told me that "crop tops are for skinny girls." I was crushed. I wore long sleeve, baggy tee-shirts and sweatshirts all spring and summer my junior year of high school.

It wasn't just my mom that contributed to my body dissatisfaction. Growing up, appearance-based comments filled my Christmases and christenings. I have had to work to not internalize other people's opinions regarding my appearance. The only person who really helped me develop a more positive body image was myself.

I definitely developed a confusing relationship with food along the way. There were perplexing messages about food in my house – some foods were "good" and some were "off limits." Sometimes only fruits and vegetables were on offer, but other times big Italian family dinners were pushed. For a while, my eating habits really suffered and across a few months I became emaciated. I eventually pushed myself to get medical help, but it was hard. One thing that really helped me rethink how I was treating myself was my doctor telling me the biological consequences of undereating and how it could put me at serious risk for developing osteopathic complications in early adulthood. Since then, I have made a sincere effort to appreciate my body for what it is, its functionality, and try to stay healthy by nourishing my body. Sometimes when I spend time with my family it's hard to keep focused on my health, but I just remember I am eating for my future self.

My advice to others is to try to evaluate yourself on qualities other than your appearance. It is perfectly OK not to love every piece of yourself; I think this is natural. It's not OK to take those insecurities and hyper fixate on them for the rest of your life; just accept them for what they are and keep moving along. If you wanted to maintain a healthy, happy relationship with a friend you wouldn't point out all of their blemishes or insecurities, so why do that to yourself? You are the only person who has to live in your body so it is important to be nice to yourself and take care of your health. It took me a while to learn that trying to be skinny can be counterproductive to being healthy.

When I talked with Alex while I was writing this book, so many pieces of her story resonated with me. I grew up feeling criticized for my appearance, too, and it took me a long time to unlearn that self-loathing. I know that it can be incredibly difficult to feel good about yourself in a world where so many messengers – your mom, your friends, your social media feed – all have ideas regarding what you should wear (crop tops or not?), what you should eat (is any food truly "off limits"?), and how you present yourself to the world.

IN THIS CHAPTER YOU'LL LEARN

- how body image is defined,
- why it's valuable to work towards a positive body image, and
- why reading this book and developing a better appreciation of yourself will improve your life.

Body image is how we think and feel about our bodies and our appearance in general. But your body image doesn't just affect your sense of self; it affects how you interact with people, the health behaviors you pursue (or skip), and your mental health in general. Body image is the extent to which you are comfortable in your own skin.

Improving your body image will not just improve your perceptions of your appearance; it will improve your day-to-day experiences and psychological well-being. Putting in effort to develop a positive body image may be difficult for some people, but the rewards are vast and sometimes even life-changing. You've picked up this book, so I'm guessing you're at least curious about what your life would be like if you had a more positive body image. I hope you'll read on and discover what the latest science, experts, and other people like yourself have come to understand about the value of improving your body image.

Is this book for you?

This book is for anyone who's ever wanted to feel better about their body image or felt interested in improving their mental health. I'm not sure that I know *anyone* who feels good about themselves all the time and is confident that their mental health is in 100% perfect, A+ shape. We all experience challenges and hardships. We all feel insecure and like we don't fit in at times. We all wish we looked a bit different (or even a lot different) than we do.

Although the scientific research and public discussions about body image often focus on women, body image concerns affect people of *all* genders. This book is for you regardless of whether you've always considered yourself female, always identified as male, or have ever been unsure of your gender identity.

Q&A:

Why does the ideal body type – for both men and women – change and why are we expected to keep up with an ever-changing standard of attractiveness?

Just as clothing styles change from year to year, so do trends in other aspects of our appearance. At one point, skinny jeans and skinny eyebrows (for women) were all the rage. Now, thick eyebrows and wide-legged jeans are back "in." For a while, referring to jeans as "mom jeans" was an insult, then those exact jeans became trendy. In the early 2000s, straight and sleek hair was preferred, and then wavy and more rumpled looking hair became fashionable. Waif-like, extremely slender female models and manly-looking men used to dominate the media, until "slim-thick" women (with slender waists but large breasts and bums) and slender, but ripped men took center stage. Then, the pendulum swung, and thin was back in.

How are we supposed to keep up?

First, it's important to consider whether or not you want to keep up with these trends. Maybe you don't mind buying new jeans every few years, but realize that this is somewhat different than trying to reshape your body every few years. Maybe you like to switch up your hairstyle regularly, but have no interest in lifting weights every day to tone and bulk up your body. You have a choice in terms of what trends you are going to care about.

However, you don't have much choice in terms of your body size and shape. We all come into this world with a particular genetic blueprint for what we will look like. Our genes determine our eye and hair color, almost completely determine our height, and have a *very* strong influence on our body size and shape. Of course, you can dye your hair and you can engage in eating and physical activity patterns that affect your body size and shape (to some extent!). You can even pursue cosmetic surgery if you really want to change some aspect of your appearance, but keep in mind that beauty trends are always changing (we'll explore this more in Chapter 9).

A central idea in this book is that I want you to think about these issues and decide for yourself if it is worth trying to "keep up" with appearance ideals. If so, which ones? I want you to realize that this takes up mental space, money, and energy. I want you to value yourself for more than your appearance and to consciously make decisions about how much time, money, and energy to invest in your appearance. I don't have all the answers for you, but I have information that is evidence based and I will help you find what works for you.

What you'll find inside this book:

- **Evidence-based information:** My primary sources of information throughout this book are scientific journal articles. Scientific research is our best bet in terms of discovering unbiased, reliable information about health issues.

- **Personal stories:** I've interviewed hundreds of people across my career as a body image scientist and include some of the latest interviews in this book.

- **Q&A:** I've been studying body image and eating behaviors for over 25 years, and I've been teaching university courses on these topics for over 20 years. Along the way, I've taken note of questions people have about the issues I discuss in this book, and I share them, along with answers, throughout the following 13 chapters.

- **Myths and misinformation:** A lot of the information about health that you see online or in other forms of the media is inaccurate, or downright dangerous. In each chapter of this book, I offer examples of the myths and misinformation about body image and other relevant health issues, along with scientific information to explain why these ideas, which are often quite popular, are wrong.

- **Expert advice:** I've had the opportunity to connect with many different types of experts, from scientists to journalists to Olympic athletes, who helped me think more deeply about the issues discussed in this book and offered words of wisdom to help you think more about these issues too.

- **Inspiration and humor:** Body image is a serious issue, but this doesn't mean that there isn't room to feel inspired or to laugh about some of these topics.

- **Surveys and activities:** There are many body image scientists who have developed ways to measure and improve body image. Some of these surveys and activities will be included throughout the book to provide you with some hands-on ways of working to understand and improve your body image.

- **Find out more:** At the end of each chapter, I direct you to good resources for learning more about these topics should you want to do so.

EXPERT ADVICE:

Katie Loth, PhD, MPH, RD, LD, Department of Family and Community Medicine, University of Minnesota, USA

"Body acceptance and self-love are so important for overall well-being. Research shows that young people who love and appreciate their bodies are more likely to take care of them by eating well, moving regularly, and avoiding risky behaviors."

MYTHS AND MISINFORMATION:

Being "body positive" means feeling good about your body all the time.

It would be nice if we felt good about ourselves all the time – in terms of our appearance, personality, intellect, and a variety of other qualities. However, it's incredibly unlikely and unrealistic to expect to feel good all the time. My goal in writing this book is to help you feel good about your body image – and yourself – most of the time. Body positivity does not mean that you'll always feel positive about yourself, but it does mean that you can appreciate, respect, and feel *mostly* positive about who you are at least *some of the time.*

What if this all feels too "positive" for me?

Some body image scholars and activists have suggested that aiming for a positive body image can keep you overly focused on your appearance. For some people, trying to feel good about how they look might involve too much thinking about how they look. If this resonates with you, then you might want to aim for **body neutrality**. Whereas the goal of body positivity is to feel good about your body, the goal of body neutrality is to just not really think about your body. For some people, body neutrality might be a stop on the way to a positive body image. For others, body neutrality is a satisfactory endpoint.

It may seem strange that the first chapter in a book about body image suggests that maybe one of your goals should be to think less about your body. I told you this stuff was complicated, but stick with me. I don't believe any of us need to love our bodies every second of every day to be happy, which is something that Liliana explains well (below). But we do need to value and respect our bodies. We should view the process of body image discovery as a journey and, above all, seek to take care of ourselves – body and mind.

Body Image Goals

The first survey in this book is the Body Image Goals activity, adapted from a book by Nichole Wood-Barcalow, Tracy Tylka, and Casey Judge. Taking the time to actually write out your responses to these questions can help you focus on your own experiences and desires.

How would you describe your current body image?

_____

_____

What thoughts and beliefs about your body image do you want to change? (*Note*: this is not what you want to change about your *body*, but what *thoughts and beliefs* you want to work on.)

_____

_____

What are three goals that you have for yourself as you work towards a positive body image?

_____

_____

I don't know if there's a moment in my life when I've felt truly good about my body. But I have come to understand that I don't have to feel good about it. I find value in myself in other ways and I appreciate myself for other qualities; I want the rest of the world to do so as well.

Growing up I felt abnormal. Everyone was skinny or trying to be skinny when I was younger and my body has never been described as "skinny." I was probably in my 20s before I came to understand that there was nothing wrong with my body. When I was growing up, I didn't feel like I fit in and I didn't see people like me in my town, in the profession I wanted to pursue (acting), nor in the media.

Today, I enjoy fashion and I only follow fashion creators that are my size or bigger online and that has made a huge difference in how I view myself. Similarly, in social media spaces I only follow people with varying body types. In this way I've been able to create a part of my world that is validating; it's such a relief!

When I was younger, online spaces weren't a strong influence on my body image but books were. Books were actually a negative influence, even though I loved to read. I always read books like the Pretty Little Liars *series. There are always mean-girl-girls in these books and a lot of fatphobia. I also read books that told the story of someone with an eating disorder. Although those books were meant to be cautionary tales, they were also instructive in a way. All these stories seemed somewhat relatable and contributed to my sense of what it meant to be a teenager. Fortunately, I think kids today have more exposure to messages that are counter diet culture.*

As an adult, books have been influential, but in a positive way. Two books really were life-changing for me. Shrill *by Lindy West was an introduction to body acceptance. Then, I read* The F*ck It Diet *by Caroline Dooner. This was really the first time I had heard of not dieting.* The F*ck It Diet *called me out in terms of food* rules and all the ideas that had clouded my thinking about food. I realized that there were so many rules in my head about food that the rules were starting to contradict each other. I didn't even know which to follow anymore and now I don't follow any. My new diet is not dieting.

I am grateful that I am able to really enjoy eating now. I think my family is a big reason why I find a lot of joy in food. My mom eats intuitively and she has helped me to find pleasure in food. I like to do my groceries because grocery shopping feels like being an independent adult. Living in New York City is amazing because I can get any food I want. Food can be incredibly fun!

If I was to offer my younger self advice, I would tell her that she doesn't have to atone for her body and she has every right to exist in her body. We all deserve respect no matter what we look like. And we can't win at the game of trying to change ourselves. I am so glad I let go of the dream of what my body could be and just let my life start. That shift in mindset changed my life.

SUMMING UP #APPRECIATEYOURSELF:

- Body image is often defined as your thoughts and feelings about your body; these thoughts and feelings have far-reaching consequences.
- This book provides scientifically based information to help you improve your body image. It also offers real people's stories, common questions and their answers, myth-busting, and activities to help you develop a greater understanding of your body image.
- Having a positive body image doesn't mean feeling good about yourself every second of every day, but it does mean that you respect and care for your body.

FIND OUT MORE:

- Nichole Wood-Barcalow, Tracy Tylka, and Casey Judge's *Positive Body Image Workbook: A Clinical and Self-Improvement Guide* (Cambridge University Press, 2021) offers a ton of great information and activities for improving your body image.
- I edited a book with my colleagues Elizabeth Daniels and Meghan Gillen called *Body Positive: Understanding and Improving Body Image in Science and Practice* (Cambridge University Press, 2018), that includes chapters on many of the topics in this book written by leading body image experts.
- References that support this chapter's content and additional resources can be found at the book's companion website: www.TheBodyImageBookforLife.com.

CHAPTER 2

LOVE YOURSELF

#Embodied

"To be yourself in a world that is constantly trying to make you something else is the greatest accomplishment."

– Ralph Waldo Emerson, *nineteenth-century American philosopher and poet*

MY STORY: Ryan Sage, 27 years old, she/her, UK

I think that my body image is pretty solid right now. I'm happy with how I present myself to the world and I don't spend a lot of time thinking about my looks. This has changed a great deal throughout my life though.

As a teen I was really dissatisfied with my body. Maybe that's true for every teen? At any rate, I am not sure I even appreciated how dissatisfied I was until I went to university and experienced a different lifestyle. I partied a lot at university and my new habits led to weight loss. Initially this just happened, but then I found myself spending a lot of time focused on my appearance. It was as if being thin suddenly made me want to keep being thinner. I wanted to stay thin, tone my body, be tanned, have the perfect make-up and clothes. I got so much positive feedback when I invested this time into my appearance that I couldn't stop. It was so validating! I got a lot of preferential treatment and everyone wanted to be my friend. It was a high schooler's dream come true!

When my university years ended, I started working and had to become a real adult with more responsibility. The partying slowly ended. I started working and then got into a graduate program and I was just too tired to go out. Initially, I started to gain some weight and I felt a lot of internal struggle about my body changing. What if people thought I was failing because I was gaining weight? But I gradually found myself skipping make-up, dressing more comfortably, and focusing on other aspects of my identity aside from my appearance.

Different facets of my identity have likely factored into my body image development. I was born and raised in Malaysia and didn't move to the UK until 2014. Growing up in an Asian family, the body ideal is really skinny. But Asian families are critical and you're always too big or too small it seems. I think being a minority and more visible in the UK has affected me. I don't feel discriminated against, but I do feel like I'm viewed as exotic or something. I also identify as bisexual and sometimes it bothers me a bit that people *tend to see me in the butch/femme binary when I either have short or long hair. I'm really just enjoying being a human and I don't want to be on display or representing any particular group of people. I am just who I am.*

If I could offer advice to my younger self, I'd tell her to focus on developing who she is and don't worry about how she looks. Of course, my younger self wouldn't have believed that advice. I think when you're younger and figuring out how you fit into the world around you, your appearance factors more into your identity than it does later in life. At some point, we outgrow some of those appearance concerns. It's like we're all swimming in this water – this culture that values appearances above all else – and we don't realize it until we outgrow it. Then we come to see how toxic that water really is.

Ryan's story is an honest reflection on the experiences so many of us have trying to fit in, wanting to be liked – and wanting to like ourselves. She reminds us that getting to know ourselves and becoming comfortable with ourselves is a process. But it's a process you can actively engage with and start or improve upon today.

IN THIS CHAPTER YOU'LL LEARN

- what it means to strive for embodiment in an appearance-focused world,
- the science surrounding the physical limits of changing our bodies, and
- strategies for improving your body image.

One of the most beautiful qualities I observe in people is a willingness to just be themselves without apology. At its best, this can look like a sort of confident contentedness. Sometimes, it may be acting goofy or silly without any care to how others will view you. Other times, it may be someone explicitly saying, "I don't care what others think about me." This very human authenticity can be contagious. When people feel good about themselves, others notice and respect that. This can also create a space for more people to feel good about themselves. But where does this begin? How do we become comfortable in our own skins?

When you were a young child, you almost certainly were accepting of yourself. You didn't know to feel self-conscious or wish you were taller or shorter or thinner or more muscular or blue-eyed, or blonder. At some point, the outside world infiltrates our minds and tells us we're imperfect and should improve ourselves – eat differently, dress differently, buy different products, try to reshape who we are physically to, in turn, like who we are psychologically. This logic is seriously misguided, however. The cultural belief that changing our exterior will improve our interior is not supported by science. We cannot dye our hair or purchase the perfect pair of jeans to achieve high self-esteem.

EXPERT ADVICE:

Drs. Lindsay and Lexie Kite, body image advocates, authors of *More Than a Body*, USA

"Positive body image is an inside job. When we keep attempting to fix an internal, psychological problem with outside, physical solutions, those quick fixes will never really solve our problem, nor will they prepare us to respond effectively to future body image concerns."

Let's talk limits

An important part of developing a positive body image is understanding that the cultural myth that your body is infinitely malleable – if you just try hard enough! – is wrong. It's an appealing myth, because who doesn't like to think that beauty, health, happiness, and success are all within reach? (Beauty, health, happiness, and success, of course, are discussed as completely interwoven, which is also wrong.) The hard truth is that there are real limits to what any of us mere mortals can do to change our appearances. Of course, if you have endless time, money, and an unusually high pain tolerance, cosmetic surgery has come a long way. But more importantly, there's plenty we can do to try to boost our mental health without relying on superficial fixes.

There are many factors that affect your height, body size, body shape, and everything else about your appearance – and *many* of them aren't within your control. One large, scientific study found that at least 80% of our height is heritable. In other words, you're however tall you are mostly due to how tall your biological parents are. Nutrition, medical care, and general health may affect your height a bit, but not a whole lot.

Although weight *may be* more easily changed than height, it's also very much influenced by our genes (up to 80% of the variation in weight in the population is associated with genes). Although advertising for diet plans and products make it seem like body size all comes down to willpower, science suggests this is a tremendous simplification of reality; our genes have a lot to do with our size and shape. Not only are our bodies' sizes and shapes mostly genetically determined, but our genes influence our tendency to store fat, fat distribution patterns, and metabolic efficiency. Recent research suggests that our body size is linked to our appetites, which are also determined by genetics. Some people feel hungry more often and have a hard time eating less, and other people don't care as much about food because they don't feel hungry as often. Being hungry is a pretty miserable experience, and it's not a good idea to ignore hunger because you risk not only feeling very cranky, but also not giving your body the nutrients it needs.

The bottom line is that our appearances are very much attributable to our genes and we cannot easily and dramatically transform them to meet cultural beauty ideals.

But what about health?

You may have accepted that not everyone will be a tall, slender, toned underwear model, but what if you have concerns about your body size and shape because you've read or been told by a medical professional that weight is associated with health? Unfortunately, a lot of what you've probably heard about weight and health is wrong – or at least incomplete.

There is a growing body of research suggesting that the links between weight (or body size) and health are *really* complicated. Scientists and doctors have argued that people who are relatively heavy are at risk of health problems such as type 2 diabetes, heart disease, and some forms of cancer. However, it is becoming clear that there are many factors that contribute to our health aside from our weight. For example, if you exercise and are in good physical shape, you may improve your heart health. Eating foods that nourish our bodies is important so that we *feel good*. Getting enough sleep is also an important way to protect our health (discussed in Chapter 12), as is avoiding substance use problems (discussed in Chapters 7 and 12). There are many steps we can take to live a long, healthy life, and it is important to focus on behaviors we can change instead of the things we can't, such as our height or body shape. Trying to change our bodies to improve our health is often nearly impossible (we're fighting our genes!) and misguided in that we would be better off focusing our efforts on factors that are somewhat more controllable.

MYTHS AND MISINFORMATION:

People who are heavy can't also be healthy and live long lives.

There is a great deal of importance placed on thinness as valuable for not just attractiveness but also health in our culture. However, research suggests that being underweight is more problematic for both our health and longevity than is being relatively heavy. Although there is scientific evidence that links weight and health, these links are *complicated* and not completely understood. Regardless, not every larger person will have health problems, and many people who are smaller may have health problems. In other words, you can't determine a person's health based on their body size and people of any size can adopt behaviors that can improve their health.

The Health at Every Size (HAES) movement encourages people to focus on healthy behaviors, no matter what their size. HAES is an anti-diet, body positivity, diversity acceptance movement that is consistent with the evidence and ideas presented in this book. Importantly, the HAES movement reminds us that all people deserve to be treated with respect and should not be discriminated against because of their size. We all should care about our health and how our body functions more than we care about looking like our favorite celebrities or influencers – and our behaviors should reflect this.

HAES presents an important counterpoint to all the fads and diets out there that can be incredibly harmful (see Chapter 4). The more we are self-accepting and supportive of others' self-acceptance, the easier it will be for all of us to reject these fads.

Embodiment

It might seem counterintuitive, but changing your appearance is unlikely to permanently transform your body image. Consider what happens when you get a great new haircut. At first, you feel like a better version of yourself, and others might comment on how wonderful your hair looks. Then, a couple of weeks pass, and both you and the people around you get used to your new haircut; it ceases to make you feel special. The same tends to happen as a result of any change to your physical appearance; the boost to your body image is likely to be short-lived.

Connecting to our physical selves is a psychological process referred to as **embodiment**. Body image scientists describe embodiment as the ways in which we engage with and experience our worlds through our bodies. Our bodies allow us to be in the world; they are containers for our personalities, intellects, thoughts, beliefs, emotions, hopes, and so much more. According to Dr. Niva Piran, the creator of the Developmental Theory of Embodiment, we experience embodiment as dynamic and complex. We relate to our bodies on a personal and psychological level but we also experience our bodies in terms of how others relate to them. It is when we try to view our bodies as others do that we tend to focus on our physical selves as a collection of parts – parts that need to be fixed to be more pleasing to others. When we focus too much on how we look and are viewed by others, we may lose attunement with how we feel. The ultimate goal is a sense of self that is empowered by a sense of embodiment – of comfort in our own skin – without relying on our appearance to feel embodied. Because our appearance inevitably changes with age, and beauty ideals are constantly changing, our appearance is not likely to be a stable source of comfort.

Q&A:

What if I just can't do it? I want to develop a positive body image, but I just don't like so much about how I look and I've never felt really comfortable with myself. What should I do?

First of all, know that you are not alone, and *many* people feel how you do. Second, I want you to know that the advice I offer in this book is not intended to invalidate these concerns or suggest that body image development is an easy process. For many of us, these are complicated and difficult issues.

Most people don't like some aspects of their physical selves and most people don't always feel comfortable in their own skin. It's important to appreciate that this is normal and that the goal isn't necessarily to wake up each day, jump out of bed, and feel madly in love with everything about who you are! As you'll read throughout this chapter, an important part of developing a positive body image is focusing in on what you *do* like about yourself and being grateful for your body's ability to move you through your life.

If you are really struggling, it may be a good idea to find yourself some extra support; there are resources at the end of this and every chapter that may help in this regard. A therapist with expertise treating body image concerns is ideal (although other therapists may also be helpful). Working through your feelings about your physical appearance and your comfort with yourself can be easier with someone else's help. You do *not* need to have a mental illness or disorder of some kind to benefit from therapy.

Strategies

Body image concerns are not merely superficial but can affect many aspects of people's lives. This also means that developing a positive body image and a sense of embodiment can have positive consequences for both mental and physical health and well-being. Unfortunately, there's no pill you can take to banish body dissatisfaction, but there are six strategies I share below that rely on your cognitive and emotional resources to help improve body image. Some of these suggestions might be easier to embrace than others; we all live in an appearance-focused world that seems to work against embodiment. But adoption of these body image-improving strategies is likely to make you both happier and healthier. I encourage you to try them out on your path to developing a more satisfying relationship with your body.

1. Reflect on your values
One strategy that body image scientists recommend for body image improvement is to "live what we value." Start by considering what it is, exactly, that

you value. You can start by thinking about what you hope to achieve in your life. Maybe you're aiming for professional success or maybe you most want to focus on your relationships with others. Consider what you want others to value about you. Are you a reliable friend or coworker? Are you fun to be around?

An appreciation of beauty or the adoration of others might be components of our value systems. However, maybe we value compassion, diversity, and equality more? Although improvements have been made recently, the beauty and fashion industries have rarely promoted images and advertisements that embrace people of all different shapes, sizes, colors, and ability statuses. It's worth considering the extent to which we want to take our cues from industries that devalue so many of us. Further, it's unlikely that the people we care about and enjoy are in our lives because of their physical appearance; we experience their (internal) beauty in a variety of ways. Living our values can mean embracing our own and other people's bodies as they are. This might begin with appreciating that some people naturally have relatively small bodies, and some naturally have larger bodies; people's body sizes are not a direct indication of their habits, health, or personality. We all have a natural body size that we're likely to hover around when we're adequately nourishing ourselves and engaging in a healthy amount of physical activity. Not everyone will be slender – even when they maintain "healthy" habits.

The psychologist Renee Engeln refers to our cultural obsession with our appearance as **beauty sickness**. It's not that she doesn't appreciate why we care about how we look. She suggests the problem is when we care about our looks more than other – arguably more important – aspects of our lives. If we spend too much time and mental energy focusing on our appearance, we might have less time and energy for hobbies, friends, or family.

2. Respect yourself
Your body is your home for the rest of your life. It's easy to get caught up in the present tense and not think long-term but you want your body to be a comfortable, healthy home for many years to come. To accomplish this, you need to treat yourself with respect and care.

Body respect is listening to your body's needs and honoring them. Body respect does *not* mean eating too little or avoiding foods that are nourishing (or entire food groups). Body respect is *not* pushing yourself too much when it comes to physical activity or leaving yourself tired out and unable to attend to other matters in your life. Body respect is *not* staying up all night or sleeping less than seven or eight hours per night; adequate rest and sleep is a critical part of showing yourself respect. Body respect is *not* abusing substances like nicotine, alcohol, or drugs that can cause lasting damage to the body (and mind). Body respect is *not* engaging in unsafe or unwanted sexual behaviors; you deserve to enjoy physical intimacy on your own terms. Body respect is *not* forgetting to take necessary medication or avoiding medical providers for regular check-ups or health care treatment.

I know you know all of this; your mom, dad, teacher, and/or medical providers have been telling you all of this for as long as you can remember. However, sometimes we hear this sort of advice so often that we don't frame it in terms of self-care. It can be surprisingly hard to take care of ourselves because we are often bombarded by cultural messages that suggest we should ignore our physical signals, such as signals of hunger or exhaustion.

Embodying Body Respect

We are all works in progress and can continue to find ways to honor and respect our bodies across our life. What are some specific activities that you would like to commit to that embody body respect? Remember, a *perfect* body and a perfect body image don't exist. Just aim for progress, not perfection!

What is something you can do every day to honor and respect your body?

_____

_____

What is something you can do each week to honor and respect your body?

_____

_____

What is something you can do each month to honor and respect your body?

_____

_____

Note: This exercise is adapted from Wood-Barcalow, Tylka, and Judge's *Positive Body Image Workbook*.

3. Focus on functionality

Our bodies are much more than a façade; they serve vital functions that allow us to live our lives and experience our worlds. Focusing more on what your body *does* as opposed to just how it *looks* can be a useful step towards body positivity.

Body functionality is a term used to describe the many physical functions of our bodies: breathing, sleeping, walking, singing, dancing, engaging with other people and anything else a body can do. Although many people feel dissatisfied with their bodies or even "at war" with them, our bodies aren't deliberately trying to hold us back from living our lives. One way to reorient ourselves towards our body's capabilities is through writing and reflection. In one study, women were asked to write statements about ten functions of their bodies and how those functions contributed to their well-being. The women who took part in this simple exercise showed improvements on measures of body image during the study.

Try concentrating on your own body functionality, and even making a list of the ways that your body serves you well. Referring back to your list later might boost your positive feelings about your body following any initial improvement.

4. Practice body appreciation and gratitude

Do you ever look in the mirror and feel grateful instead of critical? What would happen if you started to focus on the parts of yourself that you enjoy? Research suggests that expressing gratitude for our bodies can actually improve body image. Gratitude allows for an optimistic approach to the world; an appreciation of the positive aspects of your life. Gratitude may improve body image – and well-being in general – because it can lead you to focus on assets rather than deficits and to see elements of your life you may take for granted. Individuals who express gratitude have been found to be less depressed and anxious and to experience more positive relationships.

Research suggests that even a simple exercise that involves listing five qualities about your body that you are grateful for can lead to some improvement in your body image. It seems to help if you think about multiple aspects of your body – not just your appearance but your health and functionality. Also consider *why* you are grateful for these qualities.

Spend some time thinking about and listing the physical features that you do genuinely like and put this list to good use. (Are you sensing a theme here? Sometimes it seems we need to sit down and write down what we actually *like* about ourselves in order to bring ourselves away from the ledge. It's all too easy to jump into a pit of body dissatisfaction and despair without some structured tasks to refocus our thoughts about our bodies.)

You can also aim for a routine, such as expressing gratitude about your body every night when you brush your teeth. The key is to pair your gratitude exercise with another behavior that you're already in the habit of practicing daily. This way, the habitual behavior serves as a reminder to stick with the gratitude exercise.

Body Appreciation Scale

The Body Appreciation Scale is a survey used by body image scientists to determine the extent to which people feel good about and *appreciate* their bodies. Complete the survey by circling your response to indicate whether the question is true about you never, seldom, sometimes, often, or always. Scoring information is below.

	Never	Seldom	Sometimes	Often	Always
I respect my body.	1	2	3	4	5
I feel good about my body.	1	2	3	4	5
I feel that my body has at least some good qualities.	1	2	3	4	5
I take a positive attitude towards my body.	1	2	3	4	5
I am attentive to my body's needs.	1	2	3	4	5
I feel love for my body.	1	2	3	4	5
I appreciate the different and unique characteristics of my body.	1	2	3	4	5
My behavior reveals my positive attitudes towards my body; for example, I walk holding my head high and smiling.	1	2	3	4	5

	Never	Seldom	Sometimes	Often	Always
I am comfortable in my body.	1	2	3	4	5
I feel like I am beautiful even if I am different from media images of attractive people (e.g., models, actresses/actors).	1	2	3	4	5

Note: This is a revised version of The Body Appreciation Scale (BAS-2), which was created by Tylka and Wood-Barcalow in 2015. To find your score, add up your responses and divide by 10. This gives you the average number for your response. In Tylka and Wood-Barcalow's original study, the average person scored between 3 and 4; in some research examining adolescent girls, the average score was closer to 4.

5. Engage in protective filtering

An important part of developing a positive body image is navigating the array of external influences that are apt to make you feel dissatisfied with your body. There are many potential triggers of body dissatisfaction, ranging from your mom to your Instagram feed. You can benefit from becoming more aware of how a variety of different people and environments make you *feel*, and then responding to those feelings in protective ways.

Body image researchers refer to this as **protective filtering**. This is not the same as maladaptive avoidance of anxiety-inducing situations or phobic behavior; you can function in a psychologically healthy manner while still avoiding certain celebrities on social media. Some forms of media can be avoided more completely than others. For example, you might decide against watching television shows such as *Love Island* or *The Bachelor*, which feature people in objectified roles with a focus on their appearance. You can decide not to buy or flip through magazines that are full of articles and ads displaying emaciated women or selling beauty products. Social media poses particular challenges and opportunities when it comes to our body image, but I'll discuss that in more depth in Chapter 8.

We can't protect ourselves from all the people and messages that may make it difficult to maintain a positive body image, but we can practice eliminating many of our personal triggers. This can become easier when we remind ourselves that we are *protecting* ourselves and allowing our mental health to flourish; doing this is one way we can take care of ourselves.

Q&A:

I'm having a rough time. What is the fastest way to improve my body image?

You may want to start by thinking about what experiences trigger your body dissatisfaction. Is it when you are scrolling on social media? Is it when your mind is wandering, and you are thinking negative thoughts about yourself?

If you're not sure what your body dissatisfaction triggers are, I would start by limiting your time on social media and unfollowing accounts that are celebrity/beauty focused (I'll discuss this a lot more in Chapter 8). This can be an easy way to focus more on yourself and remove yourself from unrealistic appearance ideals. It may be difficult at first, but you can turn notifications on your phone/tablet/computer off so you don't know if there is something new to check and you can try to limit your social media time to a certain number of minutes (10 or 15) one or two times per day.

Another important skill to develop is redirecting your negative thoughts. We all have an inner critic that seems to zoom in on our flaws. But when this critic identifies a personal quality that it's unhappy with, redirect it. Instead of humoring these negative thoughts, tell yourself, "Stop! This isn't helpful. I deserve better than this," and work on refocusing on a positive quality that you appreciate about yourself. I know this may seem a bit silly at first, but over time it will become more natural and will have a positive impact on your body image. Taken together, these two strategies – eliminating a source of body dissatisfaction and working on how to respond to that dissatisfaction – can truly help you to feel better about yourself. It may not feel natural to begin with, but what do you have to lose? It's *free* and the benefits could be far-reaching!

6. Reframe your goals for exercise and eating

This book has entire chapters dedicated to your eating (Chapter 3) and exercise habits (Chapter 11), but it's important to mention both here as well. Not only can the health habits that you maintain affect your body image, but how you *think* about these behaviors is also important. Let me provide an example. If you go for a run, but you think of it as obligatory or as punishment (for eating? for living?), you're unlikely to enjoy that run. But if you think of running as something you do to help yourself feel good, improve your health, and take care of yourself, you might actually enjoy running more and find it easier to sustain this behavior. Further, this mindset will likely support your positive body image instead of detracting from it.

The key is to reframe our behaviors in ways that make healthy ones sustainable. Punishing or shaming ourselves for not doing all the "right" things is rarely an effective approach to health (mental or physical) and can reinforce negative body image. Easing ourselves into healthy habits can be more effective for achieving enduring change.

This is about YOU

As I mentioned in the Introduction, I can offer you evidence-based strategies for body image improvement, information about mental and physical health, and approaches to wellness that are supported by science, but your body image is about *you*. You don't owe anyone a smaller or bigger body, a different shaped body, or even a healthy body image. You get to decide how to feel about all of this and what actions to undertake *for yourself*.

Your body is not the center of your identity. I hope you think of your body in terms of the ways it allows you to connect with others, and that you can be self-compassionate and willing to continue to grow, learn, and become the best version of yourself (I'll discuss this a lot more in Chapter 13). Ultimately, it is up to you to decide what work you want to put into nurturing a positive body image. Emil's story reminds us that we may find ourselves at crossroads during our lives when we must determine if it would be advantageous to reevaluate how we think about and care for our bodies.

MY STORY: Emil Xavier, 20 years old, he/they, USA

Body image is a complicated topic for me right now. I started to model about four months ago and it has definitely had a negative effect on my body image and mental health. I've lost a significant amount of weight across this time – something I felt I needed to do to be successful in this industry. I've always wanted to model and

I decided it was time to just go for it. Now I'm really trying to work on my health while still making it as a model.

To begin this new career, I had to have marketing materials made, including professional photos and a personal web page. I've made videos that include me walking and talking about myself. I've begun to work with two different agencies. Fortunately, I haven't gotten negative feedback from them about my body. But on jobs people don't really hold back in offering feedback. Designers are picky and won't cast you if they don't think their clothes will fit you just how they want them to. I've been told that I don't have the right body type. People in the industry are often looking for a certain look. There's increasing diversity in fashion in terms of including people of color, immigrants, and people who are queer, but when it comes to weight there's not that much representation out there still.

I know that this new environment I've put myself in has toxic features, but I love fashion and design and always have. To be a model for fashion week in Philadelphia and New York this season was pretty exciting. I'm trying to figure out how to be healthy in this environment. I'm working on eating more intuitively and making sure I'm eating enough. I know that I have to take care of myself better than I have been.

I live with my mom, and she's expressed concern about me modeling. I know she is watching out for me and wants to help me. We're learning to talk about all of this in ways that are useful. I know she wants what is best for me.

I'll graduate from college this semester with a degree in psychology. I am planning to pursue a master's degree in psychology or social work at some point. I definitely want to help young people who are struggling. I know what that's like because I came to this country when I was ten years old, and I didn't even speak English. I was bullied for not fitting in. I didn't feel understood by anyone. I think I can really empathize with people from all walks of life.

Looking back on my childhood, I wish I could tell myself that those struggles to fit in will make you into a certain sort of person.

It'll help you become sympathetic and ready to help others. The challenges will make you tougher, passionate, and able to achieve whatever you really want to. I wish I had appreciated that you learn something about yourself every day. And you get stronger.
    I think I keep getting stronger.

SUMMING UP #EMBODIED:

- Body dissatisfaction is common, and people experience varying degrees of it. You can learn to feel better about your body, but it will likely require some attention to your current thought patterns and habits.
- Body image can be improved by focusing on the aspects of your body that you genuinely appreciate, are grateful for, and the ways your body enables you to experience the world.
- You can protect your body image by filtering out negative external influences, such as appearance-focused content on social media and television.
- Your body image can benefit if you think about your health habits – especially your eating and physical activity patterns – in terms of self-care rather than self-punishment.

FIND OUT MORE:

- Sisters Lexie and Lindsay Kite wrote *More Than a Body: Your Body Is an Instrument, Not an Ornament* (Harvest, 2021) to describe both their personal experiences and their research on positive body image.
- *MeaningFULL: 23 Life-Changing Stories of Conquering Dieting, Weight, and Body Image Issues* (Unsolicited Press, 2021) is a book full of stories of real-life experiences. The author, Alli Spotts-De Lazzer, is a therapist who offers motivational tips about how to develop a positive body image that she's learned through her many years working in the field.
- References that support this chapter's content and additional resources can be found at the book's companion website: www.TheBodyImageBookforLife.com.

CHAPTER 3

NOURISH YOUR BODY

#Nutrition101

"One cannot think well, love well, sleep well, if one has not dined well."

– Virginia Woolf, *British modernist author*

Averill Giana, 27 years old, she/her, USA

Right now, I'd definitely say that I feel really good about my body. I don't really have body image issues these days, but when I was a tween, it was awful. I got picked on and bullied for being too skinny. I was so self-conscious that I refused to wear anything that showed my skin. I was told that I looked anorexic, but I most definitely wasn't.

I got into modeling when I was about 17 and all of a sudden everyone loved me because I was skinny. My family used to tease that because I'm tall and lanky, I should model. Then one day, my mom took me to a model scouting event and I was signed on the spot. I really thought that we had all been only joking about modeling, but all of a sudden, I had a new career.

I think part of the allure of modeling has to do with the validation of being "chosen" for your looks. Models convince themselves that they must be among the most beautiful people in the world if people will pay to look at you. The environment in modeling is really toxic, though. One of the saddest parts about it is that you're always compared to others and you get jobs based solely off your looks; there are no other criteria. Models put up with a lot to keep working in the industry. I can remember even having my knees and elbows criticized. I left modeling when I was 21 and have not missed it one little bit.

While I was modeling, I knew that the conversation about our bodies and what we ate was really dysfunctional. Fortunately, I grew up with healthy eating habits and I ventured into the world of modeling with a great deal of resilience. I had never restricted what I ate and I grew up eating balanced meals. No one ever talked about calories or weight in my house; there was only consideration of health. But there was nothing we weren't allowed to eat. We just didn't keep bottles of soda at home. My mom used to say that, "our bodies take care of us and we take care of them." She was a firefighter and she needed to stay fit and really viewed her body as an instrument.

When I modeled, I wasn't as free or as comfortable with food. There was a lot of food restriction around me. I have good eating habits now and I don't control what I eat. I don't feel nervous or self-conscious about eating in front of people. I eat a full breakfast, lunch, dinner, and snacks. If I'm hungry I eat. I don't worry about what I've already eaten. I don't look at calories or carbs or anything.

I find myself thinking more now about setting a healthy example for young people. It's so easy for bad habits to get passed from generation to generation. I want people to start passing good habits from generation to generation. I want young people to learn to take care of their bodies for the purpose of their health and not their image. When I was modeling everything was about image, but I've become much more intentional in thinking about my health since then.

I want people to understand that everyone looks different; not bad or good but just different. It's important to treat both yourself and others with respect, no matter what anyone looks like.

Averill grew up with a healthy mindset about food and eating, but her modeling career derailed her temporarily. Her experiences remind us that what you eat can affect your health and body image. Taking care of our bodies means feeding and treating them well.

IN THIS CHAPTER YOU'LL LEARN

- all about the "what" of eating,
- basic nutritional information about different kinds of food: fat, carbs, protein, sugar, salt, fiber, fruits, and vegetables, and
- the information you need to think about food as nourishment for your body and eating as contributing to a positive body image.

The "what" of eating

What should you eat? The simple answer to this question is: anything and nearly everything. However, some foods are better for your body and health than others, but this doesn't mean that you need to completely avoid less nutritious options. Foods that are not particularly nutritious – ice cream, candy, and cake – usually taste good! In Chapter 4, I will discuss why it can actually be valuable to eat some foods that aren't necessarily high in nutrients. You don't need to totally give up any food that you enjoy, but you do want to eat foods that are nutritionally valuable so you maintain and protect your health for life.

How exactly is the nutritional value of food measured? There are a variety of ways that foods can be categorized. What I mean by **nutritional value** is that foods provide various types of nutrients through proteins, carbohydrates, fats, vitamins, and minerals, and these have an impact on our health. In this chapter, I describe different types of nutrients so you can be an educated eater, *not* because you should eliminate particular foods from your day-to-day diet, and *not* because you should feel guilty about what you eat.

EXPERT ADVICE:

Alli Spotts-De Lazzer, psychotherapist and author, *MeaningFULL: 23 Life-Changing Stories of Conquering Dieting, Weight, and Body Image Issues*, USA

"'Healthy' eating is so complex in our society, especially with so many confusing messages about what to eat and to avoid. Yet, when not allowed or seen as forbidden, food can quickly transform from being just 'food' to seeming powerful and overly desirable. That can be a tough way to live, since food and eating opportunities are everywhere. I believe that an unstressed relationship with all foods is essential to a well-rounded, full, contented life. Eating is a form of self-care."

Q&A:

What am I supposed to be eating on a day-to-day basis?

Although there is a lot of information available in popular culture to suggest that there is one specific, "correct" way to eat, research presents a much more complex picture. This is partly because although people have similar nutritional needs – for everything from carbohydrates to vitamin C – we are all also unique in what we like to eat and how much we need to eat to feel our best.

It is important that you eat foods that you enjoy and that will nourish you. For example, you don't have to drink orange juice or eat oranges, but without vitamin C, you will get scurvy (a disease caused by a lack of vitamin C, which results in weakness, fatigue, muscle soreness, and death if left untreated). Most people in industrialized countries have access to a variety of foods that contain vitamin C, such as broccoli, red peppers, potatoes, and spinach, and don't have to worry about malnutrition. If you don't eat foods you enjoy you will have a hard time sustaining a healthy diet. It's also perfectly fine to eat some foods that don't serve a significant role as physical nourishment because you enjoy them (chocolate may be psychologically nourishing).

The bottom line is that you should eat a variety of foods and include protein, carbohydrates, fruits, vegetables, and dairy in your diet. However, you should not spend a lot of energy worrying about what you eat because this can become psychologically unhealthy.

It's the pattern that matters

Because food can impact how we feel almost immediately – think how you feel after a big meal or after eating something really sweet – we tend to think in terms of specific foods or meals impacting our health. However, no single food, meal, or even several days of unusual eating habits (for example if you are sick or on vacation) are likely to affect your health. It's the pattern that matters; how you eat across weeks, months, and years will impact your health, but you need not feel anxious about any one specific day's consumption.

When you think about your eating habits in a general way and not in terms of specific meals, eating can be a lot more enjoyable. Don't worry about each meal, just be generally aware of your habits across time. For example, if you don't eat a single vegetable some days, this is hardly a problem. However, if you *never* eat vegetables, your eating habits will not be optimal for your health. And there is research to suggest that being in the habit of eating nutrient-dense foods can help you avoid a variety of health problems that creep up on people as they progress through adulthood, such as cardiovascular disease and different types of cancer.

If focusing on what you eat causes you stress or anxiety, it's important that you find support (for example, from a registered dietitian) to balance the goals of being both psychologically and physically healthy. Eating "perfectly healthy" day in and day out is not worth it if it negatively affects your *mental* health. After all, your health is not just about your physical body but your mind, your relationships with other people, and your ability to live a life that is meaningful and enjoyable. Food can be psychologically nourishing, and eating is often a social experience. The goal is not just to get the maximum amount of nutrients into your body each day!

EXPERT ADVICE:

Virginia Sole-Smith, journalist and author of *Fat Talk: Parenting in the Age of Diet Culture*, USA

"For a long time, I thought my job as a health and nutrition journalist was to tell people how to eat. But then I noticed something: The 'rules' – and the science behind them – kept changing. Like, I bet if you ask your parents, they grew up thinking fat was bad. Now, everyone freaks out about sugar, or other ingredients. We're also even more inundated with these rules, thanks to social media. Pretty much anyone can call themselves a health influencer and claim they know how you should eat. But nobody else can tell how hungry or full you are. Nobody else should be in charge of whether you eat some chips because you have a ton of studying to do and the crunching helps you focus. We eat for a million different reasons, all of them valid. Now I know that nutrition can be useful information, but it's just one piece of the puzzle. The best way to have a healthy relationship with food is to start by trusting your body."

Fat

The public discourse about fat is perhaps more confusing than the discussion of any other nutrient. It's possible that you've heard of fat as being bad for you. Or maybe you've heard of **ketogenic diets**, which suggest it's healthiest to get most of your energy from fat. If you're like most people, you may have no idea what to think about fat – how much to eat, or how much to avoid it.

You may have heard about "good fat" (**unsaturated fat**). Foods that contain unsaturated fats, such as nuts and avocados, can be good for your heart. In contrast, **saturated fats**, such as butter, cream, cheese, and most meat, raise your cholesterol, which can be bad for your heart. Eating fat is fine, unless you are eating a lot of food high in saturated fat. Although your eating habits are unlikely to affect your health in your teen and early adult years, it is valuable to establish good habits that will follow you into middle and later adulthood when you'll become more at risk of health problems.

The bottom line: It's perfectly fine to consume foods containing fat, but try eating mostly foods that contain unsaturated fats. "Natural" foods (such as salmon, olives, and avocados) are likely to contain unsaturated fats, in contrast to processed foods (such as store-bought desserts or pizza), which are likely to contain saturated fats.

Carbohydrates ("Carbs")

Carbohydrates tend to have a bad reputation. In fact, some diets (for example, **paleo** and ketogenic, aka "keto" diets) focus on reducing carbs to lose weight. However, it's nearly impossible to completely eliminate carbs from your diet and you shouldn't even try to. They are an important part of your daily food intake, providing a fast source of energy for your body and brain.

Carbohydrates such as brown rice, oatmeal, and multigrain bread are especially nutrient-dense. Many fruits and vegetables (for example, apples and spinach) are also high in carbs and other nutrients, and these carbohydrates have been found to help promote heart health.

The bottom line: Carbohydrates are a great source of energy for our bodies. According to the Mayo Clinic, a respected medical institution in the USA, nearly half of your diet should be made up of carbs. It's healthiest, however, to eat the types of carbs found in fruits, vegetables, and whole grains, rather than breads, cakes, and donuts.

Protein

Protein is an important part of a balanced, healthy diet. Protein helps your bones, muscles, cartilage (soft, connective tissue found in the body), and skin to grow. It's also important for hormone functioning. Foods that are high in protein make you feel full more quickly and for a relatively long time. According to the US Department of Agriculture, most people eat enough protein without even trying, and this is most likely from meats like hamburgers and chicken. There are other nutritious sources of proteins such as beans, peas, soy products (for example, tofu), nuts, and seeds. Seafood such as salmon can also be a healthy source of protein in your diet.

The bottom line: Protein is an important part of a healthy diet, which you're probably eating enough of, and adding "extra" protein will *not* improve your health or fitness.

MYTHS AND MISINFORMATION:

Snacking – and snack foods – are unhealthy.

Snacking is often thought to be unhealthy, in part, because snack foods can be highly palatable foods like chips (or crisps in the UK) and other salty and sweet finger foods. As a practice, there is nothing at all wrong with having a snack. In fact, if you are hungry, you should eat something!

Some interesting research looking at parents' role in feeding their kids sheds light on why snacking gets a bad rap. It turns out that when parents try to prevent their kids from eating certain types or amounts of food their kids are *more* likely to snack. Further, when kids have more processed snacks in their home, they're more likely to snack. In other words, if you grew up in a home where there was a good supply of tasty treats and/or your parents tried to keep you from eating those treats, you're likely to find yourself wanting those very foods and eating them in excess!

I'll discuss the importance of enjoying food and allowing yourself to eat all sorts of foods in Chapters 4 and 5, but it's worth mentioning here as well: no food is entirely "good" or "bad" and snack foods can be a healthy part of your diet, no matter what they are.

Salt

Salt (aka sodium on food labels) helps to preserve many foods we consume and makes most foods taste better, so it's everywhere, including in most bread, pizza, and sandwiches. If you look through the fridge and cabinets in your house and read some food labels, you may be surprised. In my kitchen I found: 1 can of black beans = 120 mg of sodium, 1 piece of bread = 210 mg of sodium, 1 serving of mozzarella cheese = 170 mg of sodium, and 1 serving of chicken noodle soup = 700 mg of sodium. You can see how it's pretty hard to avoid salt. Most people consume 3,400 milligrams daily and get 75% of their salt from processed foods such as condiments (e.g., ketchup) and canned goods.

Salt has been associated with high blood pressure and heart disease. Because of this, the American Heart Association recommends that all of us keep our daily salt intake to no more than 2,300 milligrams of salt – or approximately one teaspoon of salt. If you know that high blood pressure and heart problems run in your family, you may want to be cautious about your salt intake. Otherwise, don't stress too much about your salt intake; just don't bathe your food in salt.

The bottom line: Salt makes food taste better and last longer, but it has been associated with high blood pressure and poor heart health when eaten in large quantities. Eating fewer packaged foods is a good way to cut down on your salt intake, as is turning to other seasonings to add flavor to your food, such as garlic and ginger.

Sugar

Like salt, sugar sneaks into foods you wouldn't expect. Bread, chicken nuggets, granola bars, yogurt, and even ketchup are all surprisingly high in sugar. Sugar comes in many different forms: high fructose corn syrup, cane sugar, dextrose, and fruit juice concentrate, among many others. The average American eats 22 teaspoons of sugar per day; however, the American Heart Association suggests that we should eat no more than 6 teaspoons of sugar per day.

Sugar consumption has been linked to illnesses such as diabetes in the last few decades, which isn't to say that eating some sugar and sugary foods is a problem. The biggest concern may be that eating processed, sugary foods is likely to take the place of more nutritious options. For example, a bowl of berries would be a nutritious and healthy dessert, but that doesn't mean we can't have those berries in a pie or on top of vanilla ice cream sometimes.

The bottom line: It would be difficult to avoid all sugar and it isn't necessary to do so. It's a good idea, however, for the sake of your health, to get some of your sugar from nutritious options like fruits and vegetables, which I'll discuss next.

Fruits and vegetables

Most people don't eat enough fruits and vegetables, even though they know that they are among the most nutrient-dense food options. In fact, it's nearly impossible to eat *too* many fruits and vegetables because they're such a good source of all kinds of nutrients. The US Department of Agriculture recommends that half of *each* meal and snacks be made up of fruits and/or vegetables. Dietary guidelines recommend five to nine servings of fruits and vegetables per day. (Different recommendations are made in the USA and UK; a serving is a medium piece of fruit or about half a cup of chopped up fruits or vegetables.)

Why are fruits and vegetables this important? They contain key nutrients including folate, magnesium, potassium, fiber, vitamin A, vitamin C, and vitamin K, and they don't have the preservatives, additives, salt, and sugars that come with store-bought and packaged foods. It's also important to remember that fruits and vegetables can be delicious! You may want to explore new varieties and new ways of finding them, such as dried, frozen, or canned, and different ways of preparing them (roasting and stir frying, for example). Fruits and vegetables don't need to be fresh to be nutritious; frozen berries can taste great on yogurt.

The bottom line: Fruits and vegetables are an important part of a healthy diet. Try to eat at least some sort of fruit and vegetable each day, and ideally at most meals.

Fiber

A food that is high in fiber is slowly digested by your body, and often passes through your body without really changing much. These foods tend to be bulky, filling, and come from natural (not processed) sources. Foods that are high in fiber include apples, artichokes, barley, beans, Brussels sprouts, carrots, citrus fruits, nuts, oats, peas, prunes, raspberries, wheat bran, and wholewheat flour.

There are many benefits to eating foods high in fiber, including reduced rates of cardiovascular disease and premature death, healthy digestion, lowered risk of diabetes, heart health, lowered cholesterol, healthy blood sugar levels, and regular bowel movements.

The bottom line: Foods high in fiber are good for your health. Foods that contain a lot of fiber, such as most fruits and vegetables, tend to be good for your health in a variety of other ways, too.

Vitamins and minerals

Vitamins and minerals – otherwise known as micronutrients – are dietary components that your body needs in order to grow, develop, and stay healthy. Some of the most important micronutrients are iodine, vitamin A, iron, and zinc. Luckily, most are easily available in foods and drinks you probably consume regularly. Most salt has iodine added to it, so you're most likely getting more than enough iodine. Vitamin A is important for your eyesight and immune system, but you're likely getting enough in the milk you drink. If you don't drink milk, try kale; it's also full of vitamin A. Iron keeps your brain and your muscles functioning well, and can be found in foods like lentils (and other beans), spinach, quinoa, most meat, tofu, and even dark chocolate. Zinc is good for your immune system and nervous system, and can be found in most meat, vegetables such as spinach, broccoli, kale, beans, lentils, nuts, seeds, and whole grains.

The bottom line: Chances are, if you live in the USA or the UK, you don't have to worry about your vitamin and mineral consumption. You're likely getting what you need through the foods you eat.

Beverage science

Water and milk are often viewed as the most beneficial beverages; most other beverages – soda, juice, energy drinks, hot chocolate – are sweetened with a great deal of sugar.

MYTHS AND MISINFORMATION:

You can just take vitamins and not think about what you eat.

The vitamins and minerals that your body needs tend to be easily found in foods available to you. It is unlikely that you need to take vitamins and supplements (otherwise known as dietary supplements), which are intended to add to your diet when you are missing particular nutrients. You probably are not missing important nutrients! In fact, supplements can be more problematic than they are helpful.

Although you may see advertisements for all sorts of supplements, including protein powder and weight loss shakes, this does not mean that they are necessary or even healthy. In the USA, the Food and Drug Administration (FDA) monitors and approves food products and medications (aka drugs), but vitamins and supplements are typically not monitored. This means that many supplements are not tested to determine if they are helpful or safe before they are available to buy. When scientists examine these products, some have even been found to contain toxic or poisonous ingredients.

Other countries, such as the UK, *do* have agencies that consistently monitor the safety of vitamins and supplements, but this does not mean these products are necessary or even healthy. If you are concerned about your vitamin or mineral intake, you should talk with a health care provider. There are tests (e.g., blood work) doctors can do to check if you are having any sort of deficiencies that would warrant regular vitamin or supplement use.

Soda is often viewed as a problem because people tend to drink a lot of it, it has no nutritional health benefits, and it can have a lot of sugar and calories. Further, soda often takes the place of healthier options (e.g., water). Diet sodas don't typically contain any calories, but they contain artificial sweeteners and chemicals that aren't particularly healthy. This is partially why public health and policy officials often target soda; it has been linked to increases in people's weight more than any other single food or beverage in recent years.

The other type of beverage that is the subject of great debate and somewhat conflicting research findings is alcohol. The current science about alcohol consumption concludes that no one should *start* to drink alcoholic beverages for the sake of their health. However, among adults of legal drinking age (which varies by country), moderate alcohol consumption (one drink

per day for women and no more than two per day for men) *may* have
health benefits, in particular in terms of heart health. It does not appear
that the type of alcohol matters, whether you drink beer, wine, or liquor.
However, overconsumption or unsafe consumption (e.g., before driving a
car) of alcohol can be extremely dangerous and even deadly. (I'll discuss
addiction and alcohol consumption more in Chapters 7 and 12.) Further,
moderate consumption cannot be saved up for the weekend; if you don't
drink all week and have six drinks on Saturday, that's no longer "moderate" drinking but binge drinking, and most definitely a risky behavior.

The bottom line: It's fine to drink soda, but it's most conducive to your
health to limit daily consumption of these sugar-sweetened beverages.
Alcohol is an addictive substance, but careful, moderate alcohol consumption can limit health risks and *may* confer health benefits.

Journal: Describe your relationship with food.

We all have a relationship with food. How would you describe your
relationship? Do you look forward to eating? Do you fear situations
that involve food? Do you have a love–hate relationship with food?
Are there foods that you think you eat too often or not enough?
What do you think you could do to improve your relationship with
food? Consider how things are for you now and where you hope to
someday be when it comes to your relationship with food.

"Super foods"

Kale, avocados, blueberries, salmon, acai berries, Greek yogurt, and almonds are often touted as "super foods," as if they have super powers. It's
not an accident that these foods receive a lot of attention; they are very
nutrient-dense and contain more vitamins and minerals than the average
food. It's not a bad idea to eat these foods – at least sometimes.

However, for reasons I'll discuss more in Chapter 5, it can be problematic to think about food as "good" or "bad" or even "super." Simplistic categorizing schemes can leave you feeling like you must eat certain foods and avoid others. This is problematic because we want to enjoy the food we eat and adopt eating habits that nourish us both psychologically and physically. It's not true that some foods are so amazing that eating them is all you need to do to protect your health. Health is affected by eating and activity habits, by our circumstances, access to resources (acai berries are not inexpensive!), and many other factors.

The bottom line: "Super foods" may be worth eating if you enjoy them, but shouldn't be relied on as the key to health.

EXPERT ADVICE:

Jenna Werner, RD, cohost, *What the Actual Fork* podcast, USA

"One of the coolest things about nutrition is learning about what your body likes the most and knowing that this is different for everyone! Foods are not 'good' or 'bad,' but different meals and snacks and combinations all make each one of us feel different things. I like to tell my clients to picture themselves as explorers and consider every mealtime a mission. When it's over, check in with yourself to see how it went. How do you feel? Pleasant? Energized? Unpleasant? Uncomfortable? Happy? Hungry? Take note of those feelings, and for the less positive ones, ask yourself, 'What can I change next time?' Maybe it is the speed of consumption or the distractions around us; sometimes something small can change the outcome of your next mission! Keep learning, keep listening, and remember food is meant to be enjoyed while it nourishes your amazing body."

Now you're in charge

When you reach adulthood, your own food shopping and preparation is most likely going to be up to you. It may be tempting, assuming it's within your budget, to eat out for most of your meals, and fast food may have special appeal if you're busy with studying or work. However, it can also be fun to learn to cook and to cook with other people, such as a friend or partner.

There are ways to make food shopping and preparation relatively easy, especially with grocery delivery services and apps that help with food shopping, meal planning, and recipes. Frozen fruits and vegetables are a great way to add variety to what you eat, are relatively cheap, last a long time, and are not less nutritious than fresh produce. It can also be important to keep snack foods within reach that are easy to grab whenever you are hungry.

Food can be a lot of fun, and learning to prepare foods you like will benefit you across your life. Learn to be practical about what you like, what you'll actually eat, and what you have the time and money to prepare. Beware of online information such as *what I eat in a day* social media posts or videos, because what works for one person's appetite, budget, and preferences rarely works exactly for another person! Lakshmi's story reminds us that while our eating habits are important, we're all unique in not only our food preferences but the size and shape body we're born with.

MY STORY: Lakshmi Sita, 22 years old, she/her, USA

Growing up, I was always a skinny kid and I'm still pretty skinny. I do have big hips, so I'm sorta curvy, but people still tell me that I'm skinny. I guess because of this, I've never really worried about my weight.

My eating habits are a bit all over the place. I love fast food, but I try to eat foods that are more nutritious. I often eat eggs in the morning. My lunch somewhat depends on what my mom has made. Sometimes she makes Indian food, which is somewhat healthy. Most Indian dishes include some sort of protein, vegetables, and some sauce. It's hard to go wrong with her meals. What's not to like about Tikka Masala? For dinner, I usually eat some sort of protein, carb, and a vegetable side dish. I'll snack on chips or something if I'm hungry. I also love fruit; bananas, mangoes, and strawberries are my favorites. I'm not really a huge dessert person, but I like ice cream. I usually am happy with sweets in small portions.

I wish I had more of a "slim thick" figure. I guess almost all women I know wish they had bigger breasts and a rounder bottom. Seeing these figures on social media can contribute to my sense of insecurity, but I think I hide it pretty well. I suspect I've grown up feeling as satisfied with my body as I am and with a pretty good relationship with food because these are issues I haven't had to worry about a lot. I know that it seems sorta basic, but just not worrying about food and what I eat is a luxury.

My advice for younger kids is to appreciate that everyone is unique and you're never going to be like other people. It can take time and maturity, but I think it's important to look to yourself for validation and not to look to others for validation. Surround yourself with people that you like, that like you, and that support you. I know I'm not perfect but the people I spend time with appreciate me and that goes a long way.

SUMMING UP #NUTRITION101:

- Keep a flexible view of what you eat and provide your body with nutrients to support your physical health without compromising your psychological health by worrying about what you eat.
- You can eat any and all foods but do your best to eat a variety of foods, including plenty of fruits and vegetables.
- Eating nutritious and satisfying foods is one important way to care for your body and can help you develop a positive body image.

FIND OUT MORE:

- The US Department of Agriculture and the US Department of Health and Human Services released new dietary guidelines in 2020, which can be found here: www.dietaryguidelines.gov/sites/default/files/2020-12/Dietary_Guidelines_for_Americans_2020-2025.pdf.
- The UK's dietary guidelines, provided by the National Health Service, can be found here: www.nhs.uk/live-well/eat-well/the-eatwell-guide/.
- References that support this chapter's content and additional resources can be found at the companion website for this book: www.TheBodyImageBookforLife.com.

CHAPTER 4

CANCEL DIET CULTURE

#RiotsNotDiets

"Insanity is doing the same thing over and over again and expecting different results."

– Author unknown (although often attributed to Albert Einstein, German-born theoretical physicist and Nobel Prize winner)

MY STORY: Jenna Elizabeth, 25 years old, she/her, UK

Right now, I think my body image is the best it has ever been. Growing up, I was heavier than others in my family and I wasn't comfortable in my skin. During middle school I was teased and bullied and I struggled to feel good about myself. All of this shaped how I viewed my own body for many years. Recently, I've grown much more accepting of myself, but it was after a bit of a journey.

During my college years I lost weight in a pretty healthy way. I changed my eating and activity habits, and I received a lot of positive feedback about the changes in my body. It felt good to receive those positive comments, but at some point, I lost too much weight and became less healthy. It was confusing at first because I had always thought of thinness as healthy. My doctors had always scorned me at visits and told me that I should lose weight for the sake of my health (although I never had any problematic symptoms that were indicative of my weight being a health risk). Like so many people I had linked weight with health – I assumed they were directly related. I've had to move past that.

I've never been underweight according to a medical chart (for body mass index). But I stopped getting my period and when I went to my doctor (and later an endocrinologist, who specializes in hormone functioning) it was clear that my heart rate had dropped too low and my hormones were off. The prescription for recovery was weight gain, less exercise, and rest.

The jumpstart of my recovery was deleting the app My Fitness Pal and not keeping track of what I was eating. I think when I started college and had total control over when I ate, exercised, and what groceries I bought it was comforting to monitor my eating and activity. I had used the app for so many years that I didn't trust myself without it. I needed to learn to trust myself again and not let some app dictate what I did and didn't eat.

Getting rid of social media accounts also helped me to become healthier. When I was in college, I followed a lot of fitness accounts and food trends on Instagram. But when you are on social media you are seeing thousands more pictures a day about appearance, fitness, and eating ideals than you would otherwise. And most of what you are seeing isn't even real! It's been edited or made to look a certain way. I am happier now that I'm not on social media.

If I could offer my younger self some advice, it would be to be sure she understood that health doesn't have a certain look. In pursuing health, I created some unhealthy habits! I was a "normal" weight but still developed some pretty serious health problems. Numbers – your weight, height, what you eat, etc. – can't define your health.

Like Jenna, most of us have grown up the victims of cultural messages telling us that we can't trust ourselves. For example, it is important to control our appetites and be slender. We should monitor what we eat and how active we are. We should avoid certain foods altogether. We should "cleanse" our bodies of "bad" foods. These messages are incredibly misleading and harmful. Collectively, these maladaptive messages about food and our bodies are referred to as ***diet culture***.

IN THIS CHAPTER YOU'LL LEARN

- what diet culture is,
- why dieting is so harmful, and
- how to resist dieting when you feel the urge to change your eating habits.

What exactly is "diet culture"?

Cultural messages tell us that we can control our bodies and our health, there is one right way to have a body, and we're obligated to fix our bodies when they don't conform to cultural expectations. All these messages are pervasive and inaccurate. They suggest that we should just keep trying to achieve the body we want, one that is slender in all the right places, muscular in all the right places, and voluptuous in all the right places. (The "right places" are different for individuals who identify as male versus female.)

Here's what psychological and medical research actually indicates.

(1) We don't have total control over our health or the appearance of our bodies. With enough time, will, and money, you can exercise, alter your eating habits, get cosmetic surgery, consult with doctors and therapists, and change your appearance and health, but the alterations may not be permanent and may require a great deal of effort. Other factors – from your genes to your access to resources – play a substantial role in your psychological health, as well as your physical health and physical appearance.

(2) Every body is unique. You may have your dad's nose and your mom's vulnerability to experience an upset stomach when you're stressed, but you are your own unique person. You can try to look like a celebrity or influencer, but you won't ever be those people and you don't need to be. In fact, even if you ate the exact same things as another person, and did the exact same physical activity regimen, your body would look different!

(3) "Fixing" or changing our health or appearance-related behaviors is not obligatory. We all tend to invest some time and energy into our health, and how we look and feel. However, diet culture suggests that we really *should* do lots of things to "improve" ourselves. What if we are absolutely fine the way we are? A lot of people make a lot of money by stoking our insecurities and encouraging us to invest in these improvements, but no product, pill, or plan will produce happiness or perfection. I'll return to this theme in Chapter 9.

Dieting is big business; the "health" recommendations about our appearance, bodies, and weight are not typically offered by altruistic health professionals seeking to help us feel good about ourselves and live long, healthy lives. They're offered by unregulated companies looking to make money; they contribute to the diet culture in most industrialized countries. The *global* weight loss market was valued at 192.7 billion dollars in 2021, with projections indicating this could grow to 326 billion dollars by 2028.

Diet culture tells us we must control our bodies instead of caring for them. It leaves us feeling dissatisfied with who we are, and offers a range of "solutions" for this dissatisfaction. Often these solutions are completely maladaptive and rarely are they based on scientific evidence. As you'll see in this chapter and the chapters that follow (Chapter 5 on Intuitive Eating and Chapter 6 on Eating Disorders), *many of the recommendations we see in diet culture messages are no different from diagnostic criteria for eating disorders*. What all diet culture messages tend to have in common is a focus on the importance of individual responsibility in how we look and feel. But the real problem is with the culture, not the individual! Many of us have been gaslit into believing we just need to try harder. However, our bodies are *not* never-ending projects.

The problem with food fads and diets

Chances are you've been on a diet before or followed some sort of food fad, whether it be a juice cleanse, intermittent fasting, or a commitment to cut sugar out of your life. The majority of people dabble with this sort of behavior, and many are willing to try plans, potions, or programs again and again in the hopes of slimming or reshaping their bodies. There's nothing to be embarrassed about if this describes you. Why *wouldn't* you want to look and feel great? That's what marketing for food fads and diets suggests will happen if you just do what they recommend. The problem is that these are empty promises.

If something sounds too good to be true, it probably is! Diets and food fads are likely to encourage extreme habits, unhealthy behaviors, and they are unlikely to offer a long-term approach to taking care of your health. Below are eight specific reasons to avoid them.

1. They don't work – and they usually backfire

Let's say you decide to try a "fat melting, low-carb diet." You cut out most bread, pasta, and other grain-based foods from your diet. You'll miss those foods a lot! Assuming you replace those foods with nutritious meats and fats, you may initially feel good and you may feel like you have more energy, and maybe you'll even lose weight. For most people (including the thousands of people who have been studied), the feeling good/weight loss part of this experience lasts a few months, maybe three months if you're lucky. And then life gets in the way and "willpower" falls short. You'll be out to dinner with friends and you won't be able to resist the rolls. Your dad will make your favorite pasta dinner and you'll eat three servings. You'll have a bad day and you'll eat a cookie for lunch. Gradually, carbs will sneak back into your diet (as they should; carbs are actually good for your body and your brain!), and gradually you're likely to resort to your old eating habits and regain whatever weight you lost. In studies that follow people across time, nearly *everyone* who followed a plan that eliminated entire groups of food (carbohydrates, fats) couldn't stick with the plan long-term and gained back the weight they lost after two years, and most gained extra weight, too.

One reason food fads and diets tend to fail is because they typically involve restriction of foods that we like to eat! It's hard to avoid foods that may be among your favorites. Another reason for the predictable failure of most of these plans is because at the most basic level, our bodies don't respond to restriction in the way we typically want them to. Our bodies are hard-wired to respond to restriction as if we are starving and need to be saved. Usually, this means that restriction is met with an increase in food cravings, especially foods that provide us with fast and sustaining energy, such as carbohydrates and fats.

2. The physical consequences can be dangerous

If our bodies do not get the nutrients they need to sustain us, the physical consequences can be devastating and ultimately even deadly. As registered dietitians Evelyn Tribole and Elyse Resch said, "a dieting body is a starving body."

When we do not eat enough, our bodies respond by putting our limited resources into the most essential functions of living, depriving other physical functions, and a variety of physical symptoms may ensue. People who don't eat enough may be sensitive to cold, feel tired all the time, experience bone thinning and osteoporosis, and their reproductive health may suffer, resulting in menstrual irregularities and infertility among those born female. Our bodies are also unable to protect us and heal when we are undernourished; wounds may heal slowly and we may be at heightened risk of contracting infections. Perhaps most serious can be the cardiac risks that may result, leading to dangerously low blood pressure and even arrhythmias (irregular heartbeat).

Of course, some diets and food fads involve restricting certain *types* of foods, but not necessarily the *amount* of food. There is still danger in these approaches because our bodies need a variety of nutrients to function optimally. There are health risks associated with cutting out any category of food – including carbohydrates or fats!

MYTHS AND MISINFORMATION:

When your doctor tells you that you need to lose weight, you should go on a diet.

Most doctors want to help people achieve good health and recover from illness or injury. They make recommendations that they believe will be helpful. However, most doctors receive very little (if any) training about nutrition, diet, body image, and weight. They can document where you fall on a height–weight chart, but they may not know how to educate and support their patients concerning eating and body image. In other words, although a doctor is a good person to turn to with questions about health and well-being, they may not be the best source of advice when it comes to your weight. Medical professionals also live in our diet culture, and are vulnerable to the same misinformation that the rest of us see every single day.

If you're ever told by a doctor that you need to lose weight, get a second opinion from another medical professional. It may be most useful to talk with an expert who has been trained specifically to help people eat well and maintain a positive body image. A registered dietitian, nutritionist, or even a psychologist with this specialty could be a good person to consult.

Most important, if you believe – because a doctor told you so, or your own research leads you to believe this – that you need to lose weight, a food fad or any diet is not the answer. You could look at changing your regular habits to eat more nutritious foods or to be more physically active, but only make changes that are sustainable for the long term. A short-term diet or food fad of any kind is likely to detract from your health. It's also likely to be a miserable experience.

3. You'll be miserable

People often commit to a diet or food fad because they want to feel better. People usually expect to feel better both physically and psychologically. Research suggests that people often do feel good at the start. They tend to feel like they're committing to do something important for themselves. Janet Polivy, a researcher who has studied weight loss efforts for decades, has written that people feel so good on the day they *start* a diet that they'll report unrealistic experiences like feeling taller or thinking they're more likely to win the lottery.

The problem? These good feelings don't last very long, because none of us like to be deprived. If we've decided to avoid sugar, for example, we'll end up feeling irritable that we aren't able to eat sugar. Although this change to your diet was intended to make you feel better, within a few days you may actually feel worse.

One of the first studies to examine this phenomenon took place in the 1940s. Ancel Keys was the scientist who conducted the study that has become known as the "starvation study." Thirty-six healthy men participated and agreed to have the amount they ate each day reduced to about half of what they used to eat. The result? The men lost weight as expected. What wasn't expected was how this experiment affected participants' mental health. They became obsessed with food and some even began to steal food, dream about food, and collect recipes. They had a hard time focusing on regular activities and they became more socially withdrawn, depressed, and very, very cranky. Recent studies confirm these early findings: food fads and diets aren't good for your mental health.

4. You'll start to engage in ironic processing

Have you ever tried not to think about something and found that you couldn't get it out of your mind? Maybe you were irritated with a friend and you tried to clear your mind of this irritation to focus on a test at school, but it kept creeping back into your mind. **Ironic processing** is the scientific term used for when you're trying to clear your mind of a thought but it actually seems to have the opposite effect and you often find yourself thinking about it more. How is this related to what you eat? Well, a lot of food fads and diets are all about trying to *not* eat foods that you like and probably want to eat. The more you try to not think about these foods, the more you may actually want them! (Try not to think about chocolate for the next two minutes; how does that turn out?)

In a recent study, Traci Mann, a well-known expert on dieting, asked one group of dieters and another group of non-dieters to try to avoid eating from a box of chocolate they were given. After ten days, the *dieters* had eaten *more* of their box of chocolate. It seems that the act of trying to avoid "indulgent" food had backfired.

5. Diets and food fads encourage body hate

The diet and supplement industry attracts so many customers because it manages to convince us that there is something wrong with our bodies.

EXPERT ADVICE:

Traci Mann, PhD, Professor of Psychology at the University of Minnesota and author of *Secrets from the Eating Lab*, USA

"So many things I've heard about dieting my entire life are just plain wrong. I was told that losing weight was the hard part and keeping it off was the easy part, and that if you couldn't keep the weight off it was because you were weak and had no willpower. In fact, losing weight is the easy part and keeping weight off is the hard part. Most people are unsuccessful at this in the long term, but it isn't because they are weak. It's because dieting – calorie deprivation – leads to all kinds of changes in your body and in your thinking that make it very difficult to keep dieting successfully. The problem isn't the dieter. The problem is dieting."

The industry tells us there is something wrong with us – we're too skinny, too heavy, or not muscular enough – and they can help us fix it. Fads focus us on what we shouldn't do (and shouldn't eat) in order to be more attractive. This is an unhealthy way to think about ourselves.

A different way to think about our bodies is in a loving, caring way, which means thinking about the things we *want* to do to take care of ourselves, not the activities and foods we want to avoid. Psychologists have found that goals focusing on what we *do* want to do are usually easier to achieve than "avoidance goals," as they're sometimes called. This is a much healthier way to think about our bodies. Focusing on our health and nourishing our bodies is an important component of self-care. Plus, body hate is an unhelpful waste of energy.

6. Weight-cycling is a likely result

Any attempt to follow a food fad or diet is likely to contribute to weight cycling: you may lose some weight and then you'll gain it back (and you may gain additional weight as well) in a cycle of losing and gaining that may repeat – indefinitely – across time.

Research suggests that weight cycling decreases your metabolism and lowers your body's need for energy, making it likely that you'll maintain a

MYTHS AND MISINFORMATION:

Intermittent fasting is an effective and healthy approach to weight loss.

Intermittent fasting (also called time-restricted eating) has received attention in recent years as an approach to weight loss. It typically involves people eating as they regularly do for five days a week and then eating relatively little for a couple of days a week. Some people eat within a select window of time each day – for example, between 10 a.m. and 5 p.m. The general idea isn't always to limit the amount of food eaten, but to limit what is eaten to certain periods of time.

Research by nutritionists suggests that intermittent fasting can help people lose weight, but *not* any better than just changing the foods people eat (for example, snacking on fruit instead of less nutrient-dense snacks) or exercising more often. A recent study found that intermittent fasting led to hardly any weight loss – and the weight that was lost was muscle. One of the problems with intermittent fasting is that it leaves people hungry. It's a way of eating that can be difficult for people to stick with long term. Even if it helps people lose weight, they lose muscle, not fat, and they eventually gain weight back over time.

Intermittent fasting shares many similar qualities with eating disorders, and there is concern that intermittent fasting can lead to the development of an eating disorder. Ignoring your hunger cues for days or parts of days can eventually lead you to have a difficult time identifying when you are and aren't hungry as your body adapts to periods of "starvation." Adaptive eating habits require that you sense hunger and satiety (i.e., fullness), so I can't recommend intermittent fasting. Much more information about the importance of paying attention to your body's cues can be found in Chapter 5.

higher weight across time. It also increases the risk of disordered eating; weight gain and loss and gain can lead people to resort to more desperate, maladaptive eating habits. Weight cycling also affects basic physical processes and may contribute to cardiovascular disease, high blood pressure, and insulin resistance.

7. Food fads and diets take up a lot of mental space

What would the world be like if people used less of their valuable mental space finding and trying to adhere to fads and diets? It's still more likely for women to be engaged in these food fads and diets, and the energy

Diet or Food Fad? How to know when "health" advice is NOT actually healthy

If a celebrity, influencer, or even a doctor describes an approach to body or weight transformation with any of the below wording, it's likely to be anything *but* evidence based:

✓ *Results will be fast and easy to achieve!*
   ✗ Changing our habits to feel or look different is sometimes possible but usually takes months, or even years.

✓ *It works for everyone!*
   ✗ A simple, one-size-fits-all approach to health is rarely possible. Any prescription that claims to meet *everyone's* needs can't possibly be accurate.

✓ *Just buy my …*
   ✗ If a product is being sold, be suspicious. The seller wants to make money and probably cares little about your health.

✓ *The product will "cleanse" or "detox" you.*
   ✗ We have a natural system for detoxification; our kidneys remove waste products and excess fluid from the body. We also do not need to eat "clean" food or "guilt-free" food. No food is "dirty" (unless it literally has dirt on it!) and no food should cause you to feel guilty.

✓ *It worked for me!*
   ✗ What works for one person is not necessarily what will work for another. Just because your favorite influencer eats certain things in a day does NOT mean that's what you should do!

✓ *The ingredients are "clinically proven" or "a proprietary blend."*
   ✗ If a product doesn't offer information about how it is tested to assure that it is safe and effective, or if it refers to its ingredients as secret or "proprietary" (which means that the recipe is owned by the creator and will not be shared), walk the other way.

Don't
fall for it!

EXPERT ADVICE:

Sam Previte, registered dietitian, certified intuitive eating counselor, founder of *Find Food Freedom*, co-host, *What the Actual Fork* podcast, USA

"It is so essential that people feel unconditional permission to eat. If you've experienced 5, 10, or 20+ years of dieting, it's natural to fear that you will only consume pizza, cake, cookies, ice cream, and all the foods you have restricted across your dieting days. We know through research that restriction fuels binging, so when restriction is present we will always feel out of control around foods we've avoided. Allowing yourself unconditional permission to eat can help you neutralize your relationship with food and enjoy ALL foods, including both fun foods as well as nutrient-dense foods!"

they spend on these concerns can seriously impair their ability to invest in other areas of their lives. Food fads and diets are one more element of oppression in patriarchal societies.

That may sound a bit extreme, but think about it. If you're focusing a lot on what you can or can't eat – eating being something you're likely to do throughout the day – this is going to distract from other things that you could (and possibly should) be doing. Sometimes scientists refer to this as "attentional focus" or "bandwidth." We only have so much mental space, attentional focus, or bandwidth, but in resisting fads and diets we can preserve some of this. When you're tempted by the latest fad or diet, keep in mind that deciding to follow a fad or diet means deciding not to do other things, or not do other things as well as you could have. Is this a choice you want to make?

8. They're not a good use of your money

Many people assume that, like medical institutions and organizations, products that are supposed to promote health and wellness are created to help people, not to make a profit. But the diet industry and the Red Cross have next to nothing in common. There are many institutions, organizations, professionals, and products that may help you to improve your health, but nearly everything associated with dieting will *not*.

Products and plans can be described as "prescriptions for health" and opportunities to feel better or even look better, but this does not mean that they are any of these things. The diet and supplement industry is a multi-billion dollar industry. People who come up with and sell diet plans don't necessarily care about your health, not if you lose weight or gain weight or get healthier – they care about making money. If your body or weight doesn't change in the way you'd like it to, you may need their "product" again that much sooner. Keep this in mind the next time you're tempted to follow any sort of diet plan or food fad: there are a lot of people who want you to buy their products, plans, books, or other services. This doesn't mean they have your best interest in mind.

Your health is absolutely worth spending money on. If you love strawberries or peaches and can afford to buy them (even when they are not in season), you should. If you enjoy taking dance or karate classes, set money aside so that you can take them. If a new pillow or mattress would help you sleep better, invest in one. Your physical and mental health are valuable investments; just make investments that are evidence based and not a scam.

Q&A:

I have a hard time resisting sweet foods and always crave dessert. Should I just avoid sweets altogether?

You could certainly avoid dessert forever and still survive, but some new research examining acceptance and mindfulness strategies for managing cravings may make you rethink this approach.

Dr. Evan Forman and his team have conducted research that includes offering some participants tempting sweets and providing different participants strategies for resisting this temptation. People who were instructed to ignore their cravings, or were not offered any particular strategy, ate *more* treats than those who were instructed to accept their cravings as normal. These studies occur across days and not just minutes or hours. The implication seems to be that resisting foods we enjoy can backfire. Acknowledging cravings and even indulging them may reduce our cravings.

Do you want to live a life without sweets? Be sure to read earlier sections of this chapter and the next chapter on intuitive eating for possible explanations as to why you may feel "addicted" to sweets. There are habits you can adopt that may reduce those cravings entirely.

The role of your metabolism

People seem to think that having a fast metabolism means you can eat more than someone with a slow metabolism without gaining weight. This is an oversimplification of the complex ways in which our bodies work. Our metabolism is essentially the chemical processes that take place within our bodies to keep us alive, and these processes are dynamic. The biology that we're born with affects our metabolism, but so do our behaviors. In general, when we eat less food our metabolism slows down and our body processes that food more slowly. It's as if our bodies want to make good use of the smaller amount of food and use it more slowly. Scientists believe our bodies work this way as a result of evolution and the need for our bodies to protect us during historical times when food was scarce.

This isn't to say that we must always eat a lot to keep our metabolism working at full speed – it's not that simple. But we should listen to our bodies and eat what we need to feel full and energetic. If we try to eat *too* little, our bodies will process food slowly. This is one of the reasons why dieting to lose weight is so unlikely to work; our metabolism will work against our efforts. The best way to keep yourself and your metabolism happy is by adequately nourishing yourself.

EXPERT ADVICE:

Katy Zanville, MS, RDN, LDN, nutrition therapist, registered dietitian, and certified intuitive eating counselor, USA

"Dieting doesn't work because our body doesn't know the difference between being on a diet and starving on a deserted island. When you don't eat enough, your brain will release chemicals that tell you to crave MORE carbohydrates and high-fat foods. Instead of cutting back on foods and calories, focus on eating ENOUGH and think about how your body feels when you eat. And most importantly, don't forget to show yourself compassion."

What *should* I do instead?

You may have picked this book up because you want to know how to feel good about your body and how to eat. Following food fads and diets is a bad idea, but what *should* you do? How *should* you think about what to eat if you aren't following a plan or prescription of some sort? The general, evidence-based advice I have is below.

Focus on your health – psychological and physical

It's critical that you focus on your health and avoid fads when it comes to food. If you want to change your habits – concerning food, exercise, or anything, really – be sure you are making changes that are backed by science. No one has perfectly healthy habits all the time and no one should worry if they stop at McDonald's occasionally. You may find, however, that you do not feel your best if you stop at McDonald's every day. You may also find that you feel better when you are active and get plenty of sleep. If you've fallen away from routines that make you feel good and are good for your body and mind, it is OK to try to change your habits. The goal is a healthy *relationship* with food.

Make small, sustainable changes

The biggest mistake people tend to make when they decide to change a health habit is that they aim too high and don't focus on *sustainable* goals. People aren't always good at being honest with themselves about their current habits and about the likelihood of maintaining their desired goals. You're better off making small changes to your habits that you can stick with. If you drink juice or soda regularly, you could switch to water or milk most days. It might be hard at first, but once you are in the habit you may realize that soda doesn't even taste that good to you anymore. Because soda doesn't add any nutrients to your diet, this is a positive health swap. However, this also doesn't mean that you can *never* drink soda!

Behavioral science research supports this approach. Making small, sustainable changes to your health habits is far better than trying to cut out all sugar or carbs or count every single calorie. Most people would improve their health if they just ate one more piece of fruit or one more vegetable per day. Many people would feel better if they exercised for just 15 minutes more per day. Making these small changes to our lives is not necessarily a fast way to feel better or become healthier, but be patient! Remember, your primary goal is to improve your health and how you *feel*. Being happy, healthy, and confident is important for the rest of your life, and these factors are all part of maintaining a positive body image.

Thought Exercise: Spot Diet Culture

Once you start to notice diet culture, it's hard to stop and it can be equal parts frustrating and laughable to realize that diet culture is *everywhere*. Take a moment to think about the ways diet culture has shown up in your life. Share what you've noticed with someone else. Diet culture will only lose its power when more people stop being fooled by it!

_____

_____

The bottom line

Diet culture suggests that drastic changes to your habits – removing an entire food group from what you eat or keeping track of every morsel that passes your lips – come with rewards. Like many of us, Rosie grew up feeling the intense pressure of diet culture and was told that the rewards associated with weight loss would be real and powerful. She also grew up to believe that having a body that falls outside of cultural ideals is undesirable. In some research, girls have indicated that they are more afraid of becoming fat than they are of cancer, nuclear war, or losing their parents. Think about that for a moment. Is the size or shape of your body really *that* important?

MY STORY: Rosie Aurelie, 21 years old, she/her, UK

I'm not sure I have ever really liked my body. I'm not sure that any of the women in my family do. We all seem to have issues. As I've gotten older, I've come to accept my body a bit more, but as the summer approaches here in the UK, I hate to even think about wearing summer clothes. I'll also be leaving Uni soon and going back home and my mom seems to unintentionally always make me feel worse.

My mom has a lot of dysfunctional behavior when it comes to food. She's always said that she doesn't want me and my sister to feel the same way about our bodies as she does. She doesn't want us to feel badly about ourselves, and yet she's brought so much attention to issues of weight that she's made me aware and self-conscious about my body since I was a young child. My mom has always been on a diet; all sorts of fads and foods that aren't really foods passed through my home growing up. But in her efforts to restrict herself, my mom often ends up binging. Going clothes shopping with her was the worst when I was a kid. She would tell me and my sister if something wasn't flattering and I can literally remember crying on a shopping outing.

At about nine or ten years old, my mom sent me to a fat camp. I was weighed at school and labeled as "obese" and my parents felt they had to do something. Before I knew it, I was in a weight loss program intended for young people where they taught us about proper nutrition and exercise. There were a lot of food charts and some foods were "red foods" and some were "green foods." I'm sure my mom meant well and she just didn't want me to grow up heavy. I even think that the people at the camp meant well, but it was very humiliating. Even though I was young, I understood that people thought there was something wrong with me; I was fat and that was not OK.

I've talked with other people who participated in some sort of weight loss program when they were young – whether it be a camp or going to meetings with their mom. So many of them seem to have disordered eating now. The intention of these sorts of programs may be to create healthy kids who will become healthy adults, but the exact opposite seems to be achieved. I met one woman who was sent to Weight Watchers at age 7 because she needed to fit into a dress for someone's wedding. Why didn't they just get a bigger dress? She was 7!

I wish I could tell my younger self – and other kids who grew up hearing that there was something "wrong" with them – that people will like you for you. It's not all about what you look like, but who you are as a person. Having a good personality matters so much more than having a certain look.

SUMMING UP #RIOTSNOTDIETS:

- Diet culture prizes thinness, erroneously equating it with health and suggesting that our body sizes and shapes are changeable – if we just try hard enough.
- Dieting has been shown to be ineffective and is often more likely to lead to weight gain than loss over time.
- There are many negative consequences associated with following food fads and diets, from the distraction they create in our lives to the money they cost us.
- It is possible to change your eating and activity behaviors and doing so may improve your health, but may not necessarily change your body size and shape significantly.

FIND OUT MORE:

- To learn more about diet culture, check out Virginia Sole-Smith's book *Fat Talk: Parenting in the Age of Diet Culture* (Henry Holt, 2023). It's geared towards parents, but her research is fun to read and we can all learn a lot from her many years of writing about diet culture.
- Virgie Tovar's *You Have the Right to Remain Fat* (The Feminist Press, 2018) is a personal and cultural exploration of diet culture – and why life is better when you leave dieting behind.
- References that support this chapter's content and additional resources about dieting and diet culture can be found at the companion website for this book: www.TheBodyImageBookforLife.com.

CHAPTER 5

INTUITIVE EATING

#TrustYourBody

"There is no sincerer love than the love of food."

– George Bernard Shaw, *twentieth-century Irish playwright and political activist*

Basic principles of intuitive eating

Registered dietitians Evelyn Tribole and Elyse Resch are credited with developing the intuitive eating framework in their book *Intuitive Eating*, published in 1995. They've revised this book a number of times since then (as of this writing, it was in the fourth edition) and researchers have conducted hundreds of studies examining intuitive eating. In a little over 25 years, intuitive eating has become the gold standard in terms of how one develops and maintains a healthy relationship with food. There are specific principles that are a part of their intuitive eating framework. (The description of these principles is adapted from the writings of Tribole and Resch and supplemented with some recent research findings and insights.)

Cancel diet culture. The first principle of intuitive eating is to reject dieting. Because I wanted to tell you a lot about the psychological and physical health problems associated with dieting, I dedicated the entire previous chapter to this topic. I want to reiterate that it's not your fault if you feel a desire to diet; companies spend tons of money each year marketing diet plans and products to you. Remember that our bodies are not projects to continuously work on but should be viewed in a caring, appreciative way.

Pay attention to your hunger. How often do you eat when you are hungry? Do you even realize when you are hungry?

One approach to figuring out how much to eat is to pay attention to the signals your body provides. You can make eating decisions by attending to cues like how full your stomach feels, whether or not your stomach is making noises (different noises may signal hunger, digestion, or upset), and your energy level. Unfortunately, we tend to somewhat lose touch with our physical cues when we are quite young. Research done at the Children's Food Laboratory at Pennsylvania State University, under the leadership of one of my mentors, Dr. Leann Birch, provided some of the first scientific evidence of the importance of the social context of our eating behaviors. In this research, children's ability to eat according to physical cues was the worst when their parents were most controlling of what they ate. Having a parent tell you what you can and can't eat (and when) in early childhood tends to leave you unable to attend to your physical cues. Although parents are typically well intentioned in encouraging their children to eat nutritious foods and at mealtimes compatible with cultural expectations (i.e., eating breakfast before going to school), this tends to distract children from attending to their bodies' needs and teaches children that they should not trust their bodies.

Intuitive Eating Scale

The Intuitive Eating Scale (Tylka, 2006) measures a person's likelihood of following their body's cues for physical hunger, and determining when, what, and how much to eat. Before you read more about intuitive eating, you can test your own tendency to eat intuitively by answering these questions.

	Strongly disagree	Disagree	Neutral	Agree	Strongly agree
(1) I try to avoid certain foods high in fat, carbohydrates, or calories.	5	4	3	2	1
(2) I have forbidden foods that I don't allow myself to eat.	5	4	3	2	1
(3) I get mad at myself for eating something unhealthy.	5	4	3	2	1
(4) If I am craving a certain food, I allow myself to have it.	1	2	3	4	5
(5) I allow myself to eat what food I desire at the moment.	1	2	3	4	5
(6) I do NOT follow eating rules or dieting plans that dictate what, when, and/or how much to eat.	1	2	3	4	5
(7) I find myself eating when I'm feeling emotional (e.g., anxious, depressed, sad), even when I'm not physically hungry.	5	4	3	2	1
(8) I find myself eating when I am lonely, even when I'm not physically hungry.	5	4	3	2	1
(9) I use food to help me soothe my negative emotions.	5	4	3	2	1
(10) I find myself eating when I am stressed out, even when I'm not physically hungry.	5	4	3	2	1

also why little kids may say that they're full of dinner but have room in their stomach for dessert. They may be tired of meatloaf but happy to eat a cookie.

Although paying attention to our fullness is not always easy, it can get easier with practice and patience. It can be useful to pause during a meal and check in with yourself. (How am I feeling? Am I full?) Patiently attending to how you are feeling while you eat and after you've finished eating is an important component of becoming an intuitive eater.

No food is forbidden. Diet culture messages tell us that some foods are bad, but that's not true. Foods are not simply good or bad. Nearly all foods and drinks are energy sources, and different foods offer different benefits.

As I discussed in Chapter 4, if you view foods as forbidden and attempt to avoid them, you crave them that much more. Even attempts to avoid *thinking* about desirable foods makes you think about them more! If you allow yourself to eat foods that you once deemed forbidden, these foods lose their power. They can become both more and less interesting; you may crave them less if you know you can have them whenever you want to and enjoy them more!

MYTHS AND MISINFORMATION:

If I always let myself eat the foods I crave, such as cake and cookies, I won't be able to stop! I will end up gaining a ton of weight.

The possibility of losing control around food and eating as much as we'd like of something that feels desired or "bad" seems scary to a lot of us. It's not your fault if you maintain this concern; diet culture suggests to us all the time that we should not trust ourselves around food.

For most people, the freedom to eat whatever they want whenever they want makes it easier to turn food away. Sure, at first some people may eat a lot of ice cream or French fries, but as they become more in touch with their bodies, they are apt to learn that an entire container of ice cream doesn't leave them feeling too hot. They also come to realize that ice cream will always exist. Eating ice cream is not a now or never situation.

The bottom line is that if you've forbidden yourself from eating certain foods and then suddenly allow yourself to eat them, you may initially eat a lot of those foods, but it is most likely a temporary stop on the way to intuitive eating.

Relax around food. If you're used to restricting what you eat or avoiding certain foods, it can be difficult to feel relaxed around food. Some people avoid fast food because it seems to them to be the epitome of "unhealthy" food. Some people avoid soda because they believe it to just be "empty calories." Some people avoid sweets because sweets feel indulgent and sinful. It is worth asking yourself why you *really* avoid the foods (and drinks) you avoid. Unless you have an allergy to a particular food or follow religious or cultural norms that are important to you, maybe it's time to stop avoiding them?

To be an intuitive eater, you'll need to get reacquainted with foods you've been avoiding. Evelyn Tribole and Elyse Resch, the authors of *Intuitive Eating*, suggest making a list of the foods you like and noting the ones you've purposely avoided. They encourage you to work up to gradually trying these foods and seeing if you still enjoy them. If you do, give yourself permission to eat these foods. If it feels scary to have these foods in your house, you could start by getting them when you eat out. Little by little welcome these foods back into your life.

Enjoy food. It's important that you not only *allow* yourself to eat foods you like, but that you also work towards *enjoying* food. When I teach my Psychology of Eating course at Rutgers University, we always spend some time talking about the "meanings" of food. Food is not just a source of nutrition, but also a way that we experience our families, friends, and cultures. It's also a basic form of pleasure – or at least it should be. I often have my students list words that they'd use to describe food *and* sex. The connection between food and sex never seems obvious to the class at first and students feel (understandably) a bit shy talking about words they'd use to describe sex. But once they get going, all sorts of adjectives get thrown around: hot, fun, spicy, exciting. I've even heard "moist" and "slippery" shouted in my classroom! The point of the exercise is to help students see that both food and sex are very human, primal sources of pleasure. Why would you want to abandon such a daily, joyous experience? (The eating, that is.)

If you find it difficult to give yourself permission to enjoy food, this is not your fault; your cultural context is likely to blame. You've been taught that not only are some foods "bad," but *you* are bad if you eat them. This moralization of food and eating is not necessary and damages your relationship with food. By giving into the enjoyment – instead of experiencing tension, guilt, or a rushed experience – you will be able to eat more intuitively.

that can be of help. Research by Blair Burnette and her colleagues suggests intuitive eating self-help using books can improve eating habits and body image as well as life satisfaction. Purchasing a book focused on intuitive eating may be a great investment, as may be meeting with a registered dietitian who specializes in intuitive eating if you have the resources and access to a specialist.

An interview with Elyse Resch, nutrition therapist and co-author of *Intuitive Eating*

Charlotte: *How does diet culture impair our ability to be intuitive eaters?*

Elyse: *We get disconnected from this internal wisdom by the toxic forces of diet culture and its impact on individuals, as well as the medical community. We are told that if we follow a plan to shrink our bodies and achieve the culturally thin ideal, then we'll attain optimal health and happiness. Unfortunately, this is a trap that leads people down a path of dismay and lowered self-esteem when they inevitably fall off the diet/plan/restriction they've attempted to follow.*

Charlotte: *Why do you think diets are so unlikely to be successful?*

Elyse: *The psychological reasons that lead diets to ultimately "fail," include a sense of deprivation that occurs when people can't enjoy the foods they crave or enough of them to satisfy their physical and emotional needs. We are drawn to the forbidden or the unattainable – a force greater than the lure of the potential results of the diet.*

Charlotte: *What are your thoughts for teens and young adults in particular when it comes to dieting and intuitive eating?*

Elyse: *The feelings we experienced as our younger selves, whether from toddler years or teen years, continue to stay alive within us for the rest of our lives. Learning to access these feelings can help us understand the inner, and often, hidden motivations for our actions. Pervasive in those feelings is the great need to rebel. This force – the need to assert autonomy – is even greater than the power of deprivation. The developmental stage of adolescence is based on the need to individuate and achieve autonomy. Success in achieving autonomy is the sure sign of a healthy identity and ego as an adult. Rebelling against the rules of a diet is a sign of this success, rather than a sign of failure.*

Should you fight your cravings?

Most people crave certain foods at one time or another. These cravings are rarely for broccoli or kale, but are more likely to be for chocolate, chips, and ice cream. Being an intuitive eater means allowing yourself to enjoy these foods that you crave. But what should you do if you find yourself craving chocolate every day?

Research suggests that trying to avoid the foods you crave or distracting yourself from eating them is not always a good long-term approach. If you crave chocolate every single day, you may be best off just having a little bit of chocolate every day. However, if you have a craving that you really want to try to reduce, you may also want to try to work through it.

Working through a craving is sometimes referred to as "urge surfing" because you "ride the wave" of the craving by acknowledging your craving and accepting it. Instead of resisting it, you try to understand what might be leading to the craving. Are you hungry? Tired? Anxious? Bored? What need is the food you're craving attempting to fill? Is there another way to fill that need? Research by Traci Mann, who directs the Health and Eating Laboratory at the University of Minnesota, suggests that sometimes just the passage of time is all you need for a craving to pass. It's not necessarily days or weeks that need to pass either, but sometimes just minutes or hours.

Another option that can work surprisingly well is to find a good substitute for what you're craving. I'll offer a personal example to explain this approach. At the start of the coronavirus pandemic in 2020, I started to enjoy a glass of wine in the evenings to help me relax and manage my anxiety about the pandemic. It was always just one glass of wine, but I went from drinking one or two drinks on the weekend to drinking each night. For many people, that's a habit that is reasonable for them to maintain, but I knew that my sleep was being disrupted by the alcohol and it wasn't making me feel all that great. I looked forward to this treat every night and I craved it, so I knew I needed to find something else to look forward to instead. I've landed on a sweet treat and a particular seltzer water that I really like and only drink at night. I feel better and that's what keeps me motivated to stick with my new habit.

It is completely normal to crave certain foods. It can be valuable to try to understand your cravings and, *in some cases*, you may want to try to change them. It doesn't benefit your mental health, however, to exert mental energy trying to avoid foods or worrying about food; be mindful but not anxious about what you eat.

Bringing it back to body image

Developing adaptive eating habits is an important contributor to our body image. Research I've recently conducted with a team of scholars around the world supports this point. Young adults in Australia, Belgium, Canada, China, Italy, Japan, Spain, and the USA who are more likely to eat intuitively were also more likely to be satisfied with their bodies. We also found that intuitive eaters were more likely to feel good about themselves in general, not just their bodies. Some of the concepts in this chapter may seem challenging, but working to improve your relationship with food and your body is definitely worth it.

MY STORY: Aleja Jane, 22 years old, she/her, USA

I'm at a place where I'm content and accepting of my body. I've fluctuated a lot in how I've felt across my life, but I'm at a pretty good place right now. I felt really confident in my body when I was in the depths of an eating disorder, but I was really unhealthy at the time. Fortunately, I realized I was not healthy and through recovery I came to understand that I just have to accept that my body is not "perfect."

My disordered eating started when I was about 14 and I was trying to gain control of my life through controlling what I ate (or didn't eat). I wanted to lose weight, but I kept feeling like I had to lose more and more weight. I became really compulsive and it didn't even make sense, but I didn't see myself the way others did. I became severely underweight and was diagnosed with anorexia. I ended up hospitalized for treatment and I learned that I had a thyroid disorder, a complication from my eating disorder. I came to appreciate that I had to get my period back if I wanted to be able to have children someday. This helped me to realize that I needed to be an active participant in my recovery and I took my therapy and nutrition sessions seriously.

Intuitive eating was a huge part of what helped me during my recovery. Now I think I have a good relationship with food. It's great to be able to say that! But I don't know that I ever used to have a good relationship with food, even before my disordered eating started. As a Cuban American and the first-born child of immigrants that fled from a starving country, food always seemed like a sensitive and daunting topic.

During my eating disorder years, I really lost my sense of when I was hungry, but I was able to get that back. Intuitive eating has been really freeing. I used to schedule my meals and avoid certain foods. But intuitive eating has helped me to understand that there really are no such things as good and bad foods. You need food as fuel otherwise you can't do what you want to each day. I also pay attention to my emotions and what I feel like eating. There's so much information thrown at us through every media source and we're told that we need to control our eating and that there are food rules we have to follow. Now I see that these messages are not accurate and they're not scientific or helpful. You have to engage in intuitive eating for a long time to get it. And I think most people – even people who have never technically had an eating disorder – just can't do it for a long time because they get all of these other messages.

I think that the advice I want to offer other people is to honor their health. Take time to listen to your body and listen to your emotions and unpack them. Talk to people if you are struggling. It's OK to be different from other people. You have to learn what's best for you.

My therapist once told me, "You're not responsible for your thoughts, but you're responsible for your behaviors. Analyze your thoughts." Sometimes I still think unhealthy thoughts, but I do my best not to act on them. I know how important it is to trust my body and trust myself.

My relationship with myself has really changed. I have learned to set healthy boundaries with people. I have really worked on my relationship with myself and it's been worth it.

SUMMING UP #TRUSTYOURBODY:

- How much you need to eat depends on a variety of factors including how active you are, how tall you are, your body build, and whether you are male or female.
- Intuitive eating offers strategies for getting in touch with your body's sense of hunger and fullness and really enjoying what you eat.
- Respect and care for your body and your mind by attending to what and how much you eat without viewing food as a source of stress.

FIND OUT MORE:

- To learn more about intuitive eating, especially the basic principles, you might be interested in exploring this page on the website *Intuitive Eating*: www.intuitiveeating.org/10-principles-of-intuitive-eating/.
- The fourth edition of the *Intuitive Eating* book (2020) by Evelyn Tribole and Elyse Resch can be purchased wherever books are sold. *The Intuitive Eating Workbook for Teens* (2019) by Elyse Resch has exercises that may help you work through the principles of intuitive eating.
- For more resources about intuitive eating, see the companion website for this book: www.TheBodyImageBookforLife.com.

EVERY JOURNEY HAS HIGHS AND LOWS • ALL YOU CAN DO IS TAKE SMALL STEPS IN THE RIGHT DIRECTION EVERY SINGLE DAY

CHAPTER 6

EATING DISORDERS

#DisorderedEatingIn ADisorderedWorld

"The greatest glory in living lies not in never falling, but in rising every time we fall."

– Nelson Mandela, *twentieth-century South African political leader and philanthropist*

MY STORY: Andrea Nicolette, 20 years old, she/her, USA

I'd say I'm the most comfortable with my body that I have ever been. I certainly have come a long way, but I also feel like I have a long way to go and I look forward to continuing to feel better.

I guess things started to go downhill for me around 8th grade. I was overwhelmed and confused in a number of ways as I waded through puberty and tried to sort out who I was and who I was becoming. I started to realize I was attracted to girls and not boys around then, and that threw me for a loop. I thought if I could just control what I was eating and look conventionally attractive to boys, then I wouldn't have to deal with my sexuality. I could take charge of my life! Has anyone ever said that and had it work out? It feels like growing up is so much about relinquishing control and realizing that there's a lot you just need to accept.

But back to my eating habits. Because they have changed dramatically across the years – and sometimes within short periods of time – my body has also changed. It can feel like every time I blink, I have a new body I need to get used to. It's tempting to resort to maladaptive eating behaviors and focus on staying as thin as possible, and yet I know that's not good for me in the long run. I know my body needs nourishment and that food should also be a source of enjoyment and a part of my social life. Overcontrolling what I do (and don't) eat is not the answer. I work to keep this all in perspective each day.

Fortunately, I have had the support of good therapists and others in my life that have helped me move towards recovery, even though the path is not always linear. I also take an antidepressant, which has helped my mood but also contributed to weight gain. I'll admit that that was not easy to cope with. But I've learned that there is not one standard of beauty and I've come to appreciate appearance diversity. We are all meant to look different! Curating my social media newsfeeds so that I see diverse, accepting, mentally healthy people has helped. Sometimes diet culture and disordered eating messages sneak in (those social media algorithms don't always *seem to get it right!), but I look for information that is reassuring and helpful to me and try to block the other stuff.*

My advice to others is to make sure they find people who will support them – both in their real and virtual worlds. Some days growing up and becoming an adult is hard! If you need help, find a therapist. Therapy can change your life! Everyone is worthy and deserving of support and you don't need a specific diagnosis to "earn" it.

So much of what we learn from the media and popular news sources about eating is scientifically inaccurate. Chapters 3, 4, and 5 discussed a lot of important information about eating, and some of it may be contradictory to what you've always thought you've known. In fact, some of what you may think of as "healthy" or "normal" when it comes to eating, may be really *unhealthy*.

IN THIS CHAPTER YOU'LL LEARN

- what defines **disordered eating** and **eating disorders** and how these problems can develop,
- treatment options for disordered eating and eating disorders, and
- how to improve your way of thinking about food and adopt habits to support a positive body image.

I want to ask you to consider health as a broad and complex concept that doesn't just mean that someone isn't "sick." Being healthy means feeling well physically, but also feeling well psychologically, having satisfying interpersonal relationships, and wanting to engage with the world around you. How we eat contributes not just to our physical health but also to these other aspects of our health. Eating should be fun! You may eat only organic fruits and vegetables, grains, and lean meats but be psychologically distraught. You may also only have the time and money to eat packaged and fast food but be psychologically healthy. Although you may feel best psychologically when you are able to eat nourishing foods, these two things don't always go together in the ways you think they should.

Disordered eating and eating disorders

You've probably heard about **eating disorders** from the media or at some point in a health class at school, but you may not know that there are several different kinds of eating disorders, or that eating disorders can be *really* serious. In fact, they're the most deadly form of mental illness aside from opioid addiction. It's also likely that most of the information you're familiar with concerning eating disorders relates to girls and women. However, approximately 25% of all eating disorder patients are boys and men.

Disordered eating and eating disorders are not exactly the same. Most people probably engage in disordered eating at some time or another because most people fall prey to cultural messages suggesting they should skip meals, avoid certain food groups, or feel guilty for eating certain foods. Other disordered eating behaviors may include using medications (or illegal drugs) to try to lose weight, chronic dieting and weight fluctuations, rigidity and strict routines surrounding food and exercise, and anxiety about eating or appearance. If these thoughts or behaviors become habitual, they can lead to the development of an eating disorder.

There are significant consequences to engaging in disordered eating even if you are never diagnosed with an eating disorder. If you skip breakfast occasionally because you're in a rush in the morning, that's unlikely to become a serious problem. But if you are constantly dieting or concerned about what you eat, weigh, or how much you exercise, your psychological health and quality of life are likely to suffer. You may also experience gastrointestinal problems, low heart rate and blood pressure, and even bone loss.

I'll review the most common eating disorders below. As you read, it is important to understand that the symptoms described can apply to boys, girls, men, women, nonbinary, and transgender people, and that *anyone* who experiences these symptoms should get professional help. It's also important to realize that the criteria for an eating disorder (versus disordered eating) are not always clear cut. The categories of eating disorders are useful to clinicians and other medical professionals trying to treat patients, but in the real world people rarely fit neatly into these categories. Some people have symptoms of various eating disorders at the same time. Even if you or someone you know doesn't fit perfectly into a specific eating disorder category, this doesn't mean that treatment wouldn't be beneficial. No one should feel that they need to wait until they are *really* suffering to get help! Sometimes it may require persistence to get the help you need; do not give up!

Q&A:

I've suffered from disordered eating (although I've never been diagnosed with an eating disorder) for years. I've been working to get better, to not stress about what I eat or how I look, but some days are a struggle. When does the work stop? When am I just OK?

Recovery from an eating disorder – or even maladaptive eating habits that have not been diagnosed as a clinical disorder by a professional – can take years. Some days may feel very difficult, but across time you are likely to have fewer and fewer challenging days. There is nothing wrong with you if you feel that coping with these issues is stressful and you definitely should seek out sources of support. Working with a therapist trained in eating disorder treatment or a weight-neutral registered dietitian can make your work towards psychological and physical health feel a lot easier (also see Chapter 2 for more about the Health at Every Size perspective).

Some research suggests that eating problems can be chronic (i.e., they don't just go away like a cold does but may come and go across years). Try not to find this discouraging, but acknowledge that what you are experiencing is difficult and afford yourself compassion as you work towards improving your health. It may seem impossible to believe now, but one day you will realize you haven't thought much about what you've eaten all day and you don't worry much about your body size and shape. When you get to this point, you will experience a freedom that will make the work you are doing now worthwhile.

EXPERT ADVICE:

Cheri A. Levinson, PhD, Associate Professor, University of Louisville, Founder and Clinical Director, Louisville Center for Eating Disorders, USA

"Often times people with eating disorders have a hard time believing they are sick enough or that they really have an eating disorder. This is part of the illness. The eating disorder makes it hard to see that you are truly ill and deserving of help and support to get better."

Anorexia nervosa

Anorexia nervosa, usually referred to as anorexia, is an eating disorder that's relatively rare, but extremely serious. Individuals who develop anorexia typically eat very little and often eat only certain types of foods. They may exercise excessively and tend to be obsessed with food, calories, and other qualities of foods, such as fat content. People with anorexia often avoid social gatherings that include food and may prepare food for others that they don't eat themselves. They are usually concerned with trying to lose weight or stay lean, weigh themselves often, and tend to experience extreme body image concerns. Sometimes anorexic individuals will **purge** when they do eat. Purging can take many different forms, from vomiting to excessive exercise. Many individuals with anorexia are underweight but some are not; you can't always determine who has an eating disorder by looking at them.

The health consequences of anorexia can be very serious. When the body doesn't get enough of the nutrients it needs, a variety of problems may develop, including dramatic weight loss, stomach pain, weakness, lowered immune functioning, slowed heart rate, overall feelings of coldness, difficulty sleeping, dizziness and fainting, difficulty concentrating, and even death (often through unpredictable heart failure). Girls and women with anorexia may stop getting their periods (termed **amenorrhea**). There's also a very high mortality rate, some of which is due to suicide; about 20% – that's one in five! – people with anorexia will die due to complications associated with their illness.

Bulimia nervosa

Bulimia nervosa, or "bulimia," typically involves **binging** and then purging food. When someone binges, they eat *much* more than is typical in one sitting (defined as within two hours). You may feel really full if you eat four or five pieces of pizza, but a true binge would mean eating an entire pizza plus more, in most cases. People with bulimia tend to feel a loss of control and an inability to stop eating when they binge. After a binge, a person with bulimia often feels guilty, and then engages in some sort of purge. Purging can take different forms, including using medication that leads to vomiting or diarrhea, excessive exercise, or skipping meals. People with bulimia tend to be preoccupied with their body size and shape and may experience fluctuations in their weight as a result of their disorder.

The health consequences of bulimia are similar to those of anorexia. In both disorders, people are unlikely to get the nutrients they need, whilst the time and energy focused on food and weight is a major distraction from the rest of their lives. But unlike those with anorexia, bulimic people often develop problems with their stomachs, digestive systems, and even their teeth as a result of binging and purging. They also may have difficulty sleeping and concentrating, problems fighting infection, and muscle weakness. Purging may result in very serious issues including electrolyte imbalances, which can lead to major complications including death, often without any warning.

Binge-eating disorder

Binge-eating disorder (aka BED) is estimated to be the most common eating disorder. People with BED tend to binge at least once a week for at least three months without compensatory behaviors (i.e., purging). Binges are described as excessive in terms of how much is eaten, and they're experienced as uncontrollable. Binging may occur as a means of coping with emotional experiences and typically happens alone. When people binge, they often describe the experience as if they're in a trance. They often eat quickly and until they're uncomfortable and then feel guilty and ashamed afterwards. A binge is not a result of hunger and is not experienced as pleasant, but as distressing and physically and psychologically uncomfortable.

People with BED often experience problems with their stomachs and digestive systems. They may get cramps, constipation, heartburn, or other symptoms as a result of their problematic eating habits. They often spend a lot of time and energy thinking about food and what they will eat. It is common for people with BED to experience weight-cycling or frequent shifts in their weight and to engage in dieting to try to lose weight. People with BED are at risk of maintaining a larger body size (up to two-thirds are labeled medically "obese") and may experience stigma and shame as a result of their body size.

Other specified feeding or eating disorder

Sometimes people have unhealthy eating habits that are not as severe or as consistent as would be required to be diagnosed with anorexia, bulimia, or binge eating disorder, but their eating habits still disrupt their life. Their habits may lead to drastic weight gain or weight loss. Most importantly, these people are stressed out about their eating, body image, or weight (or all three). These individuals are often diagnosed with having an **other specified feeding or eating disorder (OSFED)**. This long name is really just a way of saying someone has an "other eating disorder."

To receive an official diagnosis of anorexia, for example, patients must have a number of specific symptoms. A patient's symptoms may fall just short of the required number of symptoms, but he or she may clearly have serious concerns and unhealthy behaviors surrounding food. This patient would likely get diagnosed as having OSFED. This diagnosis helps different health care providers to realize the seriousness of the patient's symptoms and can help organize treatment for the patient.

Body dysmorphic disorder

Body dysmorphic disorder (BDD) is not an eating disorder, but often co-occurs with eating disorders. People who have eating disorders sometimes have BDD, but it is not an eating disorder on its own. It is also more common among people who have obsessive-compulsive disorder.

BDD is a body image disorder. People with BDD are preoccupied with their bodies' defects and flaws. They are compulsive about tending to their appearance and may go to extremes to alter their appearance, such as obtaining extensive cosmetic surgery. At the heart of BDD is the inability to see oneself as others do and being extremely critical of one's body. People with BDD may experience self-doubt, anxiety, and depression as a result of their preoccupation with their bodies.

There are subtypes of BDD that are characterized by different body image preoccupations. For example, the muscle dysmorphic subtype involves preoccupation with muscle size and shape. Another subtype includes delusional beliefs about appearance; people with this subtype are completely convinced that the way they experience their physical flaws is accurate.

As I discuss throughout this book, it is typical to have some concerns about your appearance and it is normal to attend to your appearance regularly – for example, bathing, grooming, and selecting clothes you like. However, BDD goes beyond all of this and, like most mental health problems, proves disruptive to an individual's life. It is one thing to be really focused on your hair or your clothes, but it is another to never want to leave the house unless those aspects of your appearance seem perfect to you.

MYTHS AND MISINFORMATION:

You can never eat *too* healthily.

Eating nutritious foods is a good way to take care of your body. However, it is possible to become *too* concerned with healthy eating. If you find yourself spending a lot of time thinking about what you are eating and feel guilty if you eat anything that is remotely unhealthy, you may have what is referred to sometimes as **orthorexia**. The American Psychological Association does not recognize orthorexia as a clinical disorder, but it is a term used to describe an over-concern with eating only healthy foods, being rigid about food choice, and often includes body image concerns. (The diagnostic category other specified feeding and eating disorder [OSFED] would likely be used to classify most people with orthorexia.) People with orthorexia often experience anxiety and obsessive-compulsive tendencies. Although you may benefit physically from eating nutritious foods, taken to the extreme this can become problematic psychologically. People with orthorexia may avoid social situations that involve food or even eating at restaurants so that they can stick to their food rituals and routines that involve limited foods or only especially nutritious foods. Food should be enjoyed! Every meal does not need to include avocado, kale, and almonds.

EXPERT ADVICE:

Oona Hanson, MA, parent coach, family mentor at Equip, eating disorder treatment organization

"There are a lot of myths about eating disorders, including the misconception that they affect only young teens. The truth is that adults of all ages can develop eating disorders. When it comes to recovering from an eating disorder in your 20s, 30s, or beyond, know that it's OK to get support from family or friends. Even if you have a lot of motivation to recover and access to professional treatment, you don't have to go it alone just because you're an adult."

How does a person develop an eating disorder?

Like any mental health problem, no one *wants* to develop an eating disorder. Sometimes people with eating disorders describe what has happened to them as an "accident" or something they "fell into." This may seem strange if you haven't had a similar experience, but it is definitely possible to alter your eating, activity, or related behaviors and still not intend to develop an eating disorder. It's important to keep this in mind if a friend or someone you know has an eating disorder (see the Q&A, below).

Usually, people who develop eating disorders are concerned about their weight and don't feel good about their bodies. Often they're not overweight but are still worried about what they eat and the size of their bodies. It turns out that usually a person's *actual* weight is much less relevant than is a person's *feelings* about their weight in the development of eating disorders.

Many people who develop eating disorders live in families that talk a lot about food and dieting, or in which others have eating disorder symptoms themselves. Sometimes family members may tease and make a person feel bad about their food choices or weight. Sometimes parents restrict their children's access to certain foods, whether it be fast food or dessert foods or processed foods, making these foods more appealing and, in some cases, more binge-worthy. Eating disorders seem to run in families, not only because of these experiences within families, but there is evidence of a genetic predisposition to eating disorders. The genes we inherit from family members may play a significant role in our vulnerability to eating disorders (and many other mental and physical health concerns).

Media also plays a part in the development of eating disorders. As I'll discuss much more in Chapter 8, images of what the "ideal woman" and "ideal man" look like are incredibly unrealistic. Women see countless messages suggesting they should be slender, with large breasts, and curvaceous hips. This combination of features very rarely occurs naturally (without surgical intervention). Messages that equate masculinity with muscles are everywhere in Western cultures. It's easy for people to believe that they'll be happiest if they look a certain way, and to be willing to take drastic measures to achieve that look. The problem is that there are so many serious health problems associated with not taking good care of your body.

Some research suggests that people with certain personalities may be more vulnerable to developing eating disorders. People who are perfectionists or anxious are more likely to worry about things like fitting in with their peers and looking a certain way. This may lead them to be more at risk for an eating disorder. Some people with eating disorders also experience other mental health conditions, such as depression or obsessive-compulsive disorder (OCD). It's not always clear what comes first; an eating disorder may lead to depression (or another mental health condition) or depression may contribute to the development of an eating disorder.

Social experiences that accompany development and changes in hormones during puberty have also been linked to the development of eating disorders. Some people develop eating disorders and it is not clear what the causes were. It may be a combination of minor experiences or one major life event. For some, it may be an illness or travel or a break-up that led them to change their habits and ultimately develop an eating disorder. Sometimes, people can't really describe what happened or why they ended up having serious health concerns associated with eating.

Q&A:

I have a good friend who I think has an eating disorder. I don't want to offend her or seem nosey by asking her if she's OK. What should I do?

It's likely that at some point in your life you'll know at least one person who has an eating disorder. You probably want to choose whether or not you want to talk to your friend directly or talk to an adult who may be able to help (this may depend on your age and whether or not your friend lives with parents). It may make sense to do both. If you aren't comfortable approaching your friend directly, you could talk to your parents, one of her parents, or a psychologist, counselor, or teacher at your school or university. Most high schools (secondary schools) have a psychologist or counselor available and most universities have some sort of health center that includes psychological services. Sharing your concern with a caring adult can help to ease your worry and allow someone else to step in and help figure out the best approach.

If you decide to talk with your friend directly, be careful not to blame her for having a problem. No one wants to develop an eating disorder; she has an illness similar to other kinds of physical illnesses. It's often helpful to try to have a calm conversation that allows you to express your concern and worry about her. You could say, "I've noticed that some days you don't seem to eat very much. I'm concerned that you are not giving your body the nutrients that it needs." It is very possible that your friend does not think of her behaviors as an eating disorder, so she may react with surprise.

You can direct your friend to some helpful resources online, such as the National Eating Disorders Association eating disorders screening tool (www .nationaleatingdisorders.org/screening-tool). You may want to let her know that you're aware that eating disorders can be very serious – even deadly – and that you care about her getting better and enjoying food and a healthy future. Consider helping her find a way to get professional help. It can be scary for people to ask for help, even though it's probably a good idea for her to talk with her doctor and a psychologist. At the very least, she could call the National Alliance for Eating Disorders Helpline (US 866 662 1235) or the Beat Eating Disorders Helpline (UK 0808 801 0677) or chat online with professionals from The Butterfly Foundation (Australia's eating disorders help organization; go to https://butterfly.org.au/ get-support/chat-online/).

Sometimes people who need medical help aren't ready to get it, and your friend may not follow your advice. Try not to take this personally but continue to express your concern to your friend. Most important, don't ever shame someone or make them feel bad for having a problem. This is unlikely to help and may only damage your relationship. You may want to say something like, "I'm concerned about you and I'm here for you when you are ready to get help."

Self-Assessment: Eating Attitudes Test

Check a response for each of the following statements:	Always	Usually	Often	Some-times	Rarely	Never
1. I am terrified about being overweight.	3	2	1	0	0	0
2. I avoid eating when I am hungry.	3	2	1	0	0	0
3. I find myself preoccupied with food.	3	2	1	0	0	0
4. I have gone on eating binges where I feel that I may not be able to stop.	3	2	1	0	0	0
5. I cut my food into small pieces.	3	2	1	0	0	0
6. I am aware of the calorie content of foods that I eat.	3	2	1	0	0	0
7. I particularly avoid food with a high carbohydrate content (e.g., bread, rice, potatoes, etc.).	3	2	1	0	0	0
8. I feel that others would prefer if I ate more.	3	2	1	0	0	0
9. I vomit after I have eaten.	3	2	1	0	0	0
10. I feel extremely guilty after eating.	3	2	1	0	0	0
11. I am preoccupied with a desire to be thinner.	3	2	1	0	0	0
12. I think about burning up calories when I exercise.	3	2	1	0	0	0

Check a response for each of the following statements:	Always	Usually	Often	Some-times	Rarely	Never
13. I think other people think that I am too thin.	3	2	1	0	0	0
14. I am preoccupied with the thought of having fat on my body.	3	2	1	0	0	0
15. I take longer than others to eat my meals.	3	2	1	0	0	0
16. I avoid foods with sugar in them.	3	2	1	0	0	0
17. I eat diet foods.	3	2	1	0	0	0
18. I feel that food controls my life.	3	2	1	0	0	0
19. I display self-control around food.	3	2	1	0	0	0
20. I feel that others pressure me to eat.	3	2	1	0	0	0
21. I give too much time and thought to food.	3	2	1	0	0	0
23. I engage in dieting behavior.	3	2	1	0	0	0
24. I like my stomach to be empty.	3	2	1	0	0	0
25. I have the impulse to vomit after meals.	3	2	1	0	0	0
26. I enjoy trying new rich foods.	0	0	0	1	2	3

To determine your score, add the values of all the items. People who score 20 or more on the test should be interviewed by a qualified professional to determine if they meet the diagnostic criteria for an eating disorder. If you have a low score on the EAT-26 (below 20), you still could have an eating problem, so do not let the results deter you from seeking help.

EXPERT ADVICE:

Susanne Johnson, family nurse practitioner, USA

"With regard to interactions at the doctor's office – self-care looks like protecting your peace, asking for what you need, and setting boundaries. Bring a list of questions and goals for the visit and be firm if you have no desire to discuss weight, exercise, or nutrition. It is OK to communicate to medical providers that you do not want to step on the scale or that you would prefer not to see or be told your weight. Bring a trusted friend with you as an advocate and second pair of ears who can provide support, ease anxiety, and help to redirect the conversation if you feel overwhelmed."

Eating disorders treatment

Eating disorders are complex, and they're very serious. Regardless of the reasons behind a person developing an eating disorder, it isn't their fault that they're sick. People suffering from an eating disorder usually require treatment by several health care professionals including physicians, psychologists, and nutritionists. Unfortunately, not everyone gets the treatment they need. People who are heavier or who identify as male tend to be overlooked by medical professionals because it isn't expected that they will experience an eating disorder.

If you or someone you know needs body image or eating disorder treatment, you may need to talk to more than one doctor to get that help. Waiting is not the answer; early treatment is almost always more effective than waiting to see if a person grows out of an eating disorder. It's always safer to get too much help and support than not enough.

The first part of eating disorder treatment will vary depending on the severity of the disorder. Often, when someone has been malnourished or is compulsively exercising, their pulse will be quite low. (The average resting heart rate of an 18-year-old girl is 72 beats per minute and the average pulse of an 18-year-old boy is 79 beats per minute. Someone with an eating disorder may have a much lower resting heart rate.) Girls and women may stop getting their periods and those who are weak from malnourishment may faint. When physical symptoms accompanying an eating disorder are concerning, someone may be referred for inpatient treatment. In a hospital setting, the initial focus is often on nourishing patients so that they become physically stable. This can be uncomfortable to a person who is used to not eating a lot or exercising often; however, it is necessary.

After a person is physically stable and the risk of a cardiac event or other really serious health event has been reduced, other aspects of treatment get more attention. Usually this includes some form of psychotherapy including one-on-one therapy and possibly family therapy or group therapy. Therapy can help patients work through problems they are having with recovery (for example, eating enough food to support their health) and factors that may have contributed to the rise of the eating disorder. It's not necessary for patients to understand exactly what led them to develop an eating disorder, but it can be helpful to consider whether there are factors that contributed that may make recovery difficult. For example, if a parent tends to be critical of their weight, learning how to handle this may be essential to recovery. Therapy can help with many other aspects of recovery by offering social support, strategies to help manage difficult times and relapses, and by helping to shore up mental health more generally.

A nutritionist or registered dietitian may be an important part of treatment for eating disorders. Many people who experience eating disorders lose touch with their body's nutritional needs. They've ignored their body's hunger cues and those signals no longer function well. Someone with training in nutrition science can help people with eating disorders learn what their body's nutritional needs are and help them adopt habits that are mentally and physically healthy. Many nutritionists and registered dietitians have training in *intuitive eating* (see Chapter 5) and in a weight-neutral perspective and can help people appreciate that their body, weight, and eating concerns originate from a culture that offers many, many unhealthy and inaccurate messages about these issues.

Medication may also play a role in helping a person recover from an eating disorder. Often, eating disorders co-occur with anxiety, depression, or other mental health problems. Some of the medications, such as antidepressants, that are useful in treating one mental health condition can also help to alleviate eating disorders. They all affect the chemicals in our brain (aka, neurotransmitters including serotonin and dopamine) that influence our moods and emotions. Our scientific understanding of the role of psychotropic medications, such as Prozac and Zoloft, continues to expand as does their use for treating various illnesses. Some recent research suggests that a medication often used to treat attention deficit hyperactivity disorder (ADHD), lisdexamfetamine dimesylate (LDX), can be effective in treating binge-eating disorder. However, there's a lot that is not completely understood about how these medications work or why certain medications work for some people and some conditions and not for others. Regardless, medication can be an important part of treatment for many people recovering from an eating disorder.

MYTHS AND MISINFORMATION:

You can become addicted to food the way you can become addicted to drugs.

Food – especially fast food and sugary foods – is often discussed as "addictive." It is undeniable that we can get into the *habit* of eating certain foods regularly, but to say that food is addictive is more controversial. My interpretation of the research science leads me to believe that "addiction" is not the correct term to use when discussing food.

Brain science is often used to discuss food addiction because there are similarities in the parts of the brain that seem to respond to some foods and other addictive substances. Some research even suggests that some people who eat ultraprocessed foods often experience changes in their brains that somewhat parallel the types of changes experienced by people with addictions to other substances. However, just as not all people's brains respond to drugs or alcohol the same way, not all people's brains respond to food the same way. Individuals with binge-type eating disorders seem to exhibit signs of a physical response to food that can resemble an addiction.

Addiction to substances such as alcohol, nicotine, or drugs like methamphetamines (aka, meth) is different in important ways from anything resembling addiction to food, however. When a person becomes addicted to a substance like alcohol, the body becomes dependent on the substance to function. Without the substance, withdrawal symptoms kick in. These symptoms can be mild and include irritability or a headache or they may be much more serious and include body tremors and vomiting. People with these addictions will do nearly anything to get the substance that has become a part of their lives. In contrast, you may really like chocolate or Big Macs, but are you willing to lie, cheat, or steal to get either?

Another important difference is that we need food to live. We can't avoid it completely! Addiction to alcohol or drugs can be treated with abstinence, but that's just not an option when it comes to food.

How you eat is related to how you feel

How you eat – even how you think about food – has a big impact on many areas of your life. Part of the connection between how you eat and how you feel is physical; both your brain and your body react to what you eat (or don't eat). If you aren't eating nutritious foods or enough food, you're also more likely to be tired, unable to concentrate, and maybe even **hangry** (hungry + angry). Poor nutrition is also associated with an inability to fight off illness and infection.

Your eating habits are also likely to affect how you feel about yourself and your psychological health, even if you never have anything resembling an eating disorder. For example, in one recent study researchers found that lower self-esteem is associated with poorer eating habits. This may mean that people with low self-esteem don't eat as many nutritious foods, or that eating nutritious foods has a positive impact on self-esteem – likely both things are partly true. There's also emerging research that suggests that positive changes to a person's diet can improve mood and well-being.

It can be difficult to know "how to eat," given the many confusing and con-tradictory messages we are all exposed to about food and diets. Many diets essentially prescribe disordered eating. It's important to push back against these messages and appreciate that brains and bodies thrive when they get the nourishment they need. A mind preoccupied with concerns about food or deprived of food cannot flourish. Plus, you deserve to enjoy food!

MY STORY: Charlotte Kayla, 20 years old, she/her, USA

I've come to a place where I put less emphasis on my perceptions of my body and I think more about how I feel inside. I work to be in tune with my body. I try to practice mindfulness, which is helpful in creating a sense of calm.

I know that growing up I was blessed with parents who didn't struggle with their own body images. My mom in particular always set a good example in this regard. I've never looked at myself and thought of myself as ugly or fat. Somehow, in spite of this, I still struggled with an eating disorder in high school.

Things started to devolve when I got really into running and I was really focusing on eating "healthy" and "clean." I was really enjoying running and I was getting lighter and faster. This didn't seem to be problematic until I went for a regular check-up with my doctor and they checked my heart rate. Apparently, it was very low and the doctor was concerned. She recommended that I meet with a nutritionist, which I did. I had been eating, but over a few meetings with the nutritionist, she helped me to see that I needed to be eating more if I was going to keep running. I worked to adjust my eating habits, but when I went for a follow-up appointment with my doctor my heart rate was still low. This ultimately resulted in my hospitalization.

I stayed in the hospital for a week and it was a miserable experience. I didn't feel like anyone was listening to me; they were entirely focused on my vital signs. I was just a series of numbers: my pulse, my weight, caloric intake. It was dehumanizing. It also was clear that I didn't meet the typical criteria for an eating disorder – or any disorder – so they didn't know what to do with me. They wanted to save my life, but they didn't understand me.

What really saved my life was finding a therapist that I really clicked with after I left the hospital. She wasn't trying to label me as having a particular disorder. She listened to me and I'm sure I wouldn't be the person I am today without her. She has really helped me to feel more connected to myself.

If I could offer my younger self advice, I'd tell her to find things that really make her feel good: yoga, going on walks, cooking. Hold onto the things that bring you back to yourself and make those things a priority. For me, that's been the key to happiness. When you're in love with yourself, other people want to be around that energy. It will attract amazing people and bring them into your life!

SUMMING UP #DISORDEREDEATINGINADISORDEREDWORLD:

- Healthy eating habits include choosing nutritious food options from what is available to you (for example, fruits and vegetables), but also *enjoying food* and making eating a fun part of your life.
- Always denying yourself foods that you enjoy, or eating too much or too little to feel good, isn't healthy and may lead to disordered eating, or even a serious eating disorder. If you think that you or someone you know may have an eating disorder, talk with a mental health professional and seek out support and treatment.
- Treatment for eating disorders is possible, but most effective if it begins early and includes specialists with expertise in treating eating disorders.

FIND OUT MORE:

- If you have questions about eating disorders, spend some time on the Alliance for Eating Disorders and the Beat Eating Disorders' web pages: www.allianceforeatingdisorders.com and www.beateatingdisorders.org.uk.
- To find a therapist with an inclusive and/or Health at Every Size Approach, look here: www.inclusivetherapists.com/therapy/health-at-every-size.
- References that support this chapter's content and additional resources about eating disorders can be found at the companion website for this book: www.TheBodyImageBookforLife.com.

CHAPTER

MENTAL HEALTH

#MentalHealthMatters

"It is during our darkest moments that we must focus to see the light."

– Aristotle, *ancient Greek philosopher*

MY STORY: Emma Paola, 15 years old, she/her, USA

In the last couple of years, I've dealt with major depression, an eating disorder, a drug problem, and three suicide attempts. To say I'm lucky to be alive is an understatement!

I think it really started during my freshman year of high school. I'm sure that these issues were bubbling beneath the surface before then, but the pandemic struck and everything about my life went out of whack. I think I started to restrict my eating as a way to gain control over my life, which felt like it was spinning out of control. But the less I ate, the more I hated myself. My mind just couldn't function properly – for that matter, neither could my body! I really couldn't tell when I was hungry and before I knew it, I was eating very little and I was diagnosed with anorexia.

I didn't start to get treatment for my eating disorder until the first time I tried to take my own life. I'm not sure why I did it, but I really didn't want to live. That first hospitalization was short and not all that helpful. But when I ended up in the hospital again after another attempt, I started to get scared. In intensive care treatment, there were other patients in far worse shape than I was. I could see that things could get worse if I didn't actually try to get better.

My road to recovery has been rocky. It was when I ended up in a treatment center the last (third) time that healing began to set it. I really bonded with some of the providers and the other girls there. The company of the other patients was really welcome and for one of the first times in my life I felt like I wasn't the only "crazy" person I knew. One of the nutritionists at the center would eat lunch with us. She talked with us while we ate and focused a lot on how food was needed to nourish our bodies. She explained the biology and also reminded me that my body had never done anything bad to me and I needed to take care of it – not starve it. I also learned about radical acceptance during treatment and came to start to accept my body and myself.

The psychological aspects of my treatment have been important, but I think the real turning point for me was when I started to take lithium. My mom is from Afghanistan and had very strict Middle Eastern parents, which left her with very strong and adamant beliefs about some things, including medical intervention when it isn't "necessary." But it became obvious that I needed help beyond what therapy or even a treatment center could offer. When I'm not on lithium, my suicidal ideation gets worse. In an interesting way, lithium also helped my eating disorder recovery. Not only could I deal with life better, but I need to eat to take the medication, or I'll get a really upset stomach. Now my mom refers to the "before Emma" and the "after Emma" – before and after lithium. She understands how much medication has helped me (which isn't to say that this is a "cure" for everyone I know).

My relationship with my parents has been through a lot these past couple of years. My dad was always the rock in our family; he was always happy and stable. My mom and I are more similar and used to fight a lot. Through treatment, I've come to understand that when a kid does stupid stuff like develop an addiction to weed, her parents are going to try to protect her and get her to change her behaviors. I hated my parents for getting involved in my life, but I came to respect them and understand their perspective. My parents and I found a way to release our resentments and rebuild our relationship.

When I was consumed by mental illness, I was so angry. I felt anger towards everyone and everything. Recovery has required me to focus more on other people's perspectives and to have empathy for both myself and others. We're all imperfect. I had to forgive myself for being imperfect. I also had to forgive others. Perhaps, the biggest lessons I've learned are that we all struggle, we all need help, and we all deserve love and forgiveness.

Although most of us are unlikely to struggle with our mental health the way that Emma has, many of us have mental health vulnerabilities and may need support to maintain good mental health across our lives. In this chapter, I discuss mental health beyond eating disorders, because our body image and mental health are intricately linked. One inevitably affects the other. I focus on some common mental health problems that are likely to be associated with body image: depression, anxiety, and substance use disorders.

IN THIS CHAPTER YOU'LL LEARN

- about the causes and symptoms of depression, anxiety, and substance use disorders,
- how these mental health problems are associated with body image, and
- treatment options for depression, anxiety, and substance use disorders.

Prevalence

Mental health conditions are incredibly common, especially when it comes to teenagers and young adults these past few years. The pandemic that began in 2020 has had a serious effect on mental health.

Even before the pandemic, there was an increase in mental health concerns among young people. For example, from 2009–2019 the number of 14- to 18-year-olds in the USA who reported feeling sad or hopeless increased by 40%, and those that reported considering suicide increased by 36%. Some research suggests that depression and anxiety doubled among youth around the world during the pandemic; one in four reported symptoms of depression and one in five reported symptoms of anxiety. In fact, mental health issues are leading causes of illness and disability among youth and suicide is a leading cause of death among 15- to 19-year-olds.

Body image is linked with nearly every mental health concern young people experience and is important to understand because of its contributions to mental health in general.

What is depression?

I'm sure you've felt sad before, and maybe even depressed. **Depression** is the most common psychological disorder, and it can be incredibly debilitating, resulting in physical, cognitive, and emotional symptoms. Symptoms may include feeling tired all the time or being unable to sleep, extreme hunger or a lack of appetite, changes in weight, headaches and nausea, or irritability and moodiness. Depression may lead a person to have a difficult time concentrating or completing tasks. Depression is often revealed in feelings of worthlessness and despair, as if life is not worth living. It can be mild and last for a few months, or it may be severe and last for years. Sometimes depression comes and goes across a person's life and sometimes it follows intense life experiences, such as loss of a loved one. Women are much more likely to experience depression than men.

A mental health concern similar to depression that you may have heard about is *bipolar disorder* (aka, manic-depression). An individual who experiences bipolar disorder may alternate between relatively extreme mood states: sadness, low energy, and despair and periods of high energy and mania. It is also typical for people with bipolar disorder to experience periods of "normal" mood, known as *euthymia*. Bipolar disorders may manifest differently for different people and may involve a variety of complex symptoms.

Depression–body image connections

For many years, doctors and scientists have investigated connections between depression and body image. There has appeared to be a chicken and egg problem – which comes first, the depression or body dissatisfaction? It seems that both may be true; depression may cause body dissatisfaction and body dissatisfaction may cause depression. Certain personal qualities and circumstances can lead us to be vulnerable to both.

One recent study suggests that body dissatisfaction leads to depression, but this is more likely to be true for people who are relatively heavy and dissatisfied with their bodies. There is also evidence that puberty is a trigger for both body image and depression, particularly among girls. Puberty leads girls to gain weight and become curvier, but these are not necessarily welcome physical changes for all girls. It also appears that body dissatisfaction and depression are more common among women who have recently had a baby. The complex physical and hormonal changes that accompany pregnancy are likely part of why this occurs. As women age and their bodies continue to change during menopause (a transition that typically begins during women's 40s and may continue into their 50s), body dissatisfaction can contribute to depression.

Not only do physical changes heighten body dissatisfaction and depression; some of us are just more prone to experience both. Some research suggests that people who are more sensitive and prone to worry are more likely to experience body dissatisfaction and depression, while being extraverted may be protective. Further, social support – for example, loving, supportive parents and friends – may prevent or ease body dissatisfaction and depression.

Treatment options for depression

The development of depression (or any mental illness) is not a person's fault. No one wants to suffer from sadness, hopelessness, or any of the other symptoms that accompany depression. Fortunately, there are effective treatments for depression.

If you or someone you know is experiencing depression, the first treatment option worth pursuing is therapy. There are many different types of therapists and approaches to therapy, but what is most important is finding a therapist that you are comfortable with. It is valuable to ask a potential therapist about his or her training, therapeutic orientation, and experience treating depression. There is a great deal of research to suggest that *cognitive behavioral therapy* is among the most effective approaches to treating depression. This form of therapy focuses on changing thoughts (cognitions) and behaviors that contribute to depression. It is a practical approach to therapy in that it focuses on the here and now and how to improve people's current mental health. There is limited (if any) focus on early developmental experiences in cognitive behavioral therapy.

Sometimes the start of therapy can be difficult and people find discussion of their problems challenging and emotional. It is usually important to stick with therapy for several weeks (if not months or years!) to fully reap the benefits. For some people, even a few sessions of therapy may be helpful, however.

Antidepressant medication can be helpful in addition to (or sometimes instead of) therapy. You've probably heard of different brands of antidepressants including Prozac, Zoloft, Lexapro, and Effexor, but there are many other options as well. Different types of antidepressants are designed to affect different neurotransmitters in the brain (e.g., serotonin), which then tend to lead to improvements in mood. Most antidepressants can take at least four weeks to take effect. There are varied benefits and side-effects associated with different antidepressants. Common side-effects include nausea, headaches, and dizziness. Most people adjust to these side-effects and benefit from antidepressants. They may feel more optimistic, less sluggish, and of course, happier. Some people need to try a few antidepressants before they find one that works well for them without bothersome side-effects. People who experience bipolar disorder are often treated with different medications that have a more mood stabilizing effect; this is part of why proper diagnosis is so important. Although many primary care doctors will prescribe antidepressants, for some people it is helpful to meet with a psychiatrist (a medical doctor especially trained in the treatment of mental illness) to discuss symptoms, side-effects, dosage, and different types of medications.

MYTHS AND MISINFORMATION:

People only commit suicide when they are seriously depressed, so it is pretty predictable.

Depression and suicide are most definitely linked. But it isn't accurate to say that suicide is predictable or *always* a result of depression.

Suicide is viewed as a real public health concern and there's some evidence that the rates of suicide have risen in the twenty-first century. According to the Centers for Disease Control and Prevention in the USA, suicide rates increased 30% between 2000 and 2018. Further, suicide is the second leading cause of death in the USA among tweens, teens, and young adults (ages 10–34; of course, this is partly because other causes of death that become prevalent with age such as cancer, stroke, and heart disease are unlikely among young people). Further, according to the World Health Organization, every year more than 800,000 people worldwide die by suicide. Researchers suspect that for every one person who dies by suicide, 25 people attempt suicide. Suicide is preventable and it is important to know the signs to look for.

Depression, schizophrenia, and bipolar disorder are all serious mental illnesses that have been associated with suicidality. Further, substance use disorders, experiences of violence and victimization, and poverty place individuals at risk for suicidality. Improvements to social support systems and increased access to medical and mental health care can reduce the negative effects of poverty, violence, and mental health problems. These sorts of societal changes are difficult to enact, however.

If you or someone you know is struggling with serious mental illness or any of the other risk factors I've mentioned, it is critical to seek help. Both therapy and medication are likely necessary for successful treatment. It is also essential that anyone who may be considering suicide does not have access to guns or medications that may facilitate death by suicide.

How Depressed Are You?

You can assess your own depression the way that scientists measure depression using the Center for Epidemiologic Studies Depression Scale. Read each item and indicate how often you've felt this way **during the past week**.

	Rarely or none of the time (less than 1 day)	Some or little of the time (1–2 days)	Occasionally or a moderate amount of the time (3–4 days)	Most or all of the time (5–7 days)
1. I was bothered by things that usually don't bother me.	0	1	2	3
2. I did not feel like eating, my appetite was poor.	0	1	2	3
3. I felt that I could not shake off the blues even with the help from family or friends.	0	1	2	3
4. I felt like I was just as good as other people.	3	2	1	0
5. I had trouble keeping my mind on what I was doing.	0	1	2	3
6. I felt depressed.	0	1	2	3
7. I felt that everything I did was an effort.	0	1	2	3
8. I felt hopeful about the future.	3	2	1	0
9. I thought my life had been a failure.	0	1	2	3
10. I felt fearful.	0	1	2	3

	Rarely or none of the time (less than 1 day)	Some or little of the time (1–2 days)	Occasionally or a moderate amount of the time (3–4 days)	Most or all of the time (5–7 days)
11. My sleep was restless.	0	1	2	3
12. I was happy.	3	2	1	0
13. I talked less than usual.	0	1	2	3
14. I felt lonely.	0	1	2	3
15. People were unfriendly.	0	1	2	3
16. I enjoyed life.	3	2	1	0
17. I had crying spells.	0	1	2	3
18. I felt sad.	0	1	2	3
19. I felt that people dislike me.	0	1	2	3
20. I could not "get going."	0	1	2	3

To score this measure, sum up your responses. The possible range of scores is 0–60, with higher scores indicating more symptoms of depression. A cutoff score of 16 is often used to indicate mild but significant depression.

EXPERT ADVICE:

Dr. Deborah Sepinwall, clinical psychologist, Providence
Psychological Services, USA

*"As a psychologist, one of the common struggles I explore with my
clients, many of whom are college age, is the difficulty they have
seeing themselves as they are. This is especially true in the context
of body image issues. I am reminded of a bumper sticker I once
saw which read, 'don't believe everything you think.' However
well meaning, our minds are not always our most trusted guides.
Anxiety can be protective and adaptive or excessive and erroneous.
Relating to our misguided thoughts as though they are the same as
the truth creates a downward spiral of negative thinking, reactivity,
and emotional pain. My goal as a therapist is to help my clients
understand the mechanisms of their anxious minds so that they can
become more discerning consumers of it and operate from a place of
greater perspective. In doing so, they are free to live a life in service of
their values and not in service of their anxiety."*

What is anxiety?

Anxiety and depression can go hand in hand (vulnerability to one may
increase vulnerability to the other), but they are distinct mental health
problems. Being anxious about something like speaking in public does not
usually mean that you have anxiety; most people feel anxious before they
speak in public. The experience of anxiety – for example, muscle tension,
a racing heart, trouble concentrating – is familiar to most of us. If you feel
this way often, however, this is obviously a very difficult way to live.

There are different types of anxiety disorders including generalized anxiety
disorder (characterized by heightened anxiety often), panic disorder (characterized by intense panic attacks), phobias (fear of certain situations or
objects), and social anxiety disorder (anxiety pertaining to certain social
situations and interactions). Anxiety disorders share some common symptoms in that they tend to affect people's ability to concentrate and focus,
disrupt sleep, affect eating habits (leading people to eat more or less than
is typical for them), and have a negative impact on people's day-to-day

lives. People suffering from anxiety often experience a great deal of worry and muscle tension and have a difficult time keeping up with their daily routines at home, work, or school.

Anxiety–body image connections

The reasons for a link between body image and anxiety are not entirely clear. It seems most likely that when people feel uncomfortable with themselves, they are more likely to feel that the world is a frightening place. In contrast, a sense of personal security that accompanies feeling comfortable in one's own skin can make the rest of the world a lot more approachable. One large study of adolescents found that body dissatisfaction was associated with later development of generalized anxiety and panic disorder. Other research suggests that anxiety leads to body dissatisfaction.

EXPERT ADVICE:

Dr. Annie Aimé, psychologist and professor at the Université du Québec en Outaouais, Québec, Canada

"In my clinical practice with individuals who report body image concerns, I often notice a relationship with anxiety and depressive symptoms. In fact, people dissatisfied with their body tend to fear what others may think of them or to believe they will be judged for not being able to 'control' their weight. Such fears are sometimes reflective of past body shaming and stigmatizing experiences. Thus, a big part of my work is to help them feel more positive and compassionate about themselves."

Treatment options for anxiety

Similar to depression, anxiety can be treated with therapy, medication, or some combination of the two. Talking with a therapist can be a good first step towards coping with anxiety. A therapist can help you think through what's making you anxious and help you change habits and behaviors that may contribute to your anxiety. Cognitive behavioral therapy (CBT) is one of the therapeutic approaches with the most evidence suggesting its effectiveness for reducing anxiety. CBT can be effective in a relatively short period of time; even as little as a few sessions or a few months' worth of sessions can be very effective. Finding a therapist that a person likes, feels comfortable with, and has some expertise treating anxiety is important to successful treatment.

Often, antidepressants are used to treat anxiety because they are effective treatments with relatively few side-effects. *Anti-anxiety medication* may also prove helpful. Similar to antidepressant medication, anti-anxiety medication seems to alter the chemicals in a person's brain and can make a person feel calmer and, well, less anxious. There are different types of medication that can be used to treat anxiety that is either chronic (generalized anxiety) or more acute (panic attacks). Medication can work wonders to alleviate anxiety, but often needs to be taken consistently across weeks to be effective and can cause side-effects including headaches, upset stomach, and drowsiness.

Stress management techniques, such as yoga and other approaches to mindfulness, can also help to reduce anxiety, but many people need more than this to cope with serious anxiety. It's important that you consider all these options if you are struggling with anxiety and seek out the support that makes the most sense for you. Oftentimes, people may want to "wait and see" if their anxiety or other mental health problems will resolve on their own because it can feel difficult or even embarrassing to ask for help. However, it is best to pursue treatment before a psychological problem becomes worse or affects more aspects of life.

What are substance use disorders?

Addiction, or *substance use disorders*, occur when a person is unable to control their use of legal (for example, alcohol or nicotine – the substance found in cigarettes) or illegal (for example, cocaine) drugs or medication. People with these disorders most likely use the substance they are addicted to daily or even several times a day. They tend to find themselves taking more of the substance over time to get the same "high" that used to come from taking less of it. People who experience addiction spend a lot of time, money, and energy getting their drugs of choice. Their addiction tends to interfere with their relationships with family and friends and may impede their ability to stay in school or hold down a job. People with addictions often engage in unsafe behaviors, such as driving while under the influence, and they may need to keep taking the substance they are addicted to in order to avoid symptoms of physical withdrawal such as nausea, vomiting, body shakes, or body aches. Addiction may lead to accidental death (e.g., a drug overdose, alcohol poisoning, or a car accident) and is linked with a wide range of health problems such as liver disease.

Substance use–body image connections

The link between substance use and body image may not seem obvious, but substance use has been shown to be related to body dissatisfaction. Some scientists have suggested that body dissatisfaction may contribute to a lack of self-respect and self-care, which in turn can lead to everything ranging from disordered eating and sedentary habits to smoking, drinking, and drug use. When people don't value their body – or they've been taught by others that it is not valuable – they may be less inclined to engage in healthy habits and behaviors such as exercise and avoiding substances.

A more direct link between substance use and body image emerges when people use substances to try to alter their bodies, in particular, their muscularity. This is more common among boys and men than girls and women, but the use of supplements and even drugs such as anabolic steroids has become increasingly common in recent years; some research suggests that about 6% of the population uses steroids. Some people use steroids to improve their athletic performance, but others take these drugs *just* to alter the appearance of their bodies. However, at least one recent study indicates that steroid use may not even improve body image over time. Steroids are drugs with the potential to become addictive and, like all drugs, they can do tremendous physical and psychological harm to users.

Although not popularly conceptualized as "drugs," diet pills (i.e., supplements you'd find in a pharmacy or vitamin shop) and prescription medications for weight loss are increasingly used by people who are dissatisfied with their bodies. Research suggests that 8% of adolescents have used these products. However, these pills can pose a number of health risks; side-effects including severe gastrointestinal distress have been reported. The bottom line is that there are good reasons to believe that these products are not safe for use among young people (and, in many cases, people of any age), and although they may not be addictive per se, they may pose physical health risks.

MYTHS AND MISINFORMATION:

If you drink alcohol on the weekends with friends but don't drink during the week, you are just a social drinker and don't have a problem.

Problems with substance use are not always easy to define. There are definitely people who drink socially – a couple of drinks with friends a couple of times a week. However, it is easy to cross the line from social, unproblematic drinking to problematic drinking.

Just because you are drinking only on the weekends, does not mean that you don't have a problem. In particular, young people who compartmentalize their alcohol use – not drinking ever on certain days and drinking heavily on other days – may be more apt to binge drink. **Binge drinking** is defined as four drinks within two hours for women and five drinks within two hours for men. Binge drinking is sometimes referred to as alcohol *misuse* as opposed to *abuse*, but it is associated with neurobiological changes that can have serious consequences. For example, some recent research indicates that adolescents and young adults who drank more literally had smaller brains (especially the frontal lobe, which is responsible for planning, impulse control, problem solving, social interaction, and many other functions that allow individuals to become successful adults). In other words, substance use has the potential to detract from young people's ability to mature into capable, competent adults.

Alcohol consumption can lead to poor choices ranging from the decision to get in a car and drive while intoxicated to the decision to have unprotected sex. Most problematic is the link between binge drinking or alcohol misuse and later life substance use disorders. Young people sometimes think that they can just stop drinking when Monday rolls around or they graduate from college. But addiction doesn't work this way and it's hard to know when misuse will become addiction and a person's life will become seriously derailed.

If you find that drinking adversely affects other aspects of your life, leaves you feeling unwell, or seems to be a means of coping (e.g., with anxiety or body dissatisfaction), be sure you seek out treatment.

Treatment for substance use disorders

Treatment from trained medical professionals, therapists, and even treatment centers is often necessary for a person to recover from an addiction. Although some people have success giving up an addictive substance like alcohol on their own, most people need professional help. For some people, a process of detoxification is necessary at the start of treatment. Detoxification involves ridding the body of the addictive substance and can result in withdrawal symptoms that may need to be treated using medication. Mental health counseling and behavioral therapies are the most common treatments for substance use disorders, whether the substance is alcohol or steroids. The aims of these approaches include understanding what led to the addiction, what contextual factors make the addiction possible, and development of strategies to avoid circumstances that may make avoiding the substance difficult. Therapeutic approaches challenge people with addictions to adopt new patterns of thoughts and behaviors that allow for a healthy, substance-free lifestyle.

In addition to the use of medication to manage withdrawal symptoms such as insomnia, headaches, body tremors, nausea, and irritability, some drugs can be used to manage cravings and to prevent relapse. Sometimes medication for depression or anxiety is an essential component of addiction treatment. If an individual is self-medicating with alcohol or drugs to cope with another mental health problem, whether it be depression or body dysmorphic disorder, treating the other mental health problem is essential.

EXPERT ADVICE:

Dr. Diane Rosenbaum, professor, body image researcher, clinical psychologist, USA

"We often compare our bodies to others that we see – on social media, in everyday situations, in movies, you name it! Focusing on what we believe we lack compared to other people can take a toll on our mental health. Research has shown that this type of thinking is associated with more negative emotions, less satisfaction with our bodies, and disordered eating. However, we have the power to make changes in how we think about our bodies. Loving our bodies, focusing on how much they do for us each day, and appreciating how they function is associated with positive mental health and well-being."

Mental health *is* health

Although this chapter only scratches the surface in its coverage of mental health, hopefully you have picked up on some themes throughout the chapter. Mental health *is* health. Mental health problems are common, partly biologically determined, and no one should be blamed or shamed for developing a mental health issue. Mental health problems are often comorbid, meaning that vulnerability to one (e.g., depression) places a person at risk of vulnerability to other disorders (e.g., eating disorders, substance use disorders). Mental health problems often require professional treatment, just like any other health problem. You deserve to feel good about yourself and positive about your life; if you don't, you deserve help.

MY STORY: Lara Mia, 32 years old, she/her, UK

I think that my body image is better than it used to be, but probably not as good as it could be. In the past, I felt that it was a failure to not feel good about myself, but now I think that feeling neutral is a better expectation for myself. Focusing on body neutrality means just not thinking about my body as much and not letting my dissatisfaction take up so much mental space.

My body dissatisfaction began early in life, and I've struggled with my mental health for many years. I grew up in a very diet-centric household. I have a vivid memory of being only eight years old and learning how to use a Weight Watchers "diet wheel" that showed foods that were "red" (bad), "yellow" (OK sometimes), and "green" (good). Of course, this wasn't what led me to develop an eating disorder, but the categorization and moralization of foods from an early age likely didn't help.

I was diagnosed with severe depression when I was 13 and during treatment for depression it became clear that my relationship with food was dysfunctional. At 15, I experienced inpatient mental health treatment for the first time, and this was when I remember really feeling heard and understood; however, I've struggled with depression and eating disorders for nearly 20 years. For so much of my adulthood, life has felt like hard work.

At 25, I was diagnosed with bipolar disorder. I had experienced mostly depression of varying intensity for years; manic episodes were few and far between, but they became more common as I got older. My fluctuations in my moods were more apparent to others and I had some intense manic episodes in my early 20s. During one of these episodes, I didn't sleep for days, I bought a car, I redecorated parts of my home, I set up a small business on Etsy, and I started to write a children's book. Emerging from that episode was like waking up the morning after a drunken night and trying to piece together what you've done. Since then, medication has helped to stabilize my moods.

I began taking medication in my early teens for my depression, but a change in medication in my 20s helped my moods to remain more even; they fluctuate but much more like a normal person's moods. I can still feel depressed sometimes and feelings of depression definitely impact my body image and self-esteem. I also notice that when I'm depressed, I don't always want to eat because it feels like a lot of work. When I'm manic, I also don't seem to want to eat because I'm distracted and busy doing a million different things. My mood and eating disorders can affect each other in ways that require me to be vigilant and engaged in treatment.

Fortunately, these days my boyfriend is an important source of support in my recovery. It also helps that I've gotten better about talking about my mental health and asking him for help. I wish I could tell my younger self that people want to help – let them help! I also wish I'd understood that the ground can fall away very quickly when disordered eating begins. Getting help right away is important and everyone deserves help. You don't need to be really ill to deserve mental health treatment.

SUMMING UP #MENTALHEALTHMATTERS:

- Depression, anxiety, substance use disorders, and other mental health problems are often associated with body image, and are fairly common, especially among teenagers and young adults.
- Genetic and environmental factors can increase your risk of experiencing a mental health problem. It is not your fault if you have any mental health problem.
- There are effective treatments for depression, anxiety, substance use disorders and other mental health problems. Treatment can include therapy, medication, or both.

FIND OUT MORE:

- General information about mental health can be found at the Centers for Disease Control and Prevention: www.cdc.gov/mentalhealth/learn/index.htm and The Health Foundation's website: www.health.org.uk/publications/reports/improving-children-and-young-peoples-mental-health-services.
- To find a therapist you can search the directory at Psychology Today: www.psychologytoday.com/us (in the USA) and www.psychologytoday.com/gb (in the UK). Be sure to check a therapist's education, background, expertise, and cost before scheduling an appointment.
- Questions to consider before pursuing therapy and additional resources about mental health can be found here: https://therapyhelps.us/resources/.
- References that support this chapter's content and additional resources about mental health can be found on the companion website for this book: www.TheBodyImageBookforLife.com.

CHAPTER 8

IMAGE INFLUENCES

#MirrorLess

> "He that falls in love with himself
> will have no rivals."
>
> – Benjamin Franklin, *American scientist,
> inventor, diplomat, and
> political philosopher*

MY STORY: Sarah Drew, 21 years old, she/her, UK

My body image is much better now than it used to be. I think it still needs work because it can vary a lot from day to day. Some days I wake up and feel hideous and then the next day I feel pretty good.

When I was a teen, my body image concerns were pretty serious. I was diagnosed with body dysmorphic disorder (BDD) about five years ago. I was really obsessive and compulsive and engaged in a lot of body checking and surveillance. Sometimes it was hard for me to leave the house because of my BDD.

I'm sure my BDD emerged, in part, because of the importance placed on appearances in my home growing up. Throughout my childhood, my mom was very concerned with how I looked. I can remember on my first day of school (when I was five) her putting lipstick and mascara on me. Because I was valued for my appearance by others, I came to feel that my appearance was incredibly valuable. It's taken work on my part to appreciate that I have more to offer the world.

I moved out of my parents' house during the pandemic. Not long after that, I met my partner who is from Italy. I hadn't left the UK much before I started dating him, but now I've been to a number of countries with him. I think he's really helped to broaden my horizons, but not just in terms of travel. I've actually found a love of mountain climbing. In the last year, I've moved out of my comfort zone, grown, and settled into myself.

In addition to being in a healthy relationship, both therapy and medication have helped me to manage my BDD. I've benefited from CBT (cognitive behavioral therapy) and group therapy, which I can join online. The online support groups have really helped me to learn that it's not just me – other people have experiences similar to mine. The support from others who understand me has really helped. I also took anti-anxiety medication for about a year. Within a month of starting the medication, I was able to stop most of my obsessive thoughts and compulsive behaviors concerning my appearance. It was really life-changing.

> One thing that's helped me in my body image journey is to learn more of the science behind mental health. I have a better understanding of where my concerns are coming from and I have the tools to reason with negative, intrusive thoughts about body image. I may never be 100% free of these issues but I've come a long way.
>
> If I had to offer others advice for developing a healthy relationship with their body, I'd suggest they get off social media. Getting out into the world and off Instagram has helped me so much. I am so glad not to have social media imagery to compare myself to anymore. I can aim for other types of goals entirely now.

I suspect that some aspects of Sarah's story resonate with many of us. Maybe our moms weren't putting make-up on us for the first day of kindergarten, but probably all of us have had influences in our lives that encourage us to focus on our appearance. The media, in particular social media, and the broader culture that values beauty seemingly above all else, can lead us to focus on our appearance and ways we can improve our appearance.

IN THIS CHAPTER YOU'LL LEARN

- all about appearance ideals,
- why these ideals can be so harmful to body image, and
- how to protect your body image from these potentially negative influences.

How do you know what is socially desirable in terms of your appearance? How do you know that clear skin and large breasts are viewed as attractive (for female-identifying individuals)? How do you know that being tall and muscular is viewed as attractive (for male-identifying individuals)? Maybe no one that you know personally ever explicitly told you that you should whiten your teeth or straighten (or curl) your hair. Instead, you developed an understanding of these beauty ideals from the larger culture you live in, through various forms of the media and advertising.

What are the ideals?

People who live in a similar geographic place end up valuing the same appearance ideals, and as we communicate across countries more and more, thanks to the media, these appearance ideals have become more similar around the world. Although some have argued that there may be evolutionary value in maintaining certain physical features – or "cues" to physical health and youth – it seems pretty obvious that most appearance ideals are cultural creations.

For men, height, muscularity, a body build that is somewhat triangular (with broad shoulders), and angular facial features have been consistently viewed as attractive. For women, a slender build, an hourglass shape, and relatively large breasts have been consistently viewed as attractive. For both men and women, symmetrical facial features, clear skin, and shiny (but not oily) hair are usually perceived as desirable. At different times and places, a variety of specifics – ranging from how people wear their hair, to what sort of clothes are fashionable, and how people accessorize their bodies – change.

Changing ideals

Although some elements of appearance ideals seem pretty constant, part of what is so insidious about these ideals is that some aspects are constantly evolving. In other words, even if any of us mere mortals could embody these ideals, it's likely that they'd change by the time we got there. When I first started to do body image research in the 1990s, thin was definitely in. Arguably thin has been in, for women especially, for all of the twentieth and twenty-first centuries to varying degrees. A growing focus on physical female strength emerged later in the twentieth century, although women were expected to be more toned than muscular.

The twenty-first century ushered in the social media age, with MySpace launching in 2003 and Facebook following in 2004. A more "fit ideal" became part of social media "fitspiration" posts and videos (even though it turns out fitspiration is rarely inspirational; more on that in Chapter 11) and a "slim thick" or curvy ideal followed for women admiring the voluptuous bodies of celebrities like Kim Kardashian, Beyoncé, and Rihanna. Most recently, a more slender, but muscular ideal seems to be making a comeback. (I'm not sure how both are achieved at the same time for most of us!) With greater access to appearance ideals in social media and other online venues, what's popular and most prized seems to only evolve faster.

When the "slim thick" trend took hold and attracted some research attention, the results of one study surprised some people. Women viewed slim thick figures as even more of a source of angst than just thin female figures. But why wouldn't they? Women report both appreciating the unlikelihood of achieving this figure and the motivation to try to do so through diet and exercise. And yet, most women will never have large breasts and bums with a tiny waist without surgery. In other words, most appearance ideals remain totally unachievable for most people, so why *wouldn't* this seem depressing?

When it comes to changing ideals for male-identifying individuals, the twentieth and twenty-first centuries have been all about muscles and hair (or lack thereof!). When researchers have asked men about their ideal body shape, they report being most concerned about being tall and lean but muscular in their arms, chest, and abdomen. Across the twentieth century, male-identifying celebrities, media images, and even children's toys have grown more muscular. For example, researchers have measured action figures from the 1970s and 1980s compared with action figures created in the 2000s. Batman, Superman, GI Joe, The Hulk, and Spiderman all gained a significant amount of muscle across approximately 25 years. When scaled to the dimensions of a typical man, the average of these action figures used to have a chest circumference that was 115 cm, but now they have an average chest circumference of 179 cm. This is in contrast to the average man, who is more likely to have a chest circumference between 97 and 115 cm. Men also report greater attention to general grooming practices in the twenty-first century and an increasing likelihood of removing body hair; in recent studies, 41% of men reported removing some of their body hair and 51% reported grooming their pubic hair.

EXPERT ADVICE:

Dr. Kristina Holqvist Gattario, psychologist and body image scientist, University of Gothenburg, Sweden

"Many people wonder how much they should care about their appearance. Not caring at all may seem somewhat strange, but caring too much can be viewed as superficial. Depending on who you spend time with, there may be different expectations for how much, when, and why you should work on your appearance. It's not easy to navigate these expectations! It can feel like a no-win scenario. What's most important is to be your authentic self."

Appearance ideals affect body image

You may be thinking something along the lines of, "I know what you are talk-ing about in terms of beauty ideals and trends, but they don't affect me," or "How do these appearance ideals lead so many people to want to change their appearance?" It's easy to think that we're not easily influenced, but most of us *do* fall prey to wanting to fit in and look good according to current trends.

Decades of research supports the idea that we learn about appearance ideals by watching others around us, or *social learning*. We learn how we *should* look and we act accordingly, whether that means buying certain clothes or adopting certain exercise habits. Important research that has taken place in Fiji, a remote island in the South Pacific, helps to make this clear. The inhabitants in Fiji didn't have access to broadcast television until the mid-1990s. Harvard researcher Ann Becker studied Fijian teenage girls before the introduction of television and found that body image concerns and eating disorders were nearly nonexistent. Fijians valued larger bodies and did not diet or adjust their eating behaviors to try to lose weight. Three years after the introduction of television, however, eating disorder symptoms were much more likely and 74% of the girls reported that they sometimes felt "too big or fat." This most definitely is not conclusive evi-dence that watching television (replete with thin, attractive people) *causes* eating disorders, but it does suggest the potential power of media exposure in terms of how we feel about our bodies and related eating behaviors.

Another early, informative study looked at tween and teen girls' exposure to magazines. I appreciate that many of you reading this book probably don't read magazines yourself; you see them in a store but don't buy them because you can get all the information you want online or from social media. In the late 1990s, however, magazines like *Vogue* or *In Style* offered celebrity and fashion information. It turns out, they also fueled body dissatisfaction. In fact, this research found that the more time girls spent reading fashion magazines the more they endorsed thin beauty ideals and wanted to lose weight. Similar studies have found that women who read fashion magazines don't just expe-rience body dissatisfaction after looking at all of those glossy, photoshopped pictures of beautiful people; they also report feeling depressed and angry.

Although a lot of the research examining how appearance ideals in the media damage body image have focused on girls and women, the research that has examined boys and men reveals similar results. Fitness magazines for men have been found to be especially detrimental to boys' and men's body image and this is especially the case when it comes to magazines directed at gay men. These magazines tend to feature more shirtless, muscular, "perfect" men than those directed at straight men. It's somewhat ironic that these magazines are often called "Men's Health" or something similar and yet they seem to *not* be good for *mental* health.

As the media has evolved, the research has tried to keep up. Most of the current research examining appearance ideals and body image focuses on the role of social media. I'll discuss some of what's been learned most recently below.

Q&A:

Everyone knows that real breasts come in different shapes and sizes. Why are all the breasts we see on celebrities and influencers biggish and perky and perfect? How are all of us ladies not supposed to want breast implants?

You're not alone if you've ever experienced breast dissatisfaction. The majority of women are dissatisfied with their breasts. That's the takeaway from a cross-country study of almost 19,000 women from 40 different countries. Nearly half (47.5%) wanted larger breasts while 23% wanted smaller breasts. That leaves a minority of women actually satisfied with their breasts.

Celebrities and influencers may seem to have enviable breasts, but your desire for breast implants is likely a result of more than just media influences. The results of another set of experiments, which had a woman wear different bras to enhance breast size to varying degrees, found that as the woman's breasts increased, so did the number of men who approached her in a nightclub or bar. In other words, increasingly bigger breasts garnered increasingly more attention. It's no wonder that women who are dissatisfied with their breasts often pursue cosmetic surgery. Since 2006, breast augmentation has been the most popular cosmetic procedure in the USA, with nearly 5% of all women in the USA having this surgery.

My advice is to appreciate that what you are feeling is perfectly reasonable given the social world you experience. It's also important to keep in mind that we all tend to focus in on specific body parts we perceive to be flawed rather than viewing our overall appearance, but changing any one body part is unlikely to be the recipe for happiness. I discuss cosmetic surgery and the likelihood – or not! – of it improving body image more in the next chapter.

Social media and body image

It's possible that the question I am asked the most when journalists (and parents!) speak with me is: *What is social media doing to our body image?*

This concern about social media is understandable; research indicates that teenagers in the USA spend an average of 7 hours per day on screens, and a lot of that time is on social media or watching videos. Adults aren't immune to the lure of social media, with average use of around 2 hours per day (in the USA and EU). More than half of the world's population uses social media!

Of course, it is not just the amount of time, but the content that is concerning. Many people only share posts and videos that present themselves in the best possible light, and use filters and editing to share the **highlight reels** of their lives. In other words, we are all inundated with visual "proof" that other people have more beautiful, exciting, and glamorous lives than we do.

We *learn* from social media and we *compare*. We wonder why we aren't better looking, we desire to change our appearance – and we desire to change our lives to be more exciting and glamorous. It is completely normal to make these sorts of comparisons, or as psychologists call them, **social comparisons**. Most people engage in social comparison. However, body image research from the past few years suggests that when individuals compare themselves to images they see on social media, they are vulnerable to experiencing body dissatisfaction and even disordered eating. One recent investigation of tween girls even found that body dissatisfaction may increase social media checking. In other words, a vicious cycle can develop whereby social media may be damaging to body image, which then increases time spent on social media. These negative effects seem to be especially likely among people vulnerable to anxiety and depression. Although social media may be a social outlet, it is not necessarily a positive social outlet for those struggling with their mental health.

It's important to recognize that people use social media in different ways and this is relevant to understanding any one person's likelihood of experiencing negative consequences of social media use. In some of my own research at Rutgers University, my colleagues and I have found that when tweens, teens, and young adults use social media to follow appearance- and fitness-related content (e.g., make-up tutorials, fitness videos) they are much more likely to experience body dissatisfaction than if they are using social media mostly as a communication tool to connect with their friends. The number of platforms or even the amount of time on social media may not impact body image or mental health nearly as much as the types of uses and content viewed on social media.

Pros and Cons of Social Media

Some research suggests that a social media "break" has advantages for our psychological health. But obviously people wouldn't use social media if they didn't think they were getting something out of it. It may be valuable to think about whether or not there are more pros or cons to your social media use. Here are some factors you may want to consider:

PROS	CONS
Connecting with people	Distraction from other important activities
Learning new things	Advertising can be annoying and misleading
Reading the news	Social comparison can be distressing
Entertainment	Unrealistic images and lifestyles are everywhere
Enjoyment	The focus is on external/appearances of people and not their substance
A creative outlet	Emphasis is on products and consumer culture
Meeting new people	

MYTHS AND MISINFORMATION:

You will lose contact with friends if you aren't on social media.

Many people – kids and adults alike – connect with others using social media. It's easy to feel like you'll miss out on these connections if you don't use social media or don't use a particular type of social media. You've probably heard this referred to as *FOMO* – fear of missing out. It turns out that you may experience *less* FOMO if you spend *less time* on social media.

A recent psychological study investigated college students' anxiety, depression, and concerns about being left out of activities. Half of the students who participated in the study used social media as they always had, and half were required to go on social media for a maximum of 30 minutes per day. The students who reduced their social media use to no more than 30 minutes per day for 3 weeks were less anxious and depressed and reported *less* FOMO. The scientists who conducted this study believe that when these young adults spent less time on social media, they engaged in fewer social comparisons. Fewer comparisons with others made them feel *better* about their own lives and less concerned about what others were doing!

If your friends use Snapchat to make plans and you delete the Snapchat app from your phone, you may feel worried that you won't be included in their plans. However, if your friends are truly good friends, they won't have a problem calling you or sending you a text instead when they are making plans. The science seems to suggest that fear of missing out isn't a great reason to use social media.

Celebrities and influencers

Who do you follow on social media? I bet it's not just your friends and family – or even people you know personally. I bet you follow at least some celebrities and influencers. In 2024, some of the most followed celebrities in the world included Cristiano Ronaldo, Selena Gomez, Taylor Swift, Lionel Messi, Ariana Grande, and Dwayne "The Rock" Johnson. Some of the most followed influencers include Huda Kattan (aka, HudaBeauty), Zach King, Addison Rae, and Khaby Lame. Together, these influencers have over 200 million followers. What do these celebrities and influencers have in common? They are beautiful people that shape our understanding of how we should look.

Some research suggests that we'd be better off *not* following celebrities and influencers on social media. In one experiment, viewing celebrities was found to be associated with negative mood and body dissatisfaction. As some researchers put it, "exposure to celebrity images, appearance comparison, and celebrity worship are associated with maladaptive consequences for individuals' body image." Interestingly, other research suggests that when young girls (11–14 years old) follow celebrities on social media they not only seem to check social media more often but also to experience more depression and anxiety. It seems likely that girls look to the world of celebrities when they are feeling insecure, anxious, or depressed to learn about what is cool or fashionable, and unfortunately, seeing celebrities only increases their distress.

Comparing ourselves to celebrities and influencers on social media is also problematic because of the highly sexualized nature of this content. If you check out Ronaldo's Instagram page, you'll find a man with his shirt off, sporting an eight-pack (I checked so you don't have to; there's not much I won't do to write a good book!). Kim Kardashian shows off a lot of both her breasts and her bum. These celebrities are sharing content that is self-objectifying. **Objectification theory** suggests that people often view themselves and others as objects because they are treated as objects valued for appearance and not substance. **Self-objectification** occurs when we (consciously or not) appreciate that others are valued for their appearance and we internalize others' views of our own bodies and value ourselves for our appearance. Basically, in anticipation of being treated more favorably if we display our most attractive self, we display our most attractive self. When it comes to social media, there's a reason that celebrities and influencers show off their bodies; the currency on these platforms is followers and "likes" which come more easily when provocative images are shared.

Appearance-Related Social Media Consciousness Scale

When researchers want to understand people's investment in appearance culture and how affected they seem to be by media and other social messages, they sometimes use this questionnaire. See the scoring information below to gain a sense of how much you're under the influence of appearance culture.

	Never	Almost Never	Rarely	Sometimes	Often	Almost Always	Always
(1) When people take pictures of me, I think about how I will look if the pictures are posted on social media.	1	2	3	4	5	6	7
(2) I think about how specific parts of my body will look when people see my pictures on social media.	1	2	3	4	5	6	7
(3) Even when I'm alone, I imagine how my body will look in a social media picture.	1	2	3	4	5	6	7
(4) During the day, I spend time thinking about how attractive I might look when people see pictures of me on social media.	1	2	3	4	5	6	7
(5) I try to guess how people on social media will react to my physical appearance in my pictures.	1	2	3	4	5	6	7
(6) My attractiveness in pictures is more important than anything else I do on social media.	1	2	3	4	5	6	7

	Never	Almost Never	Rarely	Sometimes	Often	Almost Always	Always
(7) When I go to social events, I care more about looking attractive in pictures people might post on social media than I care about having a fun time.	1	2	3	4	5	6	7
(8) If an unattractive picture of me is posted on social media, I feel bad about myself.	1	2	3	4	5	6	7
(9) I look at pictures of myself on social media again and again.	1	2	3	4	5	6	7
(10) I zoom into social media pictures to see what specific parts of my body look like.	1	2	3	4	5	6	7
(11) If someone takes a picture of me that might be posted on social media, I ask to look at it first to make sure I look good.	1	2	3	4	5	6	7
(12) Before I post pictures on social media, I crop them or apply filters to make myself look better.	1	2	3	4	5	6	7
(13) If someone takes a picture of me that might be posted on social media, I pose in a particular way so that I'll look as attractive as possible.	1	2	3	4	5	6	7

Instructions for scoring: Sum all item answers and then divide by 13. In research using this measure among women, the average score was found to range from approximately 3.5–4.5. The average score was found to be closer to 3 among men.

Get out from under the influence

Once you understand that social media use may not benefit your body image, you may reasonably want to buffer yourself from these potential negative effects. To help you think about steps you can take to keep different forms of social media (or any media, for that matter) from affecting you, keep the acronym **FACE** (Filter, Avoid, Careful of comparisons, Evaluate) in mind.

Filter

I'm not referring to filters in a photo editing tool or Snapchat. Body image researchers refer to something called *protective filtering*, which is essentially filtering out influences in your life that negatively affect your body image. Because most forms of social media feature content that's curated based on your own interests and usage, you can shape your social media world to be protective. This might require unfollowing influencers, celebrities, and possibly even friends who embody values contrary to your development of a positive body image. Instead of engaging with those on social media who focus extensively on their own appearance – and cosmetics or clothing that they feel enhance it – you could engage with body positivity activists, mental health professionals, and others who offer tools and advice to aid you in your journey towards self-acceptance.

Avoid

We all need media breaks. Be sure you avoid your phone, tablet, or computer, for some time every day. Eat dinner without texting your friends. Do homework or work for your job without videos playing in the background. Sleep without the distraction of alerts coming from your devices. Turn alerts off so that you aren't always being distracted by your phone beeping. Remove apps from your phone to keep you from spending too much time on them. One recent study confirms the importance of this time away from media. In a study of adults in their late 20s, participants first completed surveys measuring their mental health. Then, half were asked to stop using social media for one week while the other half continued to use social media as usual. At the end of the week, the group who had a social media break was less likely to be depressed and anxious and reported better overall well-being compared to their original survey scores. Although it can be difficult to disengage from social media, most people report it gets easier across time – and there are real benefits to spending less time with our screens.

Careful of comparisons

As I've already mentioned, one of the ways that the media can be most harmful is by prompting us to compare ourselves with celebrities and other unrealistic portrayals of attractive people. Remember that these are not appropriate people to compare yourself with! The images that prompt social comparisons are usually of adults who have teams of people – fitness trainers, chefs, make-up artists, and professional photographers – who help make them look good. Most of us do not have teams of people working on our image, nor is this necessary. It's also helpful to remember that it's essentially celebrities' and influencers' *job* to look good. And they have a lot of help, so the people we see in the media rarely look like themselves in real life. And even if some of them do, it's worth recognizing that another's beauty doesn't detract from your own. Maybe it's even better to be in a position where our worth is not centered on our appearance and we aren't going to lose our jobs for not looking a certain way or for just getting older.

Evaluate

Not only do celebrities, athletes, and influencers have teams of people helping them to look good, photographers and publicists are also editing (and in some cases, distorting) images to the point that these people don't even look like themselves. Why? In the places you see these people – Instagram, TikTok, or the Internet – they are very likely trying to sell you a product or promote themselves and their "brand." Be skeptical and evaluate what you see. Why does the person look the way they do? How realistic is the image? What values and lifestyles are being presented? Why was this message created? What is for sale?

It's important that we not only evaluate what we see in the media but challenge it. In fact, one study suggests that challenging appearance ideals in the media (e.g., "does she look like that in real life?" and "he must have to spend a lot of time at the gym – and not with his friends and family – to look like that") helps people to disengage from appearance-centric media. Further, it seems pretty well established that *media literacy* – essentially adhering to the recommendations presented in this chapter – reduces the negative impact of social media use in general.

EXPERT ADVICE:

Julia Dawn, body-positive TikTokker (@lovejuliadawn)

"I felt truly represented for the first time in my life when I downloaded TikTok. Seeing people of all different shapes and sizes glowing with confidence was pretty world changing for me. I thought confidence only came from weight loss, and I didn't think I could love (or even accept) myself at the size I was. But I had never seen someone with my body type in the media and it was so healing and empowering to see beauty in a larger body. My mindset shifted and I saw that confidence comes from within. Soon after, I started making my own body-positive content, hoping to help others feel seen and heard, just like I felt. Even though it's easy to feel alone in your struggles – most of us have body insecurities. The first step to confidence is acknowledging those insecurities, accepting them, and then learning to love them. Your self-love journey can take time, but there's a whole community out there who are healing with you and cheering you on!"

Q&A:

I feel like advertisers should have to tell people when they edit or photoshop an image. Why aren't there laws about this sort of "truth in advertising"?

Some countries have adopted laws prohibiting advertisers from editing images without labeling them as edited. A law went into effect in France requiring a "*photographie retouchée*" label in 2017. In 2021, Norway adopted a similar law requiring both advertisers and influencers to label retouched images. As of time of writing, a "body image bill" has been proposed in the UK as well.

Of course, I love the idea of advertisers and influencers either being required to share realistic pictures with the world or indicate that they probably aren't realistic because they are edited. However, some research has tried to sort out how effective these labels are and this is where the bad news comes in. They aren't effective. Experiments have shown people pictures of models with no labels, labels saying the image is edited, and even labels with other information (e.g., the model is underweight). Seeing pictures of models increases body dissatisfaction and labels don't stop this from happening.

Where does this leave you? You'll have to remind yourself that when you're seeing images of models, celebrities, influencers, and even athletes, nearly *all of the time* they have been edited. Stop comparing what you are seeing to yourself because what you are seeing isn't real!

Consumer culture

An important component of becoming media literate and working on our own body image is appreciating that so many of the messages we receive about our appearance are driven by advertisements and our consumer culture. The global beauty and personal care market was estimated to be worth $511 billion in 2021 and is projected to be worth $716 billion by 2025. (This doesn't include health and wellness products, but takes into account skincare, cosmetics, and fragrances.)

This can be confusing because a lot of appearance-related messaging is disguised as wellness and self-care messaging: It's important to paint your fingernails because it's self-care. It's important to buy certain face and body wash with particular fragrances because it's self-care. Bubble bath is self-care. Face masks are self-care. Sometimes shopping is even discussed as self-care (retail therapy!).

Maybe some of these beauty regimens do feel like self-care to you, and there's nothing wrong with that. But if you don't enjoy them and they feel obligatory they probably are not really going to contribute to your sense of taking care of yourself. Instead, you are contributing to the beauty industry's profits and the maintenance of impossible appearance ideals.

Body diversity

One antidote to the body dissatisfaction that seems to be fed by the media is the inclusion of greater diversity in the media. We probably like to think that we can keep our own biases in check and logically realize that the appearance ideals we see in the media are not realistic. Yet the more we are exposed to these ideals the more they seem, well, ideal and what we should be striving for.

Researchers have conducted experiments to see how our perceptions change as the images we see change. In one study, the more times participants saw thin bodies, the more likely they were to rate "normal" sized bodies as "overweight." In contrast, when participants saw images of more "normal" bodies, they viewed these bodies as actually "normal"! The number and type of bodies depicted in these images seemed to directly influence people's perceptions of bodies. Other studies tend to support these findings; viewing unrealistically thin models fuels body dissatisfaction, whereas viewing more relatable, similar-to-us models doesn't.

The body positivity movement is credited with challenging appearance ideals and presenting more body diversity on social media. In one analysis, over 90% of bodies in body-positive posts featured "normal" to "heavy" people and 40% featured physical features that deviated from appearance ideals, such as cellulite. These images typically feature text promoting body acceptance and diversity (i.e., celebrating "normal" bodies). Some have expressed concern that this messaging may leave people feeling bad if they can't embrace their cellulite or rolls of fat. Others have expressed concern that presenting heavier people in positive images could *promote* weight gain. There is no evidence to support the idea that body diversity in the media "glorifies" or contributes to larger body sizes. Further, although it may be challenging to "love your body" no matter what size or shape it is, some body image researchers have suggested that the opposite is far worse.

EXPERT ADVICE:

Lenox Tillman, former model and America's *Next Top Model* contestant

"When I was younger, I was focused on external approval instead of internal approval. Since working hard on improving this, I have felt so much less stress about comparing myself, how I look, and what others think. Now I care what I want to wear, what I want to eat, what I think about my body, and how much I love it. Bodies are neutral to me now and my perception has totally changed since I was a young teen. This didn't happen overnight, and it wasn't a linear process, but actively catching unhealthy thoughts and replacing them with a kinder, more accepting perception of yourself and others makes a big difference over time. Your body works so hard to have you here and speaking kindly of it goes a long, long way in boosting your internal approval."

Body neutrality, redux

I discussed the concept of body neutrality in Chapter 1, but it is worth bringing up here again because an important tool in counteracting the effects of the media and appearance ideals is to just focus and value appearances less. This may be especially true if you find yourself stressed by the prospect of loving your body with all its flaws. A body-neutral perspective allows for any and all people to be beautiful because the focus is on inner beauty and not physical beauty. It can reduce the pressure to try to feel positive about or love aspects of your body that you currently might not. Instead of trying to convince yourself that you love your entire physical self, you can make a decision to not care as much about every aspect of your physical appearance.

You may not care that you are not a gifted musician, talented athlete, or charismatic public speaker. If you don't expect these things of yourself and don't care that you don't possess these qualities, you'll spend less time and energy thinking about them. Body neutrality is similar. What if you just didn't even expect yourself to have defined abs? What if you left worries about fashionable clothes to others and didn't stress about your own attire? Of course, you can choose not to play music or sports, but you can't avoid having an appearance.

One way to adopt elements of body neutrality is to utilize an approach often incorporated into cognitive behavioral therapy, called **cognitive defusion**. Cognitive defusion refers to observing negative thoughts, in this case about your appearance, but not allowing yourself to get caught up in them. Try to acknowledge thoughts such as, "I wish I was taller," but try to be emotionally detached from them. Try to accept that there's nothing wrong with wanting to be taller and there's nothing wrong with you because you aren't taller. Body neutrality allows you to know yourself and accept yourself as you are and encourages you to not dwell on body image concerns.

MY STORY: Lucas Michael, 21 years old, he/him, Spain

I have mixed feelings about my body. Some days I'm happy with it and feel comfortable with the fact that the only body I have is a decent one. Other days, I look in the mirror and wish something or other was different. As I become older, these negative thoughts are becoming less and less frequent as I come to terms with the fact that this bit of meat is mine for life!

I do care about what I eat, but not necessarily enough to change anything about my (imperfect) habits. I would like to be a healthy eater and I definitely feel better about myself when I've had a healthy meal, but as a university student it's sometimes hard to eat well. I've always had a high metabolism and I've always been pretty active. However, during the coronavirus pandemic I started to be more self-conscious as I was way less active and eating a lot more snacks and noticed a little more belly on me.

I love skateboarding and tennis purely because of the happiness they bring to me, although I like to feel like I've done my body some good at the end of the day and got my heart pumping. However, I also work out at home with weights and do abs and stuff. I would say this is purely for aesthetic reasons, although sometimes it's enjoyable. Mostly, I just do this because I don't want to have skinny arms and would prefer to see myself as sexy as opposed to skinny.

I'm probably more self-conscious about my body hair than I am about my arms, though. I remember in school we had swimming lessons when I was about 14, and none of the other boys had any real body hair, but I had hairy legs and arms, and even a little on my chest. Being different than everyone else definitely made me self-conscious, as it drew unwanted attention to my body. It's also going to sound silly, but once I read a tweet from this girl I barely knew who said something along the lines of "how could anyone find hairy chests attractive." Having a very hairy chest myself, that really stuck with me. This must have been three years ago but I still remember the girl and the tweet. Even though my girlfriend says she likes it, so it shouldn't matter what others think, I'm still conscious of the fact that many people think it's ugly which makes it more uncomfortable to be around people shirtless, as I don't know which side they are on! You never see hairy guys on TV or social media! Just ads for "manscaping" razors or wax strips. All of this sends me the message that my body hair is ugly.

I want young people to realize that everything they see nowadays is a lie! What I mean by this is that we are bombarded by "sexy" people with their "perfect" bodies and the women are always wearing make-up or have gotten Botox or fake eyelashes, fake nails, fake boobs, fake everything! The modern perfect body is fake. I think it's wrong. Personally, I like the natural look. I think the key to a good body is just to be healthy but for your own sake. It's good to feel good, but this comes from within. If you compare yourselves to others and to society's beauty standards then you're always going to want more and to want to be "better," but you'll never actually reach that. I know stunning girls who just want to be like a girl who is even more stunning. No one is happy these days. The expectations are unnatural and I just wish everyone would take a step back and say "Hey, we are all actually pretty beautiful already." I really wish society put less importance on beauty and a bit more on real things like emotions and how we treat each other. Life is not a beauty contest.

SUMMING UP #MIRRORLESS:

- We all learn about appearance ideals from the people and culture that surround us.
- Appearance ideals are overwhelmingly unrealistic and can be incredibly damaging to our body image, especially when they come at us repeatedly across the day in our social media feeds.
- General media literacy, changing our approach to how we view the media, and working to value appearance ideals less can help us to protect and improve our body images.

FIND OUT MORE:

- *Growing Up in Public: Coming of Age in a Digital World* by Dr. Devorah Heitner (Penguin Random House, 2023) is directed mostly at parents, but is an accessible resource for anyone interested in learning more about how technology impacts our daily lives.
- The *Techno Sapiens* newsletter written by Dr. Jacqueline Nesi is great for research-based commentary on social media and media use in general. It can be found online at https://technosapiens.substack.com.
- *Amaze.org* is a cool web page with health lessons intended for teens (https://amaze.org). There are lessons specifically about social media and media literacy that you may want to check out.
- *Common Sense Media* (www.commonsensemedia.org) provides research about social media use among teens. It is always being updated with new reports on everything from the effect of the pandemic on media use to race and ethnicity presentation in the media.
- For references that support this chapter's content and relevant resources see this book's web page: www.TheBodyImageBookforLife.com.

WHAT IF

 YOU

ALREADY

HAVE

EXACTLY

WHAT

YOU

NEED?

CHAPTER 9

SELF-"IMPROVEMENT"

#YouAreNotAProject

> "Life is not a problem to be solved,
> but a reality to be experienced."
>
> – Søren Kierkegaard,
> *Danish existential philosopher*

My feelings about my body are sorta confusing. I definitely think there's an expectation that Black women are supposed to look a certain way. It turns out that, mostly due to genetics, I do fit the body type aesthetic desired for Black women and I'm thick (aka, curvy). This has led to a lot of unwanted attention and sexualization from an early age. By 11 or 12 years old I was catcalled on the street for things that were very much out of my control. I feel as though it can be confusing because I didn't really ask to look like this and yet everybody who compliments my body saying things like "oh I wish I had your body" does not understand how much stress and even pressure comes with looking how I do. I feel as though because I do fit this body stereotype, I have to be a certain way, act a certain way, and dress a certain way to adhere to the stereotype.

The ideals for Black women are tricky. You have to hit this happy medium between being thick but not so thick that you are considered "fat." We have to be perfect in terms of having boobs (but they're not too big), have a small waist, and have an ass (but it can't be too big or else it's gonna look crazy). In the Black community big lashes and getting acrylics (getting your nails done) are a huge thing as is having your hair done. It's kinda like you have to hit every single item on some list. Where did this list come from? Who made this list?

Another thing that is confusing to me is that my looks evoke completely different reactions from white people versus Black people. It almost makes me question myself, "how am I supposed to be?" I feel like I've definitely changed for the better in terms of figuring out who I am and what I want to be but it's definitely difficult because I grew up going to a predominantly white school and trying to fit in there and now I go to a college where I spend time around mostly Black people. I was dressing to fit the white male gaze – Uggs, yoga pants, and skinny jeans. I was always asking my mom for sew-ins. A sew-in is when you take a straight hair extension and you sew it in so it blends with your hair so you have the look of long straight hair. I begged my mom for sew-ins and I would never get them so I just settled for straight braids. My family is from Jamaica, so in terms of Black American culture and knowing about wigs and sew-ins and all the stuff, I really didn't know as much compared to a Black woman who has grown up in Black America all of her life. My mom gets her hair relaxed. Getting your hair relaxed is basically using a chemical solution that comes in a little box that you mix together and it sits on your hair, when it burns you wash it out and then your hair is straight. Dealing with a mom who only relaxed her hair was hard because I wanted to explore other styling options as opposed to just braids. It was kinda difficult. The period of time when I had braids and a bunch of different hairstyles I was trying to figure out what worked for me and what I liked because I really didn't know.

I have come to appreciate that there is a lot of work that goes into adhering to beauty standards that were set by white people. If you are trying to get a wig, like a nice wig that is going to last you, you'll have to spend $400 + . To install it costs another $250. Installing a wig involves braiding your natural hair down underneath so they can braid it back, cornrow it, basically just get it flat so when they put the wig cap over it (the cap is the same color as your skin tone or if it's not you can use make-up and blend it to be your skin tone) you cut the cap and form it to the space of your head and you blend it down, then you have to get an adhesive (hair glue) so that everything blends seamlessly. After that you have to do your edges (baby hairs). If someone installs your wig for you it will probably take maybe 2 hours to install and an hour to style it. However, if you're doing this yourself it will probably take 4–5 hours. Wig maintenance is a lot because naturally you sweat, wash your face, you sleep, all of this can cause your wig to lift so you have to constantly reapply the glue, redo your edges to make sure that it lays flat. Wig lifting can happen at any time within however long you have your wig. It's a constant source of anxiety knowing *at any point in the day your wig could lift. Styling a wig before bed includes using rollers or braiding it so it's prepped for the next day.*

The perception of what is "natural" for Black women isn't actually natural. People don't want real, natural beauty, they want a version of reality that still adheres to beauty standards. You can't win because even when people say to "go natural" you don't know how natural to be. I think my advice for younger girls is to try to find your comfort zone. If you keep trying to make yourself look how others want you to, you'll never feel comfortable in your own skin.

It's hard to not care about how you look. Nearly everyone does, to some extent. Please don't be upset with yourself for caring. You receive all sorts of messages every day saying that it's appropriate, important, even essential to care about your appearance. I appreciated how honest Serenity was about wanting to explore her personal style and yet how she appreciated that some of what she did in the name of beauty was time-consuming, expensive, and even somewhat arbitrary.

IN THIS CHAPTER YOU'LL LEARN

- why most of us tend to focus on our appearance as much as we do,
- what the science says about different types of appearance "improvements," and
- how to think through your options when it comes to modifying your appearance.

Scroll through your social media accounts or YouTube videos and you're likely to see advertisements, influencers, or even friends telling you that there are things about yourself you should fix. You need new clothes! Adopt this year's latest hairstyle! Your skin will look better if you try a new cosmetic or cream! Have we mentioned these cute new shoes?! This sort of messaging often undermines how we feel about ourselves, and it is often intended to have this effect. What we really experience is: You're not OK the way you are! You'll be happier if you could improve how you look! You need to buy stuff!

But will we actually feel better about ourselves or experience any benefits to our lives if we change our appearance? You may be surprised by the research.

Adaptive appearance investment

Appearance investment is a term used by body image scientists to describe the amount of time, energy, money, and other resources people invest in their appearance. *Adaptive appearance investment* refers to investments that are safe and contribute to a positive body image. Basic grooming practices and the selection of clothes we like are usually considered adaptive appearance investments. Most people would probably consider hair coloring, waxing (to remove hair), and nail polish adaptive appearance investments because they are low risk, relatively low cost, and often contribute to individuals' sense of style or comfort in their own skin. Some appearance investments, such as appropriate attire (whatever that may be depending on where you spend time, where you work, etc.), are somewhat expected in most social settings and workplaces. Some of this is a matter of hygiene, while some may symbolize respect for institutions, organizations, colleagues, or clients. Showing up to work wearing pajamas and sporting a disheveled head of hair may lead coworkers to question your mental health.

Not all appearance investments are adaptive, however. In 2020, the beauty and personal care industry was valued at $93.1 billion in the USA. According to the same web page (Statistica.com), this is more than the federal education market is valued at in the USA. This makes it difficult not to wonder if appearance investment has gone too far for many of us, and if it does, in fact, undermine body positivity.

When does caring go too far?

There should be other things occupying your mental space besides concerns about your appearance. However, even scientists who study body image issues admit that it can be hard to know what qualifies as an adaptive appearance investment versus what is maladaptive. It's usually viewed as maladaptive to engage in behaviors that pose some risk to your health or well-being, like spending so much time exercising that you don't have time to do other important things (like get enough sleep) or putting your health at risk by following fad diets. Here are some questions you may want to ask yourself to determine whether your appearance investments are working for you.

(1) **Why** are you spending time, energy, or money on these appearance investments?
(2) **For whom** do you invest in your appearance? Is this something you do for yourself or because you feel obliged to please a parent, partner, or others in your life?
(3) **What do you expect** to achieve by investing in your appearance?

Some body image scientists have suggested that beauty practices may be viewed as a choice. They maintain that deciding how to treat your body – i.e., **body autonomy** – is empowering. Some common, safe, appearance-related practices no doubt result in a morale boost. Selecting comfortable clothing or styling your hair may impart a degree of confidence that makes interactions with others more pleasurable and results in flattering attention from others. Some experts, such as Renee Engeln, have warned that when the attention devoted to appearance investment detracts from investments in other important areas of your life this results in "beauty sickness." They argue that relationships with others, health behaviors, and professional pursuits should garner more of our attention than appearance-related practices.

Regarding the question of for whom we invest in our appearance, there is debate among scholars as to whether we can truly invest in our appearance for ourselves, given the social pressure we all face. Feminist scholars remind us that women are expected to adopt beauty rituals but in doing so may actually reinforce oppressive gender roles.

In terms of our expectations for appearance investments, we might expect that a new haircut, brand name clothes, or even cosmetic surgery will improve not only our body image but our relationships with others, job prospects, and quality of life. Perhaps this third question is best examined through the consideration of additional questions.

Do your appearance practices bring you joy, comfort, or relaxation? Or do they bring you anxiety, stress, or financial hardship? Does the pursuit of beauty ideals feel like self-care or does it feel oppressive?

Maybe there are some appearance-related practices that make sense for you, some you may want to reconsider, and some you'll want to avoid altogether.

Q&A:

I often feel less attractive than my friends. I don't date as much as they do and I feel jealous of the attention they receive. I don't want to be envious of my friends. How can I become more comfortable with myself?

It can be really painful to want what others have and feel that we will never have those things – whether that be a certain type of hair or a significant other. We all tend to look to others around us to evaluate ourselves, a phenomenon psychologists refer to as **social comparison**. Social comparison is normal, and yet research suggests that we tend to feel bad about ourselves when we engage in social comparisons with others that we perceive to be better than us in some relevant way, such as our physical appearance.

One way to improve our outlook about our physical appearance and our lives in general is to work on comparing ourselves less. Of course, this is often easier said than done! But when an intrusive thought leaves us wishing we had some quality that someone else has, we can remind ourselves to stop thinking this way and redirect our thoughts to some of our own strengths. (See Chapter 2 for discussion of how to focus on and appreciate your strengths.)

It's also easy to look at someone else's life and feel like it's better than your own, but that's usually because we make social comparisons on just one aspect of life. It may seem like someone else has a better life because they go on more dates. However, maybe they don't like their job at all or maybe they don't have a great relationship with their parents. No one has a perfect life, but each of us has our own strengths, whether in terms of our ability to make friends, our fashion sense, or our sense of humor. Focus on your strengths and try to be happy for your friends when you notice them thriving.

Clothes: comfort versus style

Your clothing choices may be an expression of your personality, identity, lifestyle, or other preferences. For example, you may want to wear certain brands of clothing, or clothes that feature your favorite sports team's logo or favorite band's lyrics. You may enjoy shopping for clothes and selecting items to wear, or you may not, but clothes can be fun.

How you dress has the potential to attract others' attention and people draw conclusions about others' personalities based on their clothes. Although you should dress in a way that is most comfortable for you, you may also want to consider that others' perceptions of you could have some bearing on the opportunities that are available to you. For example, you may find it most comfortable to wear jeans and a hoodie, but dressing in those clothes during a job interview could cost you the job. Your clothes can signal to others that you are professional, someone to be taken seriously, someone worthy of respect, and that you care about your body (or you don't) or that you think that being able to move comfortably is more important than just looking a certain way. There is nothing wrong with caring about your clothes and wanting to be fashionable, but make choices that make *you* feel good, not those based on your favorite Instagram celebrity.

There is often some tension between clothes that are comfortable and clothes that are fashionable. This is especially true when it comes to women's clothing. Some research suggests that women are much more likely than men to wear clothing that is painful, distracting, or limits movement. They're ten times more likely to wear uncomfortable shoes than are men. In psychologist, Renee Englen's words, "Too many women's shoes do a terrible job of being shoes."

Uncomfortable clothing isn't just uncomfortable – or possibly even painful. It can be bad for your body image. A classic psychology study asked college-aged women to participate in an experiment that involved trying clothes on and then doing activities in those clothes. The researchers told study participants that it was a study about shopping and clothes, but it was really a study about body image. Some of the women in the study were asked to try on swimsuits and some were asked to try on sweaters. There was no one else around them to see what they were doing in their "new clothes," and they were then asked to work on a math quiz while they tested the clothing's comfort (or lack of comfort). Guess what? The women wearing the swimsuits did much worse on the quiz. In fact, they got nearly twice as many of the problems wrong as did the women wearing bulky sweaters. How come? The researchers have proposed that clothing that's revealing or less comfortable is also distracting. It's not that wearing a swimsuit decreases your IQ. Most people probably feel more insecure in a swimsuit than they do in loose, comfortable clothes. Wearing revealing clothing may make it more difficult for you to focus on other tasks.

If you feel uncomfortable with what you're wearing, you are also likely to spend time in a state of **body surveillance** or monitoring your body's sensations and appearance. Body surveillance often contributes to body dissatisfaction because spending a lot of time thinking about your body can make you feel insecure about it. Uncomfortable clothing can be distracting in other ways as well. For example, have you ever worn shoes that are cute but not very comfortable on an outing that requires a lot of walking? Instead of enjoying what you're doing (especially the walking) you may have found yourself thinking that you couldn't wait to go home. In other words, your cute shoes may ruin the outing for you.

EXPERT ADVICE:

Leigh Ann Healey, influencer and self-confidence advocate, USA

"Buy that new pair of jeans. There's nothing wrong with any number or letter, and there is sure as heck nothing wrong with getting a new one (aka, sizing up – or down!) if it means your clothes will fit you better. Your clothes are meant to fit YOU, not the other way around. And no one sees the size on the tag except you!"

Hair: style, addition, and subtraction

Have you ever had a bad hair day? Maybe your hair was frizzy or sticking up somewhere or just generally uncooperative? Why is it that failed attempts to style our hair can leave us self-conscious or even grumpy?

There are scholars who study hair (really!) and they find that this attachment to our hair is a near universal experience. Hair has received a great deal of attention in societies all over the world across history and "good hair" is valued for beauty and for signaling youth; our hair is a part of our identity. In contrast, hair loss on our heads is feared and often treated with the use of chemicals or hair extensions (strands of human, animal, or synthetic hair that are attached to existing hair using glue, braids, or sewing).

As revealed in Serenity's story at the start of this chapter, hair represents a particular challenge and expression of beauty for Black women. Black people's hair differs in texture from those of other ethnic backgrounds, which often leads to time, resource, and labor-intensive hair care regimens. As Serenity points out, most beauty ideals often elevate white features, including silky, smooth hair. As a result, among Black women in particular, the styling of one's hair is often viewed as not just an aesthetic challenge but has greater meaning in terms of esteem, race, and identity.

Whereas many are interested in adding hair or making hair on their heads seem fuller, hair is often removed from other parts of the body. The removal of body hair is one of the most common beauty practices. Younger people with higher incomes who live in urban areas are more likely to remove body hair when compared to older, poorer, and more rural residents. There is a gender difference in hair removal practices; recent research shows that most adults identifying as female removed body hair but only about 40% of those identifying as male do. However, men's hair removal practices are becoming more mainstream. Although body hair was viewed as rugged and masculine for most of recent history, now men find themselves expected to "manscape" – style and/or remove hair on their faces and bodies. Manscaping seems to be more normative in gay male culture, and straight men experience more flexibility surrounding hair removal practices. Of course, all aspects of hair styling, addition, and removal represent consumer opportunities; there are an endless number of products and services we can pursue to "fix" our hair. As with all the other appearance investment practices, it remains something of an open question as to whether or not the effort, time, and resources we devote to our hair result in improvements in body image.

EXPERT ADVICE:

Julia Elliott, award-winning stylist, California, USA

"There's a reason that people tell everything to their hair stylists. I see people every day that are looking for a bit of a morale boost and usually I'm able to give that to them. Sometimes they literally leave my salon with a spring in their step. Maybe it's because people are taking the time out to do something for themselves. Maybe it's because they think they look better. A new hairstyle isn't going to solve all of anyone's problems or bring about world peace, but it definitely can be a boost."

Q&A:

I constantly see videos on TikTok of influencers and celebrities before and after cosmetic surgery. I know that there is a fine line between advertising and the content I see, but these videos make it seem so easy to alter your appearance. How do I resist the draw to do all these things to myself?

"Before and after" images are everywhere, and research suggests that time on social media leads people to be more interested in cosmetic surgery. In other words, you are right that the content you're viewing is essentially advertising.

We see appearance ideals in all forms of media, but especially social media and we compare ourselves to those ideals. Usually, we find ourselves lacking in some way. But social media doesn't only present a problem, it presents a solution; *cosmetic surgery is the answer! It is safe, easy, and acceptable!* It makes sense that you may find it difficult to resist this messaging.

It is not my goal to try to convince you that your appearance doesn't matter at all, but it's important to realize that social media oversimplifies the costs and benefits of altering our appearance (look back to Chapter 8 for more on this). And, of course, we are not helpless in the face of social media; we curate the information we see. You can change what you see by *not* clicking on, liking, or following content that makes you feel insecure about your appearance. It can also be valuable to just acknowledge and appreciate that media influences are powerful and always present; we can resist their appeal often, but this can be challenging.

Cosmetic surgery

In 2022, it is estimated that $11.2 billion was spent on aesthetic cosmetic procedures in the USA. The number of people – mostly women – who pursue cosmetic procedures has grown significantly; this is especially true of nonsurgical procedures (e.g., Botox). Further, the amount that people will invest to alter their breasts, stomachs, noses, faces, and nearly every other part of themselves has also grown. According to the American Society of Plastic Surgeons, the average cost of a nose job (aka, rhinoplasty) is more than $5,000. In 2021, the *New York Times* reported that while the average facelift in the USA costs about $9,000 some surgeons will charge over $200,000. Cosmetic surgery may not be only for the rich and famous, but some of the rich and famous are willing to invest *a lot* into their appearance.

Why doesn't everyone obtain cosmetic surgery? Possible reasons include not only the price tag, but concerns about physical safety, people's connection to their physical selves as a part of their identity, and uncertainty about the psychological benefits.

Most cosmetic surgeries are safe, but there are always physical risks associated with surgery. The anesthesia necessary for most surgeries occasionally results in serious medical complications. Infections can lead to serious and even deadly consequences. Bleeding, scarring, and nerve damage are other possible complications. Brazilian butt lifts (BBLs) are one of the fastest growing procedures around the world and they also have one of the highest mortality rates of all cosmetic surgery procedures. When fat is repurposed from another part of the body to create a fuller butt, everything from a fat embolism (fat causing a blockage in the blood, which can result in death) to torn veins can ensue. Although medical technology has come a long way, many people are unwilling to take serious risks with their health (and life) to alter their appearance.

Some of us may dislike some of our physical features but may also feel that they are an important part of our identity. Maybe you wish you didn't have your dad's nose or your mom's chest size, but you also think of these features fondly as family traits. It's possible that some of your features are culturally or racially meaningful, from the shape of your eyes to the color of your skin. You may feel that these qualities make you unique and are not worth trying to change because those changes would feel inauthentic.

Perhaps the most confusing issue when it comes to cosmetic surgery is whether or not it's psychologically beneficial. Some body image scientists believe that an important part of developing a positive body image is accepting yourself and avoiding extreme practices such as cosmetic surgery, which are not always viewed as adaptive appearance investments. Further, research suggests that plastic surgery doesn't completely change how people feel about themselves. My own studies and my review of others' research indicates that although cosmetic surgery may improve satisfaction with a particular body part, there are no long-term improvements in body or life satisfaction. In other words, if you get a nose job you might like your new nose better than your old nose, but you aren't likely to be happier overall.

In some cases, cosmetic surgery can actually make people more dissatisfied with their bodies. People with eating disorders, body dysmorphic disorder (BDD; see Chapter 6), and other mental health concerns may pursue surgery in the hopes of improving their psychological health. When these improvements don't necessarily manifest, they can feel worse than they did before surgery. For some people, this leads them to obtain additional surgery and can intensify conditions such as BDD. In fact, the American Society of Plastic Surgeons reported in 2020 that 44% of cosmetic surgery patients are "repeat patients." This seems to suggest that, for these people, their original cosmetic surgery did not improve their body image.

EXPERT ADVICE:

Dr. John Fernandez, reconstructive plastic surgeon, Trinity Health Mid-Atlantic, Pennsylvania, USA

"We have excellent patient reports verifying how important appearance is to patients. When a person has significant scarring or loss of limb or loss of functionality after cancer or a traumatic injury, they also tend to suffer from deep emotional and mental stresses that are often as significant as their physical ailment. What I have found is that restoring the physical appearance can help heal the emotional and mental struggles that go along with it. However, those mental and emotional struggles must often be separately addressed as well."

Q&A:

A few of my friends have started to get lip fillers. Are these treatments safe?

Minimally invasive cosmetic treatments including Botox and dermal fillers have become very popular in recent years. These treatments work by "freezing" or "relaxing" muscles (Botox) or by adding volume to the face where wrinkles have formed or fullness is desired (dermal fillers). The effects are temporary, usually wearing off within three to six months.

In 2020, more than 3 million dermal filler procedures were performed, mostly among women aged 40 to 54 years, although nearly half a million of these procedures were performed on people 29 years old or younger. These products have been tested extensively and have been approved by the US Food and Drug Administration for cosmetic use. Like nearly any medical drug or treatment, there can be undesirable consequences to using these products. Side-effects can range from bruising to flu-like symptoms and nausea. However, these minimally invasive procedures aren't likely to compromise general health.

There are a few other things to consider, however, when it comes to minimally invasive cosmetic procedures. First, some people feel that they have "unnatural" results and can make people look "fake" while trying to make them look different or younger. Second, these procedures are expensive, typically costing *at least* a few hundred dollars for results that will wear off within months. If you like the way you look following this sort of treatment, it will cost many thousands of dollars across time to maintain the look. Finally, some people feel very strongly that a positive body image means accepting yourself and not taking drastic steps to alter your appearance. Fillers aren't nearly as drastic or risky as surgery, but they aren't risk-free either. You'll have to decide for yourself what sorts of changes to your appearance – if any – are right for you, and at what point in your life.

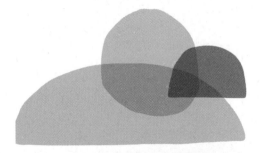

Damned if you do, damned if you don't?

Altering your appearance – even surgically – may not lead to significant improvements in body image. This is part of why body image researchers encourage self-acceptance and body appreciation as antidotes to body dissatisfaction and not physical modifications or surgery. Of course, that may be easier said than done. The marketing of cosmetics, clothes, and other appearance-related practices can be incredibly compelling and often seem to offer a happy, healthy, sexy, and exciting life. Many people feel a certain sense of *obligation* to "improve" their appearance or "look their best."

It is somewhat ironic, however, that if you choose to alter your appearance you may not always experience social approval for doing so. As much as our culture values beauty, what it really seems to value is *natural* beauty, and if your beauty appears to be inauthentic or purchased it's often devalued. Some recent research has even identified a **cosmetic surgery paradox**, whereas beauty ideals seem to encourage the pursuit of surgery and yet natural beauty is valued over artificial beauty. The confusing cultural message seems to be that if you aren't naturally beautiful then you should try to become more attractive, but only in ways that are undetectable. It can be easy to feel like you are damned if you do and damned if you don't!

Broad Conceptualization of Beauty

Most of us spend at least some time feeling that we fall short of rigid beauty ideals. But what if we had broader ideals? What if we were more flexible and open-minded about what makes someone beautiful? Body image scientists have discovered that some people are better than others at thinking outside the box when it comes to beauty ideals. And those people who can think outside the box tend to have a more positive body image! Want to see how you do? Answer these questions from The Broad Conceptualization of Beauty Scale (created by Tracy Tylka and Amy Iannantuono to assess *women's* beauty; a comparable measure has not been created for men yet).

How do YOU define beauty?

	Strongly disagree	Moderately disagree	Slightly disagree	Neither agree nor disagree	Slightly agree	Moderately agree	Strongly agree
Even if a physical feature is not considered attractive by others or by society, I think that it can be beautiful.	1	2	3	4	5	6	7
A woman's confidence level can change my perception of her physical beauty.	1	2	3	4	5	6	7
I think that a wide variety of body shapes are beautiful for women.	1	2	3	4	5	6	7
I think thin women are more beautiful than women who have other body types.	7	6	5	4	3	2	1
A woman's soul or inner spirit can change my perception of her physical beauty.	1	2	3	4	5	6	7
I define a woman's beauty differently than how it is portrayed in the media.	1	2	3	4	5	6	7
A woman's acceptance of herself can change my perception of her physical beauty.	1	2	3	4	5	6	7
I appreciate a wide range of different looks as beautiful.	1	2	3	4	5	6	7
I think that women of all body sizes can be beautiful	1	2	3	4	5	6	7

Select a response to each item. Sum up your responses and divide by 9. In previous research, the average score on this questionnaire was 5.7.

You don't need to be "fixed"

Positive body image is typically associated with the rejection of stereotypical beauty ideals. And yet, there are many reasons that you may want to alter your appearance. It's essential that you realize that you do not *need* to change your physical self; you do not need to be "fixed."

Someday you may want to color your hair. Someday you may want to change the shape of your nose. These are personal choices but make them for the right reason: because you want to do these things for yourself, not because anyone else wants you to. Always consider all the risks and consequences of these choices. Never forget that who you are and your body image aren't just a result of how you look. You're much more than your outward appearance. You have many layers of thoughts, emotions, feelings, hopes, and dreams. You can choose to pay less attention to some details of your appearance and focus that time and energy on other aspects of your life. Confidence can grow not just from how you look, but also from developing skills, nurturing meaningful relationships, and appreciating that people value many of your qualities.

Unfortunately, there is no simple answer to the question, "Can appearance investment contribute to a positive body image?" It seems likely that no two individuals will have the exact same answer.

The bottom line is this: your body should not be a to-do list of things to fix.

MY STORY: Kiara Nicole, 24 years old, she/her, USA

As a child, I was picked on a lot for my hair because my mom was white and did not know how to do biracial hair like mine. I had an older sister and she always had her hair done, but mine was a different texture that my mom just couldn't seem to figure out how to handle. She let me leave the house looking somewhat crazy. People might not think that hair is a crucial part of body image but for Black girls it means so much. I still feel anxious when I feel like my hair does not look good. I make sure that if I plan on taking pictures that my hair is done well.

As far as the rest of me goes, I guess I have a love–hate relationship with my body. I have seen my body at its most capable when I was in the military and had to work out to stay fit for my job. However, since I left the military a few years ago I stopped working out as much and I gained some weight. I hate to admit it, but it's been a blow to my self-esteem. I am overly critical of how I look in clothes and absolutely despise going shopping. In fact, I think fitting room mirrors have played far too big a role in how I view my body. I always seem to find myself buying the biggest size in "normal size" stores (Forever 21, Zara, H&M) and that's just really demoralizing. I feel like I'm always a meal or two away from moving into the plus-size section.

During the coronavirus pandemic, I started to feel like my whole day was planned around my next meal. There was nothing to look forward to; life was all about school and stress and more stress. Now, I'm starting to work out again as a way to relieve stress and get back in shape. I know this is an important part of taking care of my body. I need to exercise; it's something that I do for myself, but I am still learning how to feel good about my body.

I think the lesson I wish I could've told my younger self is to try not to compare yourself to others. Everyone is unique; no one is going to look exactly like you. Also, PUT IT ON. Whatever "it" is. If it makes you feel good, put it on! That bathing suit that you're not sure is flattering but you feel powerful in – put it on. That crop top that you've been dying to wear, but you second guess every time you're about to leave – put it on. Have confidence and you will be sure to rock it! The way that you carry yourself and the confidence that comes from within is what shines for everyone to see.

SUMMING UP #YOUARENOTAPROJECT:

- It's understandable to care about your appearance and invest some time, energy, and money into looking your best given the appearance-focused culture we live in. Don't feel bad for caring about how you look.
- Before trying to alter your appearance – especially in any permanent way – you should question why you want to invest in your appearance, for whom, and what you expect to result from this investment.
- It's important to appreciate that your physical appearance is only one part of who you are and altering your appearance will not necessarily improve your life in meaningful ways.

FIND OUT MORE:

- Renee Engeln's book *Beauty Sick: How the Cultural Obsession with Appearance Hurts Girls and Women* (Harper, 2018) is a great resource for the topics in this chapter.
- If you are trying to sort through your feelings about your body image and appearance investment, check out some of the exercises in Lindsay and Lexie Kite's *Official Workbook for More Than a Body: Daily Practices for Building Body Image Resilience in a Looks-Obsessed World* (More Than a Body, LLC, 2024).
- For scientific references and more information about appearance modification see the book's web page: www.TheBodyImageBookforLife.com.

CHAPTER 10

RELATIONSHIPS

#ThePeopleYouKeep

"You don't love someone for their looks, or their clothes, or for their fancy car, but because they sing a song only you can hear."

– Oscar Wilde, *British playwright, novelist, and poet*

MY STORY: Sam Jayden, 21 years old, he/they, USA

I appreciate and love my body, but I'm trying to navigate what it means to have my body because I don't really identify with a gender that matches my body. I am working to feel more connected to my body.

Starting when I was around 12 years old, I became hyperaware of my body and felt like I had to try to connect to some sense of femininity. I lived as a girl and was trying to fit the mold of what I thought it meant to be a girl/woman. I'm Black and was relatively tall as an early adolescent and people viewed me as more masculine. I felt stigmatized by some people for both my race and gender identity. I think I was understanding that I might not be a girl for the rest of my life and that I wasn't entirely comfortable with being a girl, but I accepted that I was a girl and that was an important part of my life.

I started becoming interested in developing a romantic relationship by mid-adolescence. I remember becoming concerned about how my clothes looked. I wanted my clothes to be tight but not too tight. I enjoyed the attention I got from boys and I had a boyfriend for a lot of high school.

I had a lot of anxiety and depression during my adolescence. I always assumed that no one liked me. I had friends in high school but they weren't always good friends. I think I didn't have the ability to form close friends yet or I just didn't know how to pick the right people. Now I have friends who genuinely want to get to know me better. I think my life is going in the right direction and I appreciate my friends even if my relationships still require work.

If I could offer my younger self advice, I'd say that you don't have to do what others expect of you. You should see yourself as a whole person with your own needs and desires. Love is not an obligation. It is something that you have a say in and something you have the ability to choose in this life. You are not stuck to anyone or anything that you do not want to be. You should trust yourself more; you might make mistakes but that's OK. People do and will enjoy you. You will find people who care about you and appreciate you. Life is hard but it is not as difficult as you may have made it out to be in your head.

Our body image does not develop in isolation and so much of how we feel about our bodies has to do with how the people around us have responded to our bodies and appearances throughout our lives. Elements of Sam's story may not resonate with all of us, but his insecurities surrounding his relationships and how he has related to others in his life likely feel familiar.

Growing up, your mom may have been critical of how your clothes fit you, or your dad may have had an affectionate but humiliating nickname for you like "chubs" or "gordo/gorda." Maybe the way that a sibling or friend teased you left you self-conscious about some aspect of your appearance. It could be a dance instructor or coach who stressed eating a certain way or maintaining a certain weight that led you to first develop concerns about your eating habits or body image. Maybe no one in your social world ever explicitly said anything to you but still had a way of making you feel inadequate. It's possible that the way your family talked about others' bodies, size, or appearance led you to believe that all of these were incredibly important. How can we ensure that the people in our lives are positive body image influences?

IN THIS CHAPTER YOU'LL LEARN

- about the critical role that our family members play in our early body image development,
- how friendships and romantic relationships are relevant to our body image, and
- how to create body-positive, healthy relationships.

Family

It's possible that no two people have the exact same family experiences. How families discuss body image, eating, exercise, and even health in general, varies widely. However, it's also likely that you can categorize your family as a primarily positive or negative body image influence.

If your family members were unconditionally accepting of your body and your appearance, did not have a lot of restrictions on what you ate, and offered support and praise for the person you were becoming, they were likely positive body image influences. In contrast, your family members may have placed importance on trying to lose weight, kept you from enjoying foods that came in any sort of packaging, and may have teased you about your appearance, making them somewhat negative body image influences. Sometimes family influences are very explicit, such as teasing or bullying, and sometimes they are more subtle. Body image research suggests that it is very common for teens to report that their parents talked about weight issues, dieted, and teased each other about their weight. In one study, about half of teen girls reported that their moms encouraged them to diet and they were teased about their weight. It probably won't surprise you to hear that these girls were also more likely to report disordered eating. In fact, the researchers concluded that, "In *no* instances were family weight talk and dieting variables associated with *better* outcomes."

Family members often love each other very, very much and have the best of intentions, yet still end up being far from supportive. For example, it may be that your parents grew up in homes where food was scarce and not to be wasted. Everyone was required to finish their meals before getting up from the table. In your home, food may not have been scarce, but being forced to eat certain foods may have led you to develop an unhealthy relationship with food because you were never left to just trust your own body's signals of hunger and fullness. Or maybe you grew up in a home where one of your parents or siblings was always attempting to lose weight by trying different diets. From a young age, you may have learned that weight loss is considered a valuable goal to your family and having a slender body is important. Again, none of this is to say that family members *intentionally* harm one another; sometimes our family members say the wrong things, model unhealthy behaviors, or just have no idea how to help us develop adaptive health habits, a positive sense of self, and a healthy body image.

Even if you feel like your family members were not supportive of body positivity, there's a decent chance they were trying to be. One of the questions I get asked most often is how moms, in particular, can help their kids to grow up with positive body images. Often this is because these women have struggled with their own body image and desperately want something better for their own children.

One recent study examined how the mother–daughter relationship can be integral to the development of not just daughters, but also *mothers'* body image. Plenty of past research suggests that mothers who have more positive body images and adaptive eating habits are likely to be good models for their children and pass on positive body image and eating behaviors to their kids. However, this new study is unique in its consideration of reciprocity between mothers and daughters; daughters were considered as influences on their mothers. The researchers found that when mothers were disparaging about their own bodies, their daughters were at risk of body dissatisfaction; mothers taught their daughters to be dissatisfied with their bodies. Interestingly, when daughters talked more positively about their own bodies, their mothers reported better body images. The researchers also found that daughters who expressed more positive body image were more likely to embrace feminist ideals. A cycle of empowerment may settle into these family dynamics, with young women's beliefs about their self-worth inspiring not only their own body image but also their mothers. I'll admit that I like this study, in part, because it reminds me a bit of my own daughter. For obvious reasons, I hope that I am a positive influence on her body image, but I also know I benefit from her strong-willed feminism and appreciate when she reminds me of the importance of both psychological and physical comfort over appearance. I was proud of her for telling me to size up for comfort on a recent shopping outing.

It's not just girls whose body images are influenced by their parents. In fact, more than one study suggests that boys' attitudes about their own and others' bodies are related to their parents' perceptions regarding body size. Fathers' opinions about what constitutes an ideal male body especially seem to rub off on their sons. Being teased about their bodies seems to lead boys to want to pursue a muscular body. Further, when fathers are more nurturing and accepting of their sons in general, this seems to have a positive effect on boys' body image.

EXPERT ADVICE:

Dr. Kristin August, Professor of Psychology, Rutgers University, USA

"Our relationships with our partners, family, friends, and even health care providers, can have a powerful impact on both our physical and mental health. For example, our relationships can have a positive (and sometimes negative) impact on our health behaviors – what and how much we eat, exercise, smoke, and drink. Our relationships also can affect how we view our bodies. We often compare the way we look to our partners, family, and friends (for good or bad), but they can also support us when we feel bad about ourselves."

MYTHS AND MISINFORMATION:

You have to love yourself before you can truly love someone else.

It is a popular belief that you must love yourself before you can really form healthy, lasting relationships. However, this belief is not well supported by science.

It is easy to see how this belief originated; if we don't view ourselves as worthy and lovable, how can others? Further, if we are self-critical or self-disparaging, do we open ourselves up to being devalued by others?

In terms of body image, it would follow that while there may be benefits to initiating a relationship once some degree of body satisfaction is achieved, this is not a prerequisite to maintaining a positive relationship with another person. Given how prevalent body dissatisfaction is, most of us wouldn't be able to maintain positive relationships if this were the case! Of course, we don't want to count on another person to develop a positive body image, but it is possible that supportive others – friends, family, or romantic partners – may actually help us to nurture a positive body image. It's also likely that spending time around people who are accepting of us and us of them is conducive to mental health in general, including body satisfaction.

Friends matter

It is typical for teenagers and young adults to feel that they are better understood by their friends and that people their own age are easier to relate to than their parents or other adults. Adults often seem out-of-touch and not particularly connected to popular culture. To some extent, this is often true and there's nothing wrong with wanting to spend time with people your own age. In fact, some research suggests that it's good for your body image!

People who have a positive body image tend to report that they have friends who feel positively about their own bodies, too. Further, positive body image is nurtured in relationships where people feel unconditionally accepted. Research suggests that when people have just one supportive friend to talk with, they tend to have greater body satisfaction. This works both ways, though, and having a positive sense of yourself may lead you to be more supportive and accepting of others.

Not all our friends are necessarily going to be accepting and reassuring, however. Sometimes friends may tease us in ways that may be intended to be affectionate but actually are hurtful. Further, sometimes conversations we have with friends about our bodies, weight, physical activity, or even our clothes can contribute to our body dissatisfaction.

Fat talk

Have you ever had a conversation with a friend that begins with her saying, "I feel fat!" You probably appreciate that the expected response to this is, "No! You don't look fat!" Maybe you'll even throw in your own, "*I* feel fat!" as well. This is such a common sort of exchange among people – especially female friends – that researchers have called it "fat talk."

Often friends bond over these conversations; they seem to flow naturally and feel harmless. However, research suggests that these sorts of body-disparaging comments contribute to body dissatisfaction, concerns about weight, and even disordered eating. These conversations aren't harmless – they perpetuate fatphobia, the idea that thinness is essential, and the belief that changing our bodies to meet cultural beauty ideals is required.

You can work to stop the cycle of fat talk conversations. First, appreciate that "fat" is not a feeling. When you find yourself on the brink of a fat talk exchange, you could try to tell your friend something positive and encouraging

("It hurts me to hear you disparage yourself or people who are fat" and "You know that's not what matters most") and change the subject or explicitly suggest that the discussion of body and weight issues is not what you want to focus on. Body image scientists and advocates have found that when there is less fat talk, there is less concern and worry about weight. And that creates space to talk and think about a whole variety of more interesting subjects.

Q&A:

I have a friend who makes subtle, but frequent, negative comments about my body size. I don't think she means anything by it, but the comments are really hurtful and I've started to avoid her because of them. I don't know if I should say something to her or just let the friendship fade.

There is so much fatphobia and appearance-centric messaging in our culture, that it is entirely possible that your friend really doesn't realize what she's saying and how it makes you feel. This doesn't make it acceptable, however. Just because many people are ignorant doesn't mean that we can't hold our friends to higher standards.

I suspect that you haven't said anything to your friend about how her comments make you feel because it feels uncomfortable to do so or you worry about the impact it will have on your relationship. If you are already avoiding her and considering letting the relationship fade, then it seems that you don't have a lot to lose by being honest. The next time you are around her and she says something negative about your body or someone else's, you could tell her that you don't appreciate what she said. You could confidently say something like, *"I know you probably don't mean to be hurtful when you say things like that, but it can be really upsetting. I'd really appreciate it if we could just not talk about my or others' bodies and appearances. I'm working on my body image and really trying to keep things in perspective; how I look is not the most interesting thing about me."*

If your friend doesn't respond well to you confronting her, it may be that she is embarrassed and defensive and will come to realize that you are correct in your evaluation of her comments. It also may be that you are just beginning to educate her about a less superficial way to view the world and you aren't on the same page yet. If she teases you in response or tells you to "lighten up," this is probably a clear sign that you aren't sharing the same worldview. It may be time to let the friendship go, but it's possible that your friend evolves and you are able to reconnect later.

Loving relationships

As a researcher, I've been interested in how our romantic relationships are relevant to our body image, eating behaviors, and health for decades. In fact, one of my first published journal articles (back in 2001) examined how married partners affected each other's attempts at weight loss. The main finding from that study was that women who reported having "worse" relationships with their husbands were also more likely to engage in disordered eating behaviors; it wasn't clear which was the chicken or the egg, but the connection between relationship experiences and eating habits existed.

I began studying romantic relationships and their connection to eating behaviors and body image when I was in my early 20s and in one of my first long-term, serious relationships. I knew that scientists had spent a considerable amount of energy trying to understand how parents influence their kids in all sorts of ways – what they eat, how they feel about themselves, how they relate to other people – but it seemed to me that our partners were also pretty important to our health beliefs and behaviors. After all, many of us will live with a romantic partner for longer than we live with our parents. How are these partners relevant to our body image development?

The start of a romantic relationship of any kind can affect how you think about yourself and may challenge who you are. You may feel like you should try to be someone different to be liked by someone you're interested in, or who is your boy/girlfriend. If you're concerned about your appearance due to your interest in another person, this is fairly normal. However, it is worth considering whether or not you should try to change your appearance in any way to attract someone else. Do you want to build a relationship with someone who doesn't like the way you *really* look?

Finding "dates"

It's been estimated that in 2021 there were over 320 million people using dating websites and apps worldwide and about 20% of people who have access to the Internet are using a dating app. Young people's preferred dating app is Tinder, which is often described as a relatively easy way to meet people. It's also very image-centric, as are most dating apps. In online dating spaces, people tend to describe themselves and what they're looking for in a partner, but they also post pictures of themselves. Obviously, if you are trying to attract a partner – whether it be for the night or the rest of your life – you'll probably share pictures that make you look your best. In fact, some research confirms that younger adults try to make themselves look more attractive in their dating profiles (in contrast, older adults are less likely to do this, instead focusing more on authenticity). In one study of men who have sex with men, nearly all the men indicated that they shared pictures of their face on their dating profiles and about one in five shared pictures of their naked torsos. That's a lot of naked abs out there on dating apps!

In some ways, online and app-based dating only seem to exaggerate people's tendency to be drawn to potential romantic partners based on their appearance. Some research has found that people who are more anxious about their appearance are more anxious about dating in general. Of course! If you feel confident about who you are and comfortable in your own skin, it's easier to meet and talk to new people. However, physical appearance is just one piece of the attraction puzzle. I'm sure you've had the experience of meeting someone and finding them physically attractive and then you get to know them, and you find them more attractive because you like their personality. You've also probably come to find someone less attractive because you *don't* like their personality.

If you're insecure about your appearance for any reason keep in mind that although appearances can take center stage early in a relationship, they tend to become less important across time (and with age). And we've all probably had the pleasure of knowing people who are not traditionally attractive but are confident or fun to be around. Often that confidence or someone's personality ends up being so much more important to how attractive you find them overall.

Q&A:

I've been involved with a partner for a few months now, but I think he's better looking than I am. I notice other people checking him out when we're together and it makes me feel insecure and jealous. He seems attracted to me, but I don't know how to deal with this sense of us being mismatched. Help?!

A significant other should be a source of support and love and only add to your positive sense of yourself. In fact, there is research to suggest that people who are in serious relationships typically feel better about their body image than people who are not. But what happens when you feel like your partner is better looking than you?

In some of my own research looking at both straight and gay couples, I've found that a difference between partners in terms of body size seems to make the heavier partners more concerned about their weight. I don't know of any research that has examined couples' overall appearance or attractiveness using the same sort of methodology, but I'd guess that something similar may occur. In other words, if you feel insecure about your appearance, body, or weight because you think your partner is more attractive than you, you are not alone. But what are your options?

Obviously, you can choose to only date people who you think are less attractive than you or an equal match to you. You can believe your current partner when he says he's attracted to you. You can work on valuing yourself for more than your appearance and appreciate it when others do as well. You can enjoy having a good-looking partner and try not to worry about it. If you believe that this experience is making you aware of body image or appearance concerns that you had even before this relationship or that were worsened in this relationship, you can pursue therapy to work on your concerns. Remember, you don't need to have a serious mental illness to potentially benefit from therapy and low-fee therapy is often available through community organizations. I'm sure I'm biased because I'm a psychologist, but I actually think that most people can benefit from talking with a professional about their insecurities and working to become more comfortable with themselves.

Intimacy and sex

Some relationships become physically intimate. Physical intimacy can take different forms and doesn't necessarily refer only to sexual intercourse or oral sex. Sometimes, just holding someone's hand can feel very intimate and exciting.

Physical intimacy can open up a variety of body image questions and concerns. For example, some research suggests that feeling ashamed of one's body may make it hard to feel sexual arousal, and women who are dissatisfied with their bodies may find it more difficult to reach orgasm. This probably makes some sense – right? If you are distracted by worries about how you look and some (or all!) of your body is revealed, it can be pretty hard to be "in the moment."

It's not your fault if you feel uncomfortable with physical intimacy. There are many reasons why this may be. Nakedness can be awkward! Most real (non-photoshopped) bodies have jiggly parts, stretch marks, bumps, and scars. These are not things to be embarrassed by, but the media messages we all see lead many of us to believe that we should be embarrassed by any physical imperfections we have. Further, if a family member made you feel self-conscious about your weight, you may worry that a romantic partner doesn't find your body attractive, and this may be preoccupying. If you've watched pornography (more on this below), you may have seen naked people with body types that look nothing like yours and this may be a source of concern. Even on social media you may see a lot of images of beautiful, sexy people that lead you to question your own sexual appeal. These are normal responses to social pressures, and it may help to keep in mind that your partner is also subjected to these social pressures and likely feels some self-consciousness as well.

Even though insecurity surrounding sexual intimacy is not your fault, it is something to remedy so that you can – should you choose to – enjoy physical intimacy. A partner can make you feel safe and comfortable by taking the physical part of your relationship slow. Communicating and even laughing about your concerns may also increase your comfort. Some research suggests the benefit of receiving positive messages from a partner in terms of increasing self-confidence, self-acceptance, and sexual empowerment and fulfillment. It is also possible that any physical unease you have during an intimate experience has something to do with who you are with and who you are attracted to. Our sexuality is dynamic and your experience with one person may not be at all the same as your experiences with a different person.

Porn

Adult movies, X-rated movies, or pornography all contain explicit nudity and sexual interactions. How could seeing people completely naked possibly pose any body image challenges?!

Porn is usually made by men for boys and men. In fact, in one recent study, the majority of men (over 90%) reported watching pornography in the last 6 months. However, some research indicates that over 70% of women have viewed porn in the past 6 months also. Although pornography watching may be common, it has the potential to be problematic.

There's a fairly obvious body image connection between watching porn and body dissatisfaction. Most of the people featured in pornography do not look like average people. In particular, their bodies are likely to be more slender, muscular, and hairless than the average person. Men who are porn stars are likely to have larger-than-average pecs and penises, while women who are porn stars are likely to have larger-than-average breasts. Many porn stars have had cosmetic surgery to look as they do. People you see in pornography are not your role models; trying to look like these people is likely to make you feel inferior and disappointed with your own appearance. Also, avoid holding other people (for example, your romantic partners) to the standards set by porn stars or you are likely to find yourself disappointed. Some research suggests that viewing porn not only decreases body image but also decreases some people's interest in having sex.

Body Exposure During Sexual Activity Questionnaire

Being in a romantic relationship often means being physically intimate and feeling vulnerable around your partner. Body image scientists have tried to understand ways that body image may impact physical intimacy using the questionnaire below. Even if you are not currently (or never have been) sexually intimate, you can see how comfortable you are with yourself (and being naked) by circling your answers to these questions and following the scoring instructions below.

	Never	Rarely	Sometimes	Often	Always or almost always
During sexual activity I am thinking that my partner will notice something about my body that is a turn-off.	0	1	2	3	4
When it comes to my partner seeing me naked, I have nothing to hide.	4	3	2	1	0
During sexual activity something about the way my body looks makes me feel inhibited.	0	1	2	3	4
I prefer to keep my body hidden under a sheet or blanket during sex.	0	1	2	3	4
When we're having sex, I worry that my partner will find my body repulsive.	0	1	2	3	4
I don't like my partner to see me completely naked during sexual activity.	0	1	2	3	4
I am self-conscious about my body during sexual activity.	0	1	2	3	4
During sex I enjoy having my partner look at my body.	4	3	2	1	0
During sexual activity I try to hide certain areas of my body.	0	1	2	3	4

	Never	Rarely	Sometimes	Often	Always or almost always
During sexual activity I keep thinking that parts of my body are too unattractive to be sexy.	0	1	2	3	4
There are parts of my body I don't want my partner to see when we are having sex.	0	1	2	3	4
During sexual activity I worry about what my partner thinks about how my body looks.	0	1	2	3	4
During sexual activity I worry that my partner could be turned-off by how parts of my body feel to his/her touch.	0	1	2	3	4
I feel self-conscious if the room is too well lit when I am having sex.	0	1	2	3	4
I am generally comfortable having parts of my body exposed to my partner during sexual activity.	4	3	2	1	0
During sex there are certain poses or positions I avoid, because of the way my body would look to my partner.	0	1	2	3	4
During sexual activity I am distracted by thoughts of how certain parts of my body look.	0	1	2	3	4
Prior to or following sex, I am comfortable walking naked in my partner's view.	4	3	2	1	0

To score: sum up your score and divide by 18. In previous research, the average score for women is a little bit over 1 and the average score for men is a bit below 1.

This questionnaire is copyrighted by Thomas F. Cash, PhD and was approved for inclusion here.

Do not reproduce. For more information, visit www.body-images.com.

EXPERT ADVICE:

Dr. Gemma Sharp, Professor of Psychology, Monash University, Australia

"Having a positive relationship with our bodies, particularly our genitalia, can really benefit our sexual relationships. Unfortunately, in more traditional sexual education programs, the structure and function of female genitalia is often neglected leaving young girls unsure about this important part of their anatomy. I would like young girls and women to know that there is no one way for your genitals to look – they are like snowflakes – no two are alike."

Respect and consent

Research indicates that one of the top five predictors of a satisfying relationship is having satisfying sex with a partner. However, when it comes to sexual encounters, **it is incredibly important that you are sure that your partner wants to have sex with you.** I know that this may seem very basic, but sometimes partners do not communicate about where their physical relationship is heading, and one person ends up feeling (or being) hurt or taken advantage of. It is a really good idea that you know your partner has consented to be sexually intimate with you, and that you have a discussion about the protection you will use to avoid sexually transmitted infections and unintended pregnancies. You can't just rely on your perception that your partner is comfortable; **you have to ask and you have to have a discussion. You also have to allow your partner to change his, her, or their mind.**

Consensual physical encounters are *the minimum* that you should expect from a partner. You have to determine what is comfortable and important to you when it comes to sex. Do you want monogamy? Do you want commitment? Do you want a casual (but safe) partner? Is it important to you to have sex in the context of love?

Healthy relationships, healthy body image

The central theme of this chapter is that our relationships affect our body image (and vice versa). So, how do we develop body-positive relationships?

Despite decades of relationship research, there remain a lot of unknowns about why some relationships work out in general and others don't. In a very large recent study that compiled findings from thousands of participants in a quest to understand what makes a relationship "good," the factors that seem most important are pretty much what you'd guess. People report that their relationship is more satisfying when they believe their partner is committed to them, they feel appreciated by their partner, the relationship is sexually satisfying, they believe their partner is happy in the relationship, and they don't fight a lot. Further, people tend to be happier in their relationships when they are happier in general; people who experience depression and aren't very happy with how their lives are going don't tend to feel great about their relationships. From this research and other research described above, we can derive some factors that seem most likely to contribute to a positive body image.

First, it is important that you feel like your relationship is a relationship (i.e., involves some commitment) and you are appreciated by your partner. This may seem like a low bar, but I guarantee that most of us will have relationships that we would not describe as committed and that don't leave us feeling appreciated. It makes some sense that we wouldn't necessarily bask in self-appreciation if our partner doesn't seem to value and respect us.

Second, it seems unlikely that you're in a body-positive relationship if it involves a lot of fighting or teasing. Again, I understand that this probably seems somewhat obvious. But we may need to step back and evaluate our relationships a bit to be sure that there aren't tense interactions we'd rather live without. Maybe your partner has started to jokingly mention your "love handles" or "muffin top" and at first you could laugh along, but now you cringe as soon as any mention of your appearance comes up. Chances are you're going to need to change this topic of discussion or change your partner if you are invested in maintaining a positive body image – and mental health.

Third, physical intimacy is important to our relationships and our body image. Physical intimacy can take many forms, but most of us seem to enjoy some types of physical affection. Most of the research examining links between body image and sexual experiences focuses on a positive body image contributing to positive sexual experiences. However, as

I mentioned above, body image and physical intimacy are linked in a variety of ways.

Finally, research suggests that the things that initially attract you to someone (e.g., their appearance) are not necessarily related to relationship satisfaction in the long term. Everyone ages, our appearances change, and we increasingly appreciate having shared interests and values with our partners. Perhaps one simple relationship goal to keep in mind is that you and your partner should enjoy each other's company. Just being with someone can be a beautiful thing.

MY STORY: Cora Elle, 26 years old, she/her, USA

I've been feeling a lot better about my body in the last year or so. I think partly this is because I just don't look at it as much! I've been working from home mostly since the pandemic started and this has allowed me to care less about how I look and to dress for comfort. It's been a nice opportunity to think about being comfortable both psychologically and physically.

I'm also in a good relationship now with a woman I hope to marry someday when this pandemic ends. We've been together for three years now but knew each other before that. We met when we were both struggling with different aspects of our lives and we've really grown a lot since then. Living together during the pandemic has actually been a lot of fun.

My last relationship was somewhat abusive; my partner was really not nice to me, although she found me attractive and complimented my appearance and I think I really needed to have that positive feedback. It's strange because I didn't really know what a relationship was supposed to be like until I experienced a healthy one. I learned a lot from my past relationship, but I've come to see that I really want to feel connected to someone and be able to share myself freely with someone. To feel truly accepted and cared for by your partner is so important.

Growing up gay in Iowa was hard. My parents and family were supportive, but I experienced homophobia. I think all of that took more of a toll on me than I realized initially. We all get so many messages about what our identity should be and how we should behave. If we don't fit that mold it can lead to anxiety; I know my body is physically affected by the stress of discrimination. I now understand and think more about systems of oppression and how hard it can be to thrive when you're the one being oppressed. Of course, you often don't even know it's happening because it's all around you; you're a fish swimming in the waters of oppression but you've never known any other water.

Our sense of gender, sexuality, and identity are interwoven and my identity has definitely affected my relationship with my body. I've internalized a lot and was not always willing to stand up for myself. I'm learning to expect people to treat me well and to treat myself well also. One way I try to honor my body now is through exercise that is not goal oriented. I've found movement to be really good for my mental health; it improves my mood, it's a reset on a bad day, and it's a form of expression. I've tried a variety of forms of activity that I've enjoyed in recent years: aerial arts, pole dancing, traditional dance classes. Sometimes I even just freestyle dance at home. I think that dancing is a good way to process emotions; sometimes you have feelings you don't have words for. Dancing and other forms of movement can really help you feel in tune with your body.

SUMMING UP #THEPEOPLEYOUKEEP:

- Our relationships with our family members, friends, and romantic partners are important to our body image and can have both negative and positive effects on our sense of self.
- Developing friendships and romantic partnerships can be an important part of your life during your teens and adulthood and can open you up to feelings of vulnerability about your appearance; experiencing some stress surrounding the initiation of relationships is common.
- Maintaining healthy relationships can contribute to your positive body image development.

FIND OUT MORE:

- Peggy Orenstein is an expert on all matters of sex among young people. Her books *Girls and Sex* (Harper, 2017) and *Boys and Sex* (Harper, 2020) are based on hundreds of youths' experiences.
- *Stronger Than You Think: The 10 Blind Spots that Undermine your Relationship … and How to See Past Them* (Little Brown, (2021) by Gary Lewandowski is a great read to help you understand relationships better. His focus on the myths that can sabotage our relationships is really useful.
- For more scholarly articles and information about relationships and body image, see the companion website for this book: www.theBodyImageBookforLife.com.

CHAPTER 11

BE ACTIVE

#JoyfulMovement

> "The journey of a thousand miles begins with one step."
>
> – Lao Tzu, *Chinese philosopher*

MY STORY: Hannah Marjorie, 25 years old, she/her, USA

I don't like my body now, but I don't actively hate it. I understand that I don't have to love my body all the time. It carries me around and allows me to live my life. I think what I've adopted is body neutrality, before I even knew that term.

As a kid I started to row on a crew team for fun. I was good at it and I started to row competitively before I had hit puberty. It became an all-consuming part of my life and I was home schooled so that I could keep practicing and competing. The culture of crew doesn't really encourage healthy lifestyles. There's a lot of focus on weight and size combined with intense exercise. I basically grew up around people who would skip meals to drop weight and sometimes wouldn't eat all day. Coaches would make comments about people's bodies. Some of the things coaches would say were really traumatic. I remember having the opportunity to go to a camp with an Olympic crew coach and I didn't even enjoy it. I was worried the whole time that he would call me fat in front of everyone. I stopped rowing at age 16 and I had a hard time figuring out how to use my time without being active 6 hours a day.

I've grown up with social media, starting on Facebook in 6th grade. I'm sure social media has had some impact on my body image experiences, but not necessarily in the ways that you'd expect. Celebrity culture and influencers on Instagram don't really affect me, but there is a lot of troubling information on social media about eating. When I left crew and was trying to live a normal life – going to a regular school, having time for friends, taking care of my health – I'd find myself looking at "what I eat in a day" posts about how little people could eat or body "before and afters" on Instagram. And there are always influencers that post about their recovery from eating disorders and how healthy they are now. Now I think that the fact that they'd keep saying they're recovered seems to suggest that maybe they weren't. At any rate, all of that sort of content really normalized the disordered eating I had been around with crew.

It's taken a long time and a lot of work, but I've come to accept that I have to be OK with my body; it's necessary for my survival. When I was younger, I didn't have a lot of perspective and I tended to think in the short term. I wasn't thinking about the rest of my life but about what I wanted in the moment. If I was to give my younger self advice, I'd say that it's really important to be patient with yourself and take care of your body. Sometimes you have to sit with discomfort, that's just a part of life.

We're only on this planet for a short time. We should all try to live our best lives.

As you've probably noticed by now, a theme in this book is that it's important to take good care of your body. One way to care for your body is to be physically active. But this doesn't mean to be active like Hannah was as a child and have our lives revolve around our physical activities. Most of us will not be professional athletes or Olympians and there's no reason for us to make physical activity our *job*; it should be an enjoyable part of our lives. My goal in this chapter is to help you think about how to take just one step towards an active life that works for you and your body.

IN THIS CHAPTER YOU'LL LEARN

- about the benefits of physical activity for your health in general,
- techniques for establishing good habits for physical activity or anything else that could benefit your health, and
- how your activity may have direct links with your body image.

Often people talk about engaging in physical activity or exercise with the goal of being fit. Fitness is a broad term with more than one definition. What counts as fitness for one person may look very different for another person. The word fitness has become popular in recent years, as has the word fitspiration (aka, "fitspo"). Fitspiration refers to images, memes, or ideas, usually shared on social media, that are supposed to inspire fitness. Unfortunately, there is some research to suggest that fitspiration isn't always inspiring. Sometimes seeing images of fit people (usually slender, muscular, and impressive) just makes us feel bad about ourselves, which is pretty demotivating. And it's not just fitspiration: much of the information about fitness that is available online lacks scientific support and may be harmful. Entire communities have developed online that promote unhealthy eating and exercise behaviors, so be sure you are only tuning into information online that is helpful and evidence based.

MYTHS AND MISINFORMATION:

Following fitness experts on social media will help motivate you to exercise regularly and get in shape.

Who doesn't like to feel inspired? Most people can use some inspiration (or "fitspiration" #Fitspo) to help them maintain good health habits, including regular physical activity. However, fitness experts on TikTok or Instagram may not be the best place to turn to for advice and inspiration. Usually, fitness "experts" do little more than work on their fitness. That's their job – to look (and be) fit! In contrast, you most likely go to school or work, hang out with your friends, have hobbies, do household chores – just to name a few of the activities that keep most of us busy every day. Most of us don't have time to exercise all day. What this means is that fitness experts, celebrities, or professional athletes aren't usually a good source of comparison (or inspiration) because the rest of us have different lives and priorities.

In one recent study, exposure to fitspiration images on social media was linked to higher rates of eating disorder symptoms. Participants not only felt bad about themselves after viewing what were intended to be inspirational images, but they may have been more likely to adopt unhealthy eating habits as well. Turns out, fitspiration is usually not all that inspirational.

How much activity is ideal?

Most kinds of movement are good for you. Obsessing about how much you exercise is *not*. The US Department of Health and Human Services recommends that kids aged 6–17 years engage in one hour of physical activity a day. It is recommended that adults be active for at least two and a half hours per week (and up to five hours per week). It is important for activity to include both aerobic and strength-training activities. Any activity that includes working up a sweat and breathing heavily – running or even a fast-paced walk – is aerobic activity. It's valuable to also take part in physical activity that's good for your muscles and bones. This can include stretching and working on flexibility, practicing yoga, doing push-ups or sit-ups, and even lifting weights.

What often gets lost in discussions of physical activity recommendations is that some people enjoy being active, and different sorts of activities, more than others. Some people have lives that more easily allow for regular physical activity. Others have health problems that may limit physical activity. Guidelines are only guidelines and should be taken into consideration in relation to your life, preferences, and circumstances.

MYTHS AND MISINFORMATION:

It's important for your health that you take 10,000 steps a day (and keep track of them)!

No one seems to know with absolute certainty where the idea that it is important to take 10,000 steps per day originated. Some have attributed it to a Japanese company that marketed a pedometer (old-fashioned step counter) back in the 1960s as a device to measure 10,000 steps. Of course, today your phone or Fitbit may include 10,000 steps as your daily goal without you even suggesting this.

Recent research suggests that you probably don't need to take 10,000 steps per day to improve your health. In fact, pretty much any exercise may improve your health and the benefits may level off at around 7,500 steps per day (at least this seems to be the case in research examining women). Some studies indicate that about 5,000 steps is a good goal in terms of lowering mortality risk. This all depends on a variety of factors, of course. If you haven't been active in a while, going out and running 10,000 steps (four to five miles) is probably not a great idea and could do more harm than good but walking half that distance may feel great.

The bottom line is that, although fitness goals may be motivating, it's important not to fixate on them. You want to enjoy being active and not spend mental energy obsessing about your exact number of steps per day.

What are the benefits of physical activity?

Why try to be regularly active? There is a great deal of scientific research to suggest that regular physical activity is good for both your psychological and physical health. Almost every part of your body benefits from physical activity: your heart, lungs, digestive system, immune system, and even the genes in your cells seem to gain protection from physical activity. With age, we all become more vulnerable to a variety of health issues, and physical activity has been found to protect against many of them (e.g., cancer, dementia, osteoporosis) and even improve others (e.g., type 2 diabetes, arthritis). Being active may also help us live longer.

Being physically active is also associated with better mental health and lower rates of anxiety and depression. It has even been found to alleviate some symptoms of severe mental health problems such as schizophrenia. Even light activity – a couple of hours per week – has been linked with better mental health, whilst being *inactive* may be associated with mental health problems like depression. Weightlifting has been studied recently as a treatment for post-traumatic stress disorder; for some, feeling greater physical strength is a powerful antidote to trauma. Of course, if you are experiencing any mental health concerns, you should talk to a medical or mental health professional; don't rely on a new exercise routine to solve what may be a complex issue requiring more than one form of treatment. Further, physical activity *may* be a part of eating disorder treatment, but should be overseen carefully given that overactivity can be a symptom of an eating disorder (see Chapter 6).

Perhaps most important, though, is that if you are regularly active you are more likely to develop an appreciation for how good you feel when you move your body. If you develop a love for swimming or running or hockey, you're more likely to appreciate the way your body feels doing these activities. Developing active hobbies that you enjoy and *want to do* can have far-reaching benefits.

EXPERT ADVICE:

Dr. Rachael Flatt, Olympic figure skater, clinical psychologist, USA

"When we are physically active or playing a sport, it's so easy to get caught up in the idea that our bodies have to look a certain way. It doesn't help that what we see on social media – from revealing workout clothes to photoshopped and filtered workout images – is often unrealistic. In those moments, I find it helpful to think about all the incredible things my body can do for me, and I remember that being inclusive and celebrating all shapes, sizes, and abilities gives us all a chance to thrive and love what we do."

Be active because it feels good and it's fun

Not everyone finds physical activities that they enjoy early in life, and some of us don't find anything that we enjoy until later in life, but it is worth trying to find an active hobby that you love. As I've already mentioned, being active has physical and mental health benefits, but it also can just make you feel good. Exercise scientists call the mood boost we can get from exercise the *feel-better effect*. Think about a time that you felt exuberant after winning a game, crossed a finish line, or couldn't stop dancing to a favorite song; that's the feel-better effect and it can be pretty amazing.

Of course, if you find yourself engaging in a physical activity that you don't enjoy or that you feel you have no natural talent for, you may find yourself feeling worse – not better. I had this experience a number of years ago when I tried to pick up tennis. At one point, the tennis instructor asked me if I usually wore glasses (which I was not wearing at the time) because I was so incredibly uncoordinated he thought I was visually impaired. Tennis turned out to be humiliating – not my true calling. If an activity you participate in makes you feel stressed out or self-conscious, you are unlikely to experience the feel-better effect and it's OK to move on to something else.

It's valuable to think creatively when it comes to ways to move your body. Maybe you'll find that you love DIY projects around the house, enjoy playing golf with a friend, or use your dog as an excuse to take walks every day. You don't have to be competitive (or even social) to be physically active, and there are an endless number of options. Be creative in thinking about ways to keep your body moving because regular, sustained activity is important and you can't expect yourself to keep doing something that results in just repeatedly getting hit in the head by a tennis ball.

Consider Your Reasons

Why are you physically active?
Check a box next to the reasons that you engage in physical activity.

☐ To reduce guilt

☐ To follow self-imposed rules

☐ To feel comfortable eating certain foods

☐ Because a friend/partner/ coach says to

☐ So that you don't feel heavy

☐ Because it is fun

☐ For physical health improvement

☐ For stress-reduction

☐ To see other people

☐ To feel good

There are many reasons why people choose to be active and some reasons are more adaptive than others. Did you check more of the reasons in the left or the right column? Arguably, the reasons in the right column are indicative of a healthier mindset when it comes to physical activity. Notice, however, that reframing your reasons – focusing on feeling good as opposed to avoiding feeling bad – may make a meaningful difference. If you notice that you are participating in physical activity for the reasons in the left column, you may want to start to shift your approach to activity by choosing some activities that you enjoy more than what you are currently doing. More advice follows below for getting into activity habits that you both like and can sustain.

There's a direct link with body positivity

Of course, this is a body image book and not a general health book. I wouldn't be bringing up physical activity if there wasn't a direct link with body image. As you read in Hannah's story (and you'll read in Marieke's story later in this chapter) the physical activity–body image link is not always positive. But it can be! Physical activity can increase positive feelings about your body.

You may recall the discussion of body functionality from Chapter 2. Basically, the idea is that focusing on how our bodies work or function is an important part of nurturing positive body image. Recent body image research suggests that playing sports *decreases* negative feelings some people have about their bodies and *increases* the positive feelings they have about them. Feeling good about your body can also increase participation in sports. This may be a cycle that occurs for some people, with physical activity improving their body image, which in turn leads them to participate in more physical activity.

One cool study called *This Girl Can* examined links between viewing a video campaign of diverse women (in terms of size, shape, age, and ethnicity) exercising and body image. When women in their 20s saw the video campaign of diverse – in other words, relatable! – women being active they were more likely to appreciate their own bodies and feel compassion for themselves. This is important because when we feel appreciative of our bodies and not judgmental of ourselves, we're more likely to try new activities. This study also may help to explain why some of the fitspirational imagery on social media is *not* inspirational. Typically, personal trainers and fitness gurus are not especially relatable and we tend to view ourselves as inferior. However, we don't need to be athletes or gurus to reap the rewards of physical activity.

Any movement that we do regularly can help us think more about the many amazing things that our body can *do*, and focus less on how our body looks.

EXPERT ADVICE:

Dr. Katy Milkman, University of Pennsylvania, Wharton Professor and author of the national bestseller *How to Change*

"As a university student, I found it incredibly difficult to motivate myself to exercise after a grueling day of classes. All I wanted to do was curl up on my couch and binge-watch lowbrow TV shows. But I knew that for my mental and physical health, moving my body was important, so I came up with a trick that changed everything: I started reserving certain indulgent entertainment for gym-only access. This strategy, which I now call "temptation bundling," was a huge success. I started craving trips to the gym to find out what would happen to my favorite characters, and time flew while I was exercising. When my workout finished, I was rejuvenated and ready to get home and do my classwork. My grades improved, my stress dropped, and I was more physically fit, too. As an assistant professor, I ran a research study to test the benefits of temptation bundling on a larger population. I found that giving people gym-only access to tempting entertainment to pair with their workouts significantly increased people's levels of exercise."

Establishing activity habits

Maybe as you're reading this chapter, the idea of becoming more active is growing on you. How do you get in the habit of being more active? It's often difficult for people to change their habits, but there are some evidence-based practices that will help.

First of all, don't aim too high. That may sound pessimistic, but it's easy to set an unreasonable fitness goal and then find it impossible and give up altogether. Set a small goal that you know that you can achieve. Maybe your goal is to walk your dog for 10 minutes each day, or join a karate class with a friend each week. Do something that will be fairly easy to accomplish. Once you do this new activity for a few weeks, consider adding another change. Maybe walk your dog for 15 minutes per day, or run with your dog instead of walking. Maybe add in a second karate class per week, or sign up for a different sort of fitness class. When you set small, achievable goals and you're successful, that success will motivate you to do more. If it doesn't, then reconsider your goals. Maybe you don't really like karate. Maybe you'd rather go to a gym instead of walking your dog.

Another important consideration if you're trying to add physical activity to your regular routine is that you may have to take something else out of your regular routine. There are only so many hours in the day. If your schedule is already packed full, you may need to drop something to add physical activity. Be sure you don't drop other valuable activities like spending time with your significant other, or getting enough sleep. If you'd rather binge Netflix shows than go to the gym, try Professor Milkman's strategy that she calls "temptation bundling." In other words, save your temptation (Netflix) for your time *at* the gym and you may find it easier to get motivated.

Another tactic that may be helpful is to do what is sometimes called ***stacking***. Take a habit you already have and stack another one onto it. For example, I am in the habit of watching television in our family room at night. So, I've left five-pound weights in the family room and I try to do about 10 minutes of weightlifting while I watch TV. It's not enough to build big biceps, but it's helped me to develop some upper body strength and is pretty painless to do while watching a show. If you think of habits you are in every day – even something as simple as brushing your teeth, which you could add a yoga pose to – you may also be able to think about stacking a new habit onto your old habit. The idea is not to lessen the enjoyment of one habit (e.g., TV watching) but to combine habits when it can work for you.

Telling people about your goals and asking for help in achieving them can also be helpful. Scientists call this a **commitment strategy**. We tend to be more likely to stick with a goal if other people know about it because we don't want to feel embarrassed if others realize we didn't. It can also be valuable to ask people for help in meeting our goals. Maybe you'd like a parent or a friend to remind you of your activity goals, or maybe you want a friend to exercise with you. Either way, it can be useful to have supportive people in your life helping you achieve any of the goals that you have.

Finally, be patient with yourself and don't give up. If you don't follow through with whatever activity goal you've set for yourself, don't throw in the towel forever. Maybe your life feels too busy right now, but once summer rolls around you'll have more time and you can work on setting new activity goals. Once you establish a habit for two to three months it tends to stick, but you have to keep at it before the sticking happens. People tend to be creatures of habit and changing those habits isn't easy. Be patient with yourself if you don't meet your goals the first time you try. Most people have to try more than once to change any habit.

MYTHS AND MISINFORMATION:

It's important to treat yourself with "tough love" in order to achieve your fitness goals.

There are a lot of cultural messages that suggest the importance of being hard on yourself to stay motivated to achieve your goals. For example, we may feel that we want to avoid being "lazy" as opposed to doing something active because it is fun or will make us feel good. It's almost as if fun goals don't count.

There is actually a fairly extensive psychological literature on goal setting and achievement that suggests that when we frame goals in terms of things we want to do (called *approach* goals) versus things we want to avoid (called *avoidance* goals), it's typically easier to achieve our goals. A number of explanations have been offered for this, but one is that it can be difficult to avoid certain thoughts or behaviors entirely, making avoidance goals less satisfactory and less easily achieved.

How is this relevant to body image? It's unlikely that you'll be able to always avoid *all* the behaviors that contribute to body dissatisfaction. If your goal is to completely avoid sitting on your couch, then you're likely doomed to fail. But if your goal is to go on a walk with a friend, you stand a better chance of meeting that goal. Try to think of physical activity in terms of approach goals or things you want to do, not as punishment or something obligatory.

Can you exercise too much?

Watching professional athletes and people who enjoy being active can make us want to devote more of our time and energy to achieving our own fitness potential. Physical activity is incredibly good for our body and our mind, but as with anything, there can be too much of a good thing.

It's important to listen to *your* body. If you're tired all the time, really hungry from exercising, or not enjoying exercising anymore, then you're probably overdoing it. It's also possible that your body will respond in a very serious manner to physical overexertion. For example, in extremely rare cases, when people exercise for long periods of time every day for months, muscles can break down and kidney damage can occur; this condition is called rhabdomyolysis and it can lead to permanent disability or even death.

It also seems pretty clear that too much exercise can have a negative effect on your mental health, especially if exercising feels like an obligation and not like something that you enjoy. Psychologists sometimes refer to exercise that feels necessary, especially more than one time per day, as **compulsive exercise**. It has become trendy, especially among men, to compulsively exercise and focus on weightlifting in an attempt to build muscle. This is sometimes referred to as bulking (eating excessively while lifting heavy weights), cutting (reducing body fat while maintaining muscle), and shredding (working on muscle definition or getting ripped). Fitspirational posts and videos often encourage these trends, but it's important to keep in mind that most of the "plans" that you see online or on social media for building muscle or getting in shape are not developed by scientists with the education and training to offer good advice. Avoid any sorts of plans or recommendations that seem extreme. Extreme approaches to exercise can absolutely do more harm than good for your health.

If you feel like you're scheduling your day around exercise, worrying about how much you exercise, feeling guilty if you don't exercise, not eating unless you exercise a certain amount, or eating more to support your exercise habit, you may be a compulsive exerciser. Compulsive exercise can be dangerous for your mental health and you should talk to a mental health professional with relevant expertise if you think this describes you. Being regularly physically active can be great, but if you push yourself all the time and are not enjoying your activity, it's time to step back and rethink things.

Q&A:

For as long as I can remember, I've kept track of what I eat and my exercise using *MyFitnessPal*. I try to stick to a set number of minutes of physical activity per day and a set meal plan. I find myself skipping meals if I can't fit in my workouts and I know this is not healthy. How can I adjust my habits so that I don't feel like I have to earn my food through exercise?

What seems most important to me is that you already *know* you *don't* have to earn your food through exercise – even if sometimes you *feel* like you do.

There is research that has examined the use of *MyFitnessPal* and other apps for exercise and nutrition monitoring. At least one study suggests that *MyFitnessPal* is helpful to people who are not particularly motivated or who have a hard time sticking with their health goals. But if you are already pretty motivated, which it seems that you are, *MyFitnessPal* doesn't actually increase your odds of sticking with your health goals. Further, research suggests that fitness app use is associated with disordered eating behaviors. In other words, you may be better off not using this or any other app to track your exercise and nutrition habits; you're already motivated and you don't want to maintain maladaptive thoughts or behaviors about how much you eat or exercise.

You may recall from Chapter 5, which focused on intuitive eating, that an important element of developing a healthy relationship with food and your body is *trusting your body*. Relying on an app instead of your own physical signals, including your hunger, satiety, and tiredness, makes it hard to be in touch with your own body. A great deal of scientific evidence suggests that people naturally adjust their food intake depending on their activity level. Instead of monitoring your behaviors with an app, what if you just listen to your body's needs?

EXPERT ADVICE:

Amanda Sobhy, professional squash player, USA #1
and World #4

"At the start of my career, my mindset was solely fixated on working out to have my body look a certain way. I was a high performing athlete, so I felt like I needed to 'look the part' like the other top professional squash players. Over time, I shifted my mindset from how my body should look to all the incredible things it can do for me as an athlete. After many years of hating my body for what it looked like, I have learned to finally appreciate my body."

It's never too late

Maybe you aren't particularly interested in being more physically active than you already are, or you just don't have the time, with school, work, or other activities you're involved in. During your teens and 20s you may feel pulled in many different directions and your schedule may be chaotic. School, work, friends, and family may all take up time and it may be that you just can't find the time to do *one more* activity. As you get older, your schedule may become more predictable (depending on your job) and you may find more occasions and opportunities to engage in physical activity of all types. So even if you don't get into a particular form of exercise now, this doesn't mean that you won't when you're older. Physical activity will benefit your mind, body, and body image, even if you don't make it a habit until later in life. Just be sure to stick with movement that brings you joy.

MY STORY: Marieke Judith, 29 years old, she/her, the Netherlands

I've been feeling uncomfortable in my body lately. I had been an over-exerciser and then last year I tripped and broke my ankle. I had to have surgery to repair my ankle. Across the past year I have not been able to exercise much at all.

My devotion to exercise goes back to my early childhood when I began studying gymnastics. Starting at the age of four, I was in the gym a lot and I was good, but I was not the typical skinny gymnast. I can still remember being only eight years old and having a coach tell me to lose weight so that I could improve a particular skill. I wanted to go to the Olympics, so there wasn't much I wouldn't do. I started by just skipping cookies, but then I would only eat part of my meals or skip lunch at school altogether. When my parents became concerned about my weight loss, my general doctor reassured them that I had a healthy BMI and was fine. I was anything but fine.

Fortunately, my parents pursued treatment for me and I regained some weight. My eating habits became more regular, but I turned to exercise to manage my weight. I would exercise in addition to my gymnastics workouts. At 19 years old, my knee was seriously injured and my gymnastics career ended. I had encountered physical and mental abuse as a gymnast, so it was for the best. I turned to cross-fit to fill my exercise compulsion.

After years of maladaptive eating and exercise habits, I sought further treatment this past year. I live in the Netherlands and our health care for physical health problems is amazing. But because my BMI doesn't suggest that I'm in danger, I couldn't get eating disorder treatment here; treatment for psychological issues is much less available. I spent seven weeks in South Africa in a treatment center. By the time I got there I was so weak I was in a wheelchair – but my BMI was fine!

The providers at the clinic in South Africa saw me as a person, not just a BMI. I still get support remotely from them. I work with both psychologists and dietitians. I also see other patients from the clinic in remote group therapy. It's a sort of digital family, although I wish sometimes that we were able to be together in person. I also go to meetings most days online for support with people around the world. Some are in recovery and some are still struggling, but we work together to support each other. It is nice to have people who care and understand all that I've been through.

My advice to my younger self would be to learn to listen to your body; it will tell you what it needs, so pay attention if you are hungry, tired, or in pain. We live in a society where being high functioning and on, on, on all the time is so important. But sometimes we need to be off. We need to just rest.

SUMMING UP #JOYFULMOVEMENT:

- Being regularly physically active is an important part of taking care of your body and nurturing a positive body image.
- Physical activity can improve not just how you feel about yourself, but also your mental and physical health.
- There are direct links between physical activity and body image, with activity likely to help you value your physical functionality and appreciate all the wonderful things that your body can *do*.

FIND OUT MORE:

- The Centers for Disease Control and Prevention's website includes information about physical activity: www.cdc.gov/physicalactivity/index.html.
- Tally Rye's *Train Happy: An Intuitive Exercise Plan for Every Body* (Pavilion Books, 2020) is a wonderful exploration of physical activity that's compatible with positive body image development.
- For more scholarly articles and web pages with information about physical activity, see the companion website for this book: www.theBodyImageBookforLife.com.

CHAPTER 12

PHYSICAL HEALTH

#HealthMatters

"When health is absent, wisdom cannot reveal itself, art cannot become manifest, strength cannot be exerted, wealth is useless, and reason is powerless."

– Herophilus, *ancient Greek physician*

MY STORY: Emma Rene, 20 years old, she/her, USA

It has taken me a long time to accept my body for what it is. However, going to college has really helped change my level of confidence in myself. I started stepping outside of my comfort zone all around, including wearing clothes I would have never typically worn in high school. I remember the first time I wore a tube top to a party. I would have never worn a tube top in high school, especially not without a bra. For a girl who wears a 36D bra, sometimes you're told "oh you can't wear that, your boobs are too big." For me, my boobs were not the hardest part of wearing a tube top, it was my stomach. Even in high-waisted jeans I was still concerned about how my stomach looked. It wasn't just about my stomach being fat, it was about the continuous glucose monitor I wear on my stomach for my diabetes that clearly sticks out like a sore thumb when I'm out. Sometimes I'll get lucky enough and I'll have placed it in a good enough spot that my jeans will come up high enough to cover it, but sometimes it still shows. It took me a while to be completely comfortable with wearing my glucose monitor on my stomach because I always worried about looking like a complete robot. I also wear an insulin pump on my arm that is completely noticeable 90% of the time, so I did not want to have to wear anything else to make me stand out even more. But after a while of being on campus and seeing girls wear what they wanted to confidently, I decided to give it a try myself. One day I went out and started buying different clothes that I would not have worn before. Now my closet is full of super cute clothes that make me look and feel good.

My mom has always been my biggest supporter and very best friend. I think for her it all goes back to her own insecurities and making sure I never feel about myself the way she did about herself. Everyday my mom finds some way to remind me how beautiful I am even if I look like I have just crawled out from under a rock.

To take it a step further, when I am feeling down on my body specifically, she tells me that my body is beautiful. She doesn't push me to do anything differently, she doesn't talk down to me or ever minimize how I'm feeling, she just supports me. Sometimes when I am wearing an outfit that looks really good on me she'll ask me if people threw rose petals down on the ground for me when I walked in the room. I just laugh and tell her, "no." There are other times where she'll think an outfit looks really good on me and then ask me if anyone else has told me how beautiful I was today. Again, I just laugh. It's so cute how she thinks that everyone I will ever meet will think I am as beautiful as she thinks I am. But even if no one else besides her thinks that, that's all I need.

Being a girl is hard enough without having body image insecurities. I think it's really important to teach young girls to be nice to each other – and nice to themselves. It's our responsibility to be kind to one another. It doesn't need to be a competition with each other about who is more successful than the other. Instead share your successes and accomplishments with other girls. Make your confidence your favorite accessory each day. Wear your beauty with pride and a big smile and hold your head up high. When I feel a little down on myself, I remember my favorite quote, "Confidence looks good on you girl!"

I've already discussed some health behaviors in earlier chapters, including eating (Chapter 3), physical activity (Chapter 11), and substance abuse (Chapter 7), but there are other behaviors relevant to your health that are worth considering such as your sleep, screen use, and substance use. Further, some of us, like Emma, will experience chronic health conditions that warrant paying extra attention to our health behaviors. Even if we are lucky enough to maintain good health across most of adulthood, we all age and our bodies change. How do you take care of your physical health as your parents and family do less of this for you?

IN THIS CHAPTER YOU'LL LEARN

- some health habits to aspire to and some to avoid so that you can protect your health in general and body image in particular,
- some considerations if you have or develop any chronic health conditions that require extra attention to your body and health, and
- body – and body image – changes that may accompany your normally-aging body.

Most health psychologists (such as myself) endorse a **biopsychosocial model** of health. What this means is that people's biology, psychology, and social circumstances are all important in understanding their health. In other words, someone like Emma, who has diabetes, likely had a biological vulnerability to diabetes. Her experience of diabetes – for example, how under control it is – is affected by her thoughts and her behaviors (aka, her psychology). For Emma, her mom, an important component of her social environment, has been key in helping her to adapt to having diabetes. A biopsychosocial approach to health appreciates that health is not just about physical health. Similarly, our body image is complex and results from our biological, psychological, and social experiences.

In this chapter, I discuss some of the health issues and concerns that are common during the late teen and early adult years. My goal is to help you to appreciate that there are some ways to be proactive when it comes to your health. Taking care of your body is essential to nurturing a positive body image. However, there are so many factors that affect your health in general and your body image in particular; not all of these factors are under your control.

Sleep is so good for you

It's important to your health that you make sure your body gets enough rest. More than half of all high schoolers (ages 14–18 years approximately) and 35% of adults in the USA don't get enough sleep. Think about what time you usually get into bed, when you usually fall asleep, and when you usually wake up. Are you sleeping *at least* 7–8 hours of sleep each night?

The Centers for Disease Control and Prevention recommends that 13- to 18-year-olds sleep 8–10 hours each night. Adults should sleep *at least* 7 hours per night. These recommendations aren't arbitrary but are important because sleep is related to pretty much every aspect of your health and well-being. Although the relationship between sleep and different sorts of diseases is complicated, not getting enough sleep may place you at risk for illnesses including type 2 diabetes, heart disease, and even depression. There is even evidence to suggest that sleep-deprivation can disrupt the hormones responsible for feelings of hunger and fullness; people tend to eat more when they are tired. At the very least, not sleeping enough is a way to feel miserable, tired, and short-tempered. Some research suggests that adults who get less than seven hours of sleep even have a more difficult time regulating their emotions (i.e., find it more difficult to exhibit appropriate emotions for any given situation). Making sure you get enough sleep is one thing you can do to take care of yourself and protect your mental and physical health, including your body image.

EXPERT ADVICE:

Lisa L. Lewis, MS, author, *The Sleep-Deprived Teen*

"It's so easy to get overscheduled, but make sure you leave enough time for sleep. Up until age 18, teens should be getting 8–10 hours. (And after that point, it's still 7–9 hours.) If you're regularly not getting enough sleep, everything becomes more difficult! You may have figured out how to manage, but you're not doing yourself any favors. If you're learning or studying for a test, you won't be as effective. And if you're working out or preparing for a big game, your coordination, accuracy, and even your recovery time will be impacted. There's also an important connection between sleep and mood, with sleep-deprivation linked to depression, anxiety, and suicidality. Being well-rested boosts your emotional resiliency and your well-being and makes it easier to deal with whatever stressors come your way."

Power down your phone

According to my phone, I spend over three hours per day using it. Three *hours!* I am pretty sure this is not entirely correct, or if it is, it's only because I use my phone to listen to music, books, and podcasts while I do other things (walk the dog, make dinner, drive to work, etc.). Still, I probably spend too much time on my phone, and you probably do too.

Why am I talking about our phone use in a chapter on physical health in a book about body image? Our phones (and tablets and televisions and laptops and video games) are often barriers to being both physically active and sleeping enough. How often do you watch TikTok videos on your phone when you know you should be going to sleep? Or maybe you spend time binge watching a show on Netflix or texting with your boyfriend or girlfriend when you know you'd feel better if you went for a walk? It's important to find some sort of balance. Watching shows or videos and playing video games can be entertaining but taking good care of your body means moving it most days and also letting it rest. Of course, *some* screen use is relaxing and not at all problematic. (More direct links between media use and body image are discussed in Chapter 8.)

Alcohol, smoking, vaping, and pot

I discussed substance use disorders and addiction in Chapter 7, but many people will use substances and not *necessarily* develop a problem or addiction. Alcohol, tobacco products, and weed are likely to be a part of your life – directly or indirectly. I don't want this book to take on the flavor of a stereotypical school health class, so I'm only going to briefly provide some information about substances you're likely to encounter or consider trying during your teens or early adulthood, and I'll explain how substance use can be related to body image.

Alcohol

Alcohol can be consumed responsibly by many people, depending on health status and vulnerability to addiction. Responsible consumption is sometimes characterized as not more than one drink per hour, not more than one or two drinks in a day, and not drinking every day.

There is some research to suggest that women (but not necessarily men) who are dissatisfied with their bodies are more likely to consume alcohol. It's been hypothesized that these women may drink to help manage their insecurities. Regularly drinking alcohol to manage any negative feelings – anxiety, depression, or insecurity – is unlikely to be a good long-term strategy. A much more adaptive strategy would be to talk with someone, whether it be a relative, friend, or a professional, about these negative feelings so that you can work to reduce them as opposed to "treating" them with alcohol.

Smoking

The number of people who smoke (i.e., cigarettes and similar products like cigars) has decreased significantly since the 1960s. Although over 40% of adults were smokers in the 1960s, the current prevalence of adult smokers in both the USA and the UK is about 14%.

The long-term effects of smoking are decidedly negative. According to the World Health Organization, at least eight million people die each year of diseases resulting from smoking. In addition to the known cancer risk, smoking increases the likelihood of heart attack, stroke, and lung disease. Although those risks may feel far off (most smokers don't die of cancer or a heart attack in their 20s), more immediate risks include bad breath, irritability, problems concentrating, and sleep disturbances.

Some people start smoking because they find doing so decreases their appetite. In fact, research suggests that body image concerns may increase the likelihood of picking up a smoking habit. I probably don't need to tell you that smoking to try to control your eating behaviors or your concerns about your body is not a good idea. If you find yourself willing to pick up a potentially deadly habit because of body dissatisfaction, this is a clue that you could use some support to work on your body image. And, over time, therapy is likely to be much cheaper than a smoking habit!

Vaping

E-cigarettes (aka, e-cigs or vaping) were introduced as a "safer" alternative to smoking in the early 2000s. However, we now know that not only is vaping most definitely unsafe, but it often leads to smoking cigarettes; one-third of teens who vape end up smoking within six months. Vaping has also been associated with disordered eating behaviors. Recent research suggests that flavored cartridges in particular are popular among young people who are looking to lose weight. Vaping to try to avoid eating is a pretty terrible idea.

Marijuana

Marijuana (aka, pot, weed, or cannabis) is legal for medical purposes in many states in the USA and is increasingly legal for recreational purposes. In the UK, marijuana is illegal for recreational use but legal for medical use. However, like any other similar substance, the legality of marijuana doesn't necessarily make it safe. Of particular concern is the increasing frequency with which marijuana products are mixed with other "stronger" substances such as fentanyl, which can have deadly consequences for users. Even marijuana sold in a dispensary or medical establishment is not always well regulated enough to make it safe for responsible use and marijuana does lead to addiction for many and has serious, detrimental effects for countless others. Even limited use can have negative effects on memory, motivation, and judgment. Further, brain science makes it clear that our brains continue to develop well into our 20s; marijuana use (and other substance use including alcohol use) can interfere with this brain development.

Some research suggests associations between marijuana use and body dissatisfaction, especially among young women. Marijuana is sometimes used to try to alter appetite or lose weight, but this is not a healthy nor sustainable strategy! Scientists have been studying medication approaches to weight loss for decades, but most are either not effective or not an option for long-term use because of side-effects like nausea and gastrointestinal issues. If marijuana was the secret to weight loss, trust me, we'd know by now!

An important part of becoming an adult is thinking about your future and the long-term consequences of your behaviors. *Any* substance use can impact your life both today and in the long run. Substances (as well as prescription medications) can interact in potentially fatal ways. It's important to respect and care for your body and make responsible decisions when it comes to substance use.

Performance and image-enhancing substances

Although this section is called "Performance and image-enhancing substances," that title is somewhat misleading. For the most part, any substance marketed as capable of helping you to build muscles, become leaner, or lose weight is not going to accomplish any of those physical changes. As much as you may wish there was a magic pill that could help you to lose weight, build muscle, or remedy a variety of other concerns, magic pills rarely exist in real life. Perhaps most concerning is that in most states in the USA there is no age restriction on the purchase of dietary supplements. Even young kids who don't necessarily know better can purchase potentially dangerous supplements.

Anabolic steroids, on the other hand, can increase muscle size. Our bodies produce natural steroids, which are hormones that help to promote growth and development. Anabolic steroids are a synthetic version of steroids that can be taken as pills or injected into the body. They are illegal unless prescribed by a physician, and their use is not allowed among professional athletes.

Steroids may increase muscles, but their use also can have really serious, negative consequences. Steroids can shrink boys' and men's testicles, thicken breast tissue, cause mood swings and even depression, and keep young people from growing taller. Steroid use is also associated with relatively minor issues such as hair loss, oily hair, and acne, as well as serious issues such as heart attacks and cancer. Anabolic steroid use can become addictive, meaning it can be difficult to stop taking steroids once a person starts. Given all the serious risks associated with steroid use, no one should ever use them unless prescribed by a doctor, but children, teens, and young adults especially should avoid them given the risks associated with growth and development.

EXPERT ADVICE:

Julie Lythcott-Haims, speaker, activist, and author of *Your Turn: How to be an Adult*, USA

"When I was embarking on adulthood, I wish I'd known that it gets better. YOU get better. I came to know and love myself fully in my early forties. I had no idea what a relief it would be to one day not feel I had to constantly apologize for my Blackness."

Ages and changes

You can do everything right. You can get plenty of sleep. You can avoid spending hours on your phone every day. You can never smoke, vape, drink alcohol, or use any sort of dietary supplement or drug. And yet, your body will not always be healthy and functional. We will all experience viral and bacterial infections, from the common cold to Covid-19. We will all experience injury, whether it be a sprained ankle or a concussion. And, if we're *lucky*, we'll get older, and our bodies will change with age.

There are a lot of messages – and products! – thrown at us to suggest that we should fight aging and changing. If you are ever ill, injured, or pregnant, you'll hear loud and clear that you should aim to "bounce back." Although it is valuable to do what feels possible and reasonable to maintain your health, and it is natural to resist physical change, it's also psychologically healthy to appreciate that change is not always bad. As a teen and young adult, you will experience a lot of changes. You may move out of your parents' house and need to prepare all your own meals. You may find yourself in a committed relationship that brings with it new experiences and habits. You may even find yourself starting your own family and parenting others. All these changes will impact you psychologically and possibly physically. It is likely that you will gain weight in adulthood; with age we stop growing taller and our metabolism slows, making weight gain typical. Your body shape may also change if your activity habits change, you experience pregnancy, injury, or other changes to your health. These changes can be unsettling and even upsetting, but do not always have negative consequences for body image.

In fact, there is some research to suggest that people's body image does *not* get worse with age; it often improves! Our culture may value youth, but age often brings wisdom. This includes the wisdom to respect your body and feel gratitude for what it's been through and what it's capable of. Perhaps, with age we also come to understand that body perfection doesn't exist; there's some benefit to accepting our bodies and even lowering our standards! Being body positive means feeling comfortable in our own skin. In other words, not just being comfortable with our appearance but with *who we are.*

Q&A:

What does my normal body look like? When will it stop changing?

Advertisements and other media messages typically seem to imply that if you just work hard enough, eat the "right" foods, and do the "right" exercise, your body will look great – and stay that way. This, however, is an oversimplification of reality!

Our bodies continue to change as we age – sometimes in ways that we (and others) notice and sometimes in subtle ways – and we are always aging. There are so many factors that affect the appearance and functionality of our bodies: how much sleep we get, the extent to which we are physically active, our stress level, normal hormonal changes, our mental health, whether or not we experience acute (short-lived) or chronic illness, and even our interpersonal relationships. We have limited control over many of these factors, but we can do our best to take good care of ourselves by getting enough sleep, nourishing our bodies, being active, and maintaining connections to other people we care about and enjoy. And we can work towards adopting an accepting mindset so that when we notice changes in our bodies, we don't feel self-critical or concerned, but appreciate that this is completely normal.

MYTHS AND MISINFORMATION:

When students begin going to college, they tend to gain weight – the "Freshman 15" (pounds).

Life transitions may lead to changes in habits, including eating and activity habits. Many people stop living with their parents when they go to college and their health habits change. Some people may gain weight as a result of their change in habits and some people may lose weight. Some universities have dining centers with buffet style meal options that may contribute to eating more, because when faced with unlimited food, people do tend to eat more.

However, research suggests that the average college freshman does not gain 15 pounds (~7 kg). In fact, *if* weight is gained, it is typically less than 4 pounds (less than 2 kg). Many college students – especially boys – are still growing, so weight gain is completely normal and healthy, not something to be feared.

It may take you some time to settle into habits that are comfortable for you when you first move away from your parents' house. Try to be patient with yourself during this transition and enjoy ordering pizza with your friends!

Challenging changes

Sometimes our bodies change in ways that are especially challenging. I don't necessarily mean gaining a couple of pounds or kilos your first year away at college but experiencing an illness or injury that forces you to reevaluate what your body is capable of and maybe even how you feel about it. Being diagnosed with a physical health condition or disability becomes increasingly common in adulthood, can be distressing, and can affect body image.

As an adult, more than half of all people experience some type of chronic, long-term health condition. These conditions may be somewhat minor, such as seasonal allergies, or they may be more complicated and serious, such as diabetes or heart disease. Most chronic conditions require extra medical attention, doctors' appointments, and some lifestyle changes in order for people to function optimally. Chronic health problems may necessitate dietary changes or extra sleep.

Sometimes mental health and physical health conditions are related; people with chronic health problems are more likely to experience depression, for example. Some research suggests that individuals with physical disabilities are found to experience as much as three times the number of depressive symptoms as people who do not have disabilities. In these circumstances, it's normal for people to feel let down by their body, or to wish that they didn't have to deal with these things.

Health problems don't have to lead people to view their bodies negatively. In recent research looking at body image among people who experience chronic pain, people who are more accepting of their pain tend to have more positive body images. It really matters how people think about their health. If they're accepting of their health problems – after all, most people will have some kind of health problem at some point – it's less disruptive to their feelings about their body overall. This isn't to say that you should feel glad about having to deal with a health problem, but if you do experience a health problem or disability, there are things you can do to help yourself cope. Never feel like you need to deal with this sort of thing alone. Encouragement or even resources (like food or money) from caring others can be important if you find yourself in need of an extra dose of support. There are also psychologists who are trained to help people who are dealing with challenging health issues; they can be a huge help if you find yourself having a tough time.

EXPERT ADVICE:

Kelly Devos, writer and author, *Eat Your Heart Out*

"I've come to believe that loving yourself and wanting to change yourself are two feelings that should be able to peacefully coexist."

Acceptance and change

As you've probably noticed, I believe that having a positive body image requires at least some self-acceptance; even accepting body changes that you may not always like. We all have things about ourselves that we'd like to change or improve. I'd like to get more sleep and I'd like to understand international politics better. I often try to make myself get in bed earlier so that I can accomplish the goal of getting more sleep. I don't get upset with myself when it doesn't work out – as it often doesn't – because I know that is counterproductive. I just try again the next day. Someday, I'll try to read more about international politics so that I have a deeper understanding of issues that I care about but I just don't have the time to invest in reading about at this time in my life.

It is OK to be working towards self-acceptance and self-improvement at the same time. Feeling some amount of contentment allows us to be comfortable in our own skin, but it also can allow us to get joy out of activities intended to improve ourselves. Self-change efforts should never be about punishing ourselves, but about doing what is best for our health – both body and mind.

MY STORY: Darcy Sophia, 26 years old, she/her, UK

Both my body and my body image have changed a lot in the past year or so and it's something I've been thinking about a lot. I was always really slender growing up, but I've gained weight as I've been focusing on getting a doctoral degree (University of Bristol) and school takes up so much of my time. I no longer have the same time for myself and it is hard to be regularly active. I've been pondering how all of this affects how I move through the world.

I didn't think that much about my body when I was thinner. I was comfortable with how I looked. I went for a routine doctor's appointment last year and when the nurse checked my weight, she said that I had gained a lot of weight and she asked me about it. That felt really awful and I felt shamed even though part of me appreciates that bodies change across time and there is nothing "wrong" with me. I messaged my boyfriend when I came home from that appointment, but he doesn't seem to care at all about my weight. We've been together for two years now, but we were friends before we started to date. I'm glad he doesn't seem to care about my weight, but also wish he was a bit more supportive of my concerns. I suppose it's a no-win situation for him because if he was to indulge my concerns, I would feel like he was unhappy with how I look.

I'm a vegetarian and I'm a pretty healthy eater so I don't really aim to change my eating habits as much as to just be mindful of eating fruit and veg each day. During the pandemic I did the couch to 5 k program, and I liked gradually taking up running, but I didn't stick with it. I also started to do yoga at home using videos and I really enjoy that and think that's more sustainable for me. I've always been really flexible, so yoga comes naturally to me. Yoga gives me a sense of achievement because I can see what my body is capable of and I feel proud that I can get myself into these complicated poses. I also think it helps me to feel in touch with my body; the mindfulness piece of yoga is really great.

My mom has always told me not to worry about weight or weighing myself; you'll know if your body changes by the fit of your clothes. I still think that is good advice and that measuring your body is not healthy or helpful. I also really want younger people to appreciate that normal bodies are diverse and they change across time. There's so much fake imagery all around us; I wish the media presented more authentic images. It would make it easier to accept our normal bodies if we saw more of those bodies. It is so easy to get caught up in trying to look like these images that aren't even real. It's sad to think of how many people miss out on life while trying to make themselves more like unrealistic ideals.

SUMMING UP #HEALTHMATTERS:

- Sleep is an incredibly important contributor to maintaining physical and psychological health; positive body image may be difficult to achieve if you are sleep-deprived.
- Substance use – from drinking alcohol to vaping – may seem fairly common, but can be incredibly detrimental to your health. Being body positive includes treating your body well and not misusing substances.
- Our bodies change with age; this is completely normal even if it is sometimes very uncomfortable.
- Many of us will experience health concerns and even chronic health conditions as we age. This makes it extra important to take good care of our bodies and approach them with acceptance.

FIND OUT MORE:

- Lisa Lewis' book *The Sleep-Deprived Teen* (Mango Publishing, 2022) offers all sorts of interesting information about the importance of sleep not just for teenagers, but also for adults.
- *The Ultimate College Student Health Handbook: Your Guide for Everything from Hangovers to Homesickness* by Dr. Jill Grimes (Skyhorse Publishing, 2022) contains so much information about nearly all of the topics in this chapter.
- *High: Everything You Wanted to Know about Drugs, Alcohol, and Addiction* (Houghton Mifflin Harcourt, 2019) is a really cool book written by a father/son team, David and Nic Sheff. They provide both personal experience and a lot of easy-to-read factual information about substance use, abuse, and addiction.
- For more research articles and web pages relevant to the information in this chapter, see the companion website for this book: www.theBody ImageBookforLife.com.

CHAPTER (13)

SELF-CARE

#Compassion

> "Stay close to anything that makes you glad you are alive."
>
> – Hafez, *Persian lyric poet*

MY STORY: Meera Aashvi, 22 years old, she/her, USA

I don't feel bad about my body, but I guess I wouldn't say it's ideal. I've always been pretty hard on myself and in the past few months I really just decided that I need to take that energy and channel it into being more productive.

I graduated from college recently and I've had more time to think about what I'm doing with my life. I read the book Atomic Habits, *and it helped me rethink how to establish longer-term habits. I've come to see that focusing on short-term goals can be most productive in the long run. It's important to me to feel healthier and to create a sustainable lifestyle.*

I've started to walk on a treadmill most days and I've also been trying to get into yoga and Pilates. I've found some videos online and on TikTok that make beginner Pilates pretty fun. The more I exercise, the more I think of my body in terms of how I feel and not just how I look.

I'm also trying to find more foods that I like and that are nutritious that I can eat more often. I love fruit and making smoothies and fruit bowls like açai bowls. I am Indian and a lot of Indian food consists of carbs and some sort of protein, so I try to have one Indian meal a day and then be sure to eat fruits and vegetables.

I've been really working on gratitude practices and creating a healthy mindset. I try to think about what I'm grateful for each day and I'm trying to journal at least three times per week. A quote that I've been thinking a lot about lately is "life is coming from you not at you."

I really do believe that what you put out into the universe is what you get back.

When I was growing up, the bodies viewed as most attractive were the skinniest bodies. Then a shift started to happen and there were more different bodies in the media. The Kardashians and more curvaceous bodies became more popular. I think that has helped me to view my own body more favorably because I see that you don't need to just be skinny to look good.

If I had to offer my younger self advice, I think I'd say that you can't always change what is going on around you, but you can change your own behavior. It's important to take control of how you react to things and do what's best for yourself.

Nearly every day of our life contains some sort of stressor. Maybe it's something small like not being able to find a parking space. Maybe it's something big like a fight with a loved one. We weather most of these stressors without too much trouble. Human beings are amazingly resilient. As Meera describes in her story, how we react when things aren't easy is really important. Further, how we take care of ourselves day-to-day is essential.

Developing a positive body image is not something we wake up and do one day. It's something we do every day. It's built on consistently adaptive thoughts and behaviors and it requires us to direct a caring, compassionate attitude towards ourselves. In this chapter, let's consider how you "talk to yourself" and how this is related to sustaining a positive body image across time.

IN THIS CHAPTER YOU WILL LEARN

- why taking care of yourself and being self-compassionate is essential to the development of a positive body image,
- the importance of embodiment to your well-being, and
- other ways to conceptualize and foster self-care.

Body image is an important component of your overall well-being. And, as I've discussed in other chapters, particularly Chapter 7, body image not only contributes to your mental health, but your mental health also contributes to your body image. In this chapter, I discuss some approaches to caring for your well-being, and thus, your body image. I call the chapter "Self-care" because it is an all-encompassing title for the chapter, but

I actually find the term self-care somewhat annoying. I think it's been coopted by commercialism and influencers who would like us all to buy more bubble bath. I have nothing against baths (or even bubble baths), but I think that self-care is about much more than treating yourself here and there. It's about self-respect, appreciating your self-worth, and taking care of yourself each and every day. To do this, you need to be aware of how you talk to yourself and offer yourself plenty of self-compassion.

EXPERT ADVICE:

Dr. Niva Piran, psychology professor and author of *Journeys of Embodiment at the Intersection of Body and Culture*, Canada

"Be compassionate with your body! Don't hold a critical mirror to your body, but, instead, to the culture that may have disrupted the way you live and feel in your body. Further, take social action and assure a constructive environment for you and others!"

Self-compassion

Research has consistently established links between self-compassion, eating behaviors, and body image. What is **self-compassion**? If you're compassionate, you're concerned about others and you show them sympathy. Self-compassion is treating yourself with this same sort of concern and sympathy. People who think of themselves with kindness are more likely to have more intuitive and healthy eating habits than people who think poorly of themselves. Self-compassion is also linked with positive body image.

If we're honest with ourselves, we know that we treat ourselves worse than we treat nearly anyone else. We may think critical thoughts ("you are the stupidest person in this room!") and try to motivate ourselves to maintain maladaptive behaviors ("you need to walk 20,000 steps every day or you're never going to be able to wear those pants again!"). Self-compassion research suggests that this self-criticism rarely accomplishes what we hope it will and it is not motivating or good for our psychological health. What should we do instead?

Self-kindness

One of the core tenets of self-compassion research is that we need to challenge our critical self-talk. Instead of being judgmental and harsh towards
ourselves, we need to be more understanding. For example, if we usually
like to exercise most days, but we choose not to exercise one day, instead
of thinking of ourselves as "lazy," we should try to understand our behavior. We should appreciate that we probably were tired and needed a rest
day. We don't need to feel guilty or condemn our behavior; we can accept
it and work on viewing ourselves with kindness.

We all get messages that we shouldn't be kind to ourselves because being
hard on ourselves is viewed as more effective, but research shows this
isn't true. Feeling down on ourselves or guilty is usually not motivating
in the long run. These negative emotions may inspire some short-term
behavior changes, like a long run after a rest day, but they don't usually
inspire sustainable, healthy thoughts and behaviors. We need to think
of ourselves with a gentler, patient approach and greater acceptance of
who we are.

Common humanity

We all suffer, even though our suffering may look different. We all feel inadequate and disappointed in ourselves sometimes. All too often, suffering
and feelings of inadequacy or disappointment lead us to isolate ourselves.
We feel bad, so we don't want to be around other people. Adopting a
self-compassionate view means appreciating that everyone is imperfect
and it is important to look to others for support when we feel bad. In
self-compassion research, this is referred to as appreciating our ***common
humanity***.

Have you ever heard the saying, "misery loves company"? One interpretation of this saying is that our imperfections can be sources of connection
with others. Cultural messaging tends to focus on our individualism – how
we can be the best version of ourselves. What if we focused more on our
shared experiences? We don't need to compare ourselves with others and
feel bad when we come up short. We can instead recognize that perfection
is both impossible and boring; being human means failing, learning, and
growing. Being compassionate towards others can allow for connection,
but being compassionate towards ourselves can also.

Self-Compassion Scale (Short Form)

Are you wondering how self-compassionate you are? Take this survey designed by psychologists to find out.

	Almost never	Seldom	Sometimes	Often	Almost always
(1) When I fail at something important to me, I become consumed by feelings of inadequacy.	5	4	3	2	1
(2) I try to be understanding and patient towards those aspects of my personality I don't like.	1	2	3	4	5
(3) When something painful happens, I try to take a balanced view of the situation.	1	2	3	4	5
(4) When I'm feeling down, I tend to feel like most other people are probably happier than I am.	5	4	3	2	1
(5) I try to see my failings as part of the human condition.	1	2	3	4	5
(6) When I'm going through a very hard time, I give myself the caring and tenderness I need.	1	2	3	4	5

	Almost never	Seldom	Sometimes	Often	Almost always
(7) When something upsets me, I try to keep my emotions in balance.	1	2	3	4	5
(8) When I fail at something that's important to me, I tend to feel alone in my failure.	5	4	3	2	1
(9) When I'm feeling down, I tend to obsess and fixate on everything that's wrong.	5	4	3	2	1
(10) When I feel inadequate in some way, I try to remind myself that feelings of inadequacy are shared by most people.	1	2	3	4	5
(11) I'm disapproving and judgmental about my own flaws and inadequacies.	5	4	3	2	1
(12) I'm intolerant and impatient towards those aspects of my personality I don't like.	5	4	3	2	1

Circle the answer to each item and sum up the numbers. Then divide by 12. If your total score is 4–5, you are high in self-compassion, 3–3.9 is indicative of moderate self-compassion, and a score below 3 suggests that you need to work on your self-compassion!

(This measure was originally published by Raes, Pommier, Neff et al. in 2011)

Q&A:

I'm so used to being hard on myself and pushing myself to do more and accomplish more, that I don't know how to stop. What is the best way to quiet that self-critical voice?

Changing our thoughts and behaviors can be difficult, so it is important that you are patient with this process. The first thing that is important is to work on recognizing when you are being self-critical. Pay attention to your internal dialogue or how you talk to yourself. Are there some things that you routinely say to yourself? Where do you think that this dialogue comes from? Are you repeating something that your mother or a teacher once said to you? It may make sense to literally make some notes (in a journal or even using the notes feature on your phone) about what you say to yourself and when as you become more familiar with this internal critical voice.

Once you begin to recognize events that trigger self-criticism and the specifics of this critical dialogue, it's important to work on changing the voice in your head to be nicer. Challenge that voice and tell yourself that judgment and condemnation are not helpful. Think of ways to change your internal dialogue. Could you tell yourself that you understand why you are upset but that being harsh towards yourself is not helpful? Can you avoid some of the triggers of this critical voice? For example, if looking in the mirror becomes a time to critique your appearance, can you look in the mirror less?

It's important that you not just monitor your self-criticism but get better at replacing it with supportive internal dialogue. Tell yourself that you tried your best. Tell yourself that you are not where you want to be, but you are getting there. Tell yourself that some days are better than others, and that's OK! Think of what you'd tell a friend who was feeling down about skipping a work-out, sleeping in, or having a second helping of dessert. You'd tell them that they were probably tired, needed rest, and should enjoy some comfort food – right?

It's valuable to work on creating a positive body image because it can allow us to stop viewing others as competition or people we need to look as good as (or better than). Instead, think of everyone as doing their best to look and feel good in a society where messages constantly fuel our insecurities. Everyone sees and hears commercials, social media, and other messages suggesting we need to change ourselves and buy products to fix ourselves. Exercising compassion towards others and ourselves allows us to appreciate how difficult it can be to cope with those messages and how we all have this struggle in common. An added benefit to adopting this mindset is that it allows us to view both ourselves and others with greater kindness. In other words, when we practice self-compassion, it often results in *more* positive feelings towards and increased energy for others.

Mindfulness

Another way to nurture self-compassion is to be **mindful** of your physical, psychological, social, and emotional needs. Mindfulness actually has two related definitions. To be mindful means to be aware. It's important to spend some time thinking about your needs; for example, you may find that you value some time alone each day. Or maybe you realize that you feel better when you get at least eight hours of sleep each night.

Mindfulness also refers to being present in the moment, accepting your thoughts and feelings, and paying attention to yourself. There are different ways to try to achieve this sort of mindfulness, including yoga and meditation. One recent study supports the usefulness of mindfulness for improving body image. In this study, young women were shown a series of brief videos about mindfulness, including videos about mindfulness in general, breathing exercises, and eating mindfully. At the end of the study, women's body image ratings showed some improvement, suggesting that learning about mindfulness was helpful.

Practicing **yoga** is another way to increase mindfulness. Through stretches, poses, and breathing exercises, yoga can help promote body awareness. Yoga can also encourage a focus on body functionality and acceptance. Because of all of this, researchers have begun to explore yoga practice as a way to improve body image. Some research findings suggest that practicing yoga can increase mindfulness, improve how people view themselves, and positively impact body image. There is no guarantee that a weekly yoga class will dramatically alter how you feel about your body, but there is hardly any downside to trying yoga. You may improve your flexibility and strength as well as your general well-being. Feeling better about your body could just be icing on the cake.

Meditation is another approach to mindfulness that can help you to nurture self-compassion. Meditation techniques aim to train the mind, just as physical activity aims to train the body. Meditation practices often involve breathing techniques to relax the body and calm the mind. Some forms of meditation involve stillness and focusing attention on a particular object while trying to clear thoughts from the mind. Sometimes the goal is to not think about *anything*. Meditation can also focus on acknowledging thoughts or concerns and working on accepting them or distancing yourself from them. The goal can be to let thoughts flow in and out of our minds; notice and observe thoughts without judgment. Meditation can include listening to music that's enjoyable and soothing, and can even include reading or writing/journaling. The goal of any sort of meditation is to feel calm, relaxed, and "centered."

What does this have to do with body image? For some people, meditation can help them feel not only calmer, but more in touch with their bodies. As I've mentioned before (see Chapter 2), this sense of "being in touch with" or "happily living in" our bodies is sometimes referred to as **embodiment** (which I discuss more below). This may seem obvious, but we *are* our bodies. We cannot escape them. Feeling comfortable and accepting of our bodies is an important part of developing a positive body image.

Overall, self-compassion has been found to be strongly related to well-being, in terms of motivation, mental health, and health behaviors. It is also linked with body image and related behaviors. In a review study that examined all of the research on self-compassion and body image a number of explanations are offered as to why self-compassion is protective against body dissatisfaction. People who have more self-compassion seem less concerned about appearance ideals or maintaining the bodies of models and celebrities. Further, people who have higher self-compassion are less prone to comparing themselves to others, so are less likely to feel like they have bodies or appearances that are inferior to others; they seem to appreciate themselves more. In fact, people with more self-compassion are even less likely to spend a lot of time "checking out" their appearance, or engaging in what is often called body surveillance among body image scientists. Of course, this research doesn't unequivocally indicate that increasing your self-compassion will increase your body positivity, but it just might.

MYTHS AND MISINFORMATION:

When we accept or forgive ourselves, we are letting ourselves off the hook.

We tend to believe that we need self-criticism to motivate ourselves. But self-criticism actually undermines us. Self-criticism can also contribute to a sense of loss and even hopelessness. If you were talking to a coworker and called them lazy, fat, or bad at their job, how would you expect them to respond? They likely would not respond well! In fact, it seems likely that they'd no longer want to work with you.

Attacking ourselves is not all that different than attacking a coworker; it is a waste of time and energy. In fact, it is likely to be counterproductive. When we judge and criticize ourselves, we can actually trigger a stress response; there can be a physical, hormonal consequence. When we offer ourselves compassion, we actually may be able to quiet our stress response and reduce our level of cortisol, a hormone involved in stress regulation. This can be both psychologically and physically restoring.

If you are having a difficult time offering yourself self-compassion, you may want to write yourself a letter. I know this may sound a bit silly, but some recent research suggests that this can be very effective. But you can't write yourself just any sort of letter, it has to be a self-compassionate letter. Write about your strengths, weaknesses, and imperfections but as an unconditionally loving friend would describe you. You can focus on your body and body image in particular, or another aspect of yourself that you are having a difficult time with. Your letter can't be critical but should be kind. Multiple studies suggest that this sort of an exercise could both boost your mood and your body image.

Embodiment, reconsidered

Whereas self-compassion allows us to perceive and talk to ourselves with kindness, embodiment allows us to feel connected to our physical selves. As I mentioned in Chapter 2, embodiment is a term used to describe our experiences of our bodies and the extent to which we feel in touch with and comfortable with our bodies. Many of the strategies that tend to promote self-compassion and self-care may also promote positive embodiment. For example, relaxation breathing and yoga can help us attend to both our minds and our bodies.

There are overlapping philosophies that underlie both research on positive body image and practices such as yoga. Both are concerned with the development of a sense of contentedness or peace. Although an individual with positive body image is often viewed as feeling good about their body all the time, this is not necessarily the case. Acceptance, trust, and respect of the body are central to a positive body image. The practice of yoga is also focused on self-awareness and enlightenment. Both philosophies suggest that we can choose how to respond to our realities; we can focus on that which contributes to our suffering or we can move towards a sort of freedom – from others' expectations and from our own misperceptions of reality. In other words, we can choose to take care of our bodies and our minds and move away from cultural and personal ideals and expectations that burden us, such as unrealistic beauty ideals.

Our abilities to experience embodiment may result from practicing something like yoga, but may also be more likely when we make a conscious decision to shift our world views. What I mean by this is that we may benefit from adopting views that run somewhat counter to many popularly held beliefs such as the importance placed on physical appearances. People who identify as girls/women may benefit from resisting the idea that they should be submissive, not too assertive, and small. We are also likely to feel more connected with our bodies when we experience social situations where we are valued and considered an equal (as opposed to being devalued or considered lesser than). Feeling empowered lends itself to feeling embodied, but sometimes we need to commit to our own empowerment when it is not offered to us.

Other approaches to self-care

For some, nurturing self-compassion and a positive sense of embodiment may be a difficult or slow process. For example, typical mindfulness techniques are not for everyone. Maybe you've tried yoga and meditation but find it boring. Some people are naturally fidgety and then, ironically, inclined to feel bad if they can't be calm and enjoy relaxing. It's possible that more experience with yoga or meditation may lead you to get more enjoyment out of these practices. It's also possible that these approaches to relaxation are never going to be relaxing to you. There are other ways to practice self-care, feel in touch with yourself, and work on developing a positive body image.

Exercise can be a great way to relax for some people. Of course, you have to be doing some sort of exercise that you enjoy in order for it to relax you. But even just short walks, enjoying the scenery around you, and taking a break from the rest of your day can be a good way to de-stress.

For some people, grooming and hygiene practices can be a source of relaxation. A long, warm shower or a hot bath can feel soothing and relaxing. Getting a massage or having someone paint your nails may feel like a helpful break from your daily routine. Spending time washing your hair or cleaning your face can even be a way to feel like you're caring for yourself. After all, that's what self-care is: nurturing yourself in ways that you enjoy and make you feel good.

Self-care can be social

Self-care and relaxation practices are often described as solitary activities that you must do alone. I don't think this is necessarily true. If I meet a friend for lunch and we talk and catch up and spend an hour or so just ignoring the stressors in our lives and enjoying each other's company, I feel relaxed afterwards. I'm sure I'm not the only one who finds socializing to be a source of relaxation at times, and talking with others a way to rethink things in life that may be bothersome.

There is substantial research to back up the importance of what psychology professors, Drs. Waldinger and Schulz, call **social fitness**. Exercising our bodies is important, and attending to our minds most definitely

EXPERT ADVICE:

Dr. Nichole Wood-Barcalow, psychologist, body image scientist, and co-author of the *Positive Body Image Workbook*

"Moving towards positive body image is about accepting who you are *versus trying to* change what you are. *It's being kind with yourself versus being judgmental. It's fueling yourself properly instead of counting calories or restricting what you eat. It's offering yourself permission to exist just as you are without scrutinizing what you should be."*

Q&A:

I want to be accepting of myself, but I am relatively heavy and I feel like the rest of the world is not accepting of me. How do I work on self-compassion and acceptance in this hyper-critical, appearance-driven world?

Of course, it is difficult to accept ourselves when the world doesn't seem to! This can be extremely difficult when it comes to body size given that even most medical providers – the people we entrust with our physical and mental health – exhibit **weight stigma** (sometimes called **anti-fat bias**). Weight stigma is a term used to describe any bias against people because of their body size. We are all exposed to countless messages indicating that thinness is an important contributor to attractiveness, thus it is difficult for most of us to *not* have some weight stigma. Further, there are misunderstandings held by many medical providers that include a focus on weight as an important contributor to health. However, the latest research makes it clear that there are many other contributors to our health that we should focus on.

Given these popular beliefs, it makes sense that we would want to be thin! Why wouldn't we want to fit in, be liked, and be perceived as healthy and attractive?

Unfortunately, there are only a couple of options for managing this situation. You could try to change your body to be more acceptable to others, but this may only be possible by engaging in extreme physical activity or disordered eating behaviors. As I've stressed throughout this book, our body size is not totally under our control, but largely determined by our genes. Changing ourselves to please others may not be a good coping mechanism in general, and is a strategy that is unlikely to succeed when it comes to our weight. Further, it doesn't make much sense to go to unhealthy measures (e.g., skipping meals) to achieve health (or, what some would perceive as healthy, a lower weight).

The only other option really is to accept ourselves, while appreciating how difficult the world may make this for us. A supportive therapist may be helpful in the journey towards self-acceptance. And, *total* self-acceptance isn't even necessarily the end goal. I'm not sure I know anyone who experiences complete self-acceptance, but a strong dose of self-compassion can get us closer to acceptance and farther from the desire to change ourselves to accommodate others. It's important to remember that there isn't anything wrong with you, but plenty is wrong with our culture that stresses such narrow standards of physical attractiveness and a limited perception of health.

The bottom line: Even if others aren't willing to accept us, we benefit immensely from offering this to ourselves.

matters, but it is equally essential that we engage with others if we want to be healthy and happy. Whereas loneliness has been found to be detrimental to both our psychological and physical health, social relationships protect our health. People who are more socially connected not only live longer but are also more likely to fend off mental and physical illness.

We don't necessarily need to have long, therapeutic lunches with close friends to reap some wellness benefits of socializing. In fact, even casual, social interactions can be enriching. Maybe it's the person you always see at the coffee shop, the person who paints your nails, or a person who works in the same building as you, but it's been shown that warm interactions with these acquaintances improves well-being. Interestingly, most of us tend to underestimate how much others like interacting with us, a phenomenon referred to as the **liking gap** by psychologists. Conversations with others benefit us, but also benefit the barista whose child we ask about regularly. What does this have to do with body image? In as much as body image is a component of our identity derived, in part, from our social experiences, increasing the number of positive social encounters we have regularly may have consequences for our development of a positive body image.

Meaning-making

For most of us, feeling really good about ourselves means feeling good about our lives and that our lives are meaningful. Our relationships – the people in our lives – are typically a critical component of our sense that life has meaning. But there may be other factors that contribute to your well-being, or sense that life is meaningful.

Eudaimonia (pronounced u-day-monia) is a term first introduced by Aristotle to describe the importance of living in tune with our potential in order to achieve happiness and a "good life." We all can strive towards becoming the best version of ourselves. If you're not sure what that would look like, ask yourself these questions:

What do you do well?
What do you *want* to do well?
How will the world look different because of you?

Meaning-making happens when we allow ourselves to attend to our feelings and motivations and think about what we stand for and who we want to be.

I'll return to some of these themes in the next chapter when I discuss the importance of contributing to social change that empowers all people. However, it is important to also keep in mind that we should strive for self-improvement only in the ways that it makes sense and serves us. Perfectionism is not the answer. Products and purchases are not the answer. Living up to others' standards is not the answer. Becoming comfortable in our own skin and developing a positive body image does not happen overnight, but you can decide to start the journey today.

MY STORY: Jess Emily, 25 years old, she/her, UK

I haven't been at my best in the last year or so when it comes to my body image. As we were coming out of (pandemic) lockdown in the UK, I ended a serious relationship. This led to some binge eating, especially when I couldn't sleep at night. I've had a long history of using food as a coping mechanism.

My father was really emotionally abusive when I was growing up. In my teens, I often had a hard time eating when I was upset and I suffered from disordered eating. It's probably not a coincidence that he was always really critical of my body and my appearance. He would compare me to other girls my age and tell me I didn't look as good as them. Making myself smaller was a form of self-punishment.

When I was 17 years old, my parents split up. My mom tried to kill herself when my dad left. Even though he was abusive, she had been so dependent on him for so long that she didn't know how to manage without him. The antidepressant that she's on has helped somewhat and so has some counseling. I'm close with my mom now and I feel like we take care of each other.

When I turned 25, I started to write a list of 25 things to do while I was 25. I want to go camping because I've never been. I want to get a couple more tattoos. I want to go to Scotland. The list is still evolving, but one thing I'm doing now is donating my eggs. This process has really inspired me to appreciate my body for the things it can do. It's pretty incredible to think that my eggs are going to be able to help someone else have a baby. The female body is amazing!

If I had to offer my younger self advice, I'd tell her to find people who will support her. Don't worry what others are doing – do your own thing. And be 10% braver. Imagine what we could all accomplish if we were just that much braver.

SUMMING UP #COMPASSION:

- Practicing self-compassion – kindness towards ourselves, an understanding of our common humanity, and mindfulness – can be an important contributor to the development of a positive body image.
- There are many ways to practice self-care that extend beyond grooming practices and may include nurturing our social relationships.
- Examining what it is that adds meaning to our lives and working to enhance our eudaimonic well-being can also enhance our body image.

FIND OUT MORE:

- Dr. Kristin Neff is the originator of the concept of self-compassion and has written a number of books on the topic. I recommend starting with *Self-Compassion: The Proven Power of Being Kind to Yourself* (William Morrow, 2015).
- For more exercises you can do to improve your own self-compassion, you may want to check out *The Mindful Self-Compassion Workbook: A Proven Way to Accept Yourself, Build Inner Strength, and Thrive* (by Kristin Neff and Christopher Germer; Guilford Press, 2018).
- For more references and information related to body image, self-compassion, and self-care, see the web page for this book: www.TheBodyImageBookforLife.com.

WE CAN

CHANGE

THE WORLD

TOGETHER

CHAPTER 14

CHANGE THE WORLD

#BeTheChange

> "Never think that a small group of committed people can't change the world. Indeed, it is the only thing that ever has."
>
> – Margaret Mead, *American cultural anthropologist*

My relationship with my body is complicated. Very complicated.

I began to develop an eating disorder when I was a preadolescent. The beginning of my eating disorder was like a gradual movement towards a cliff and then falling over it. It was never a traditional eating disorder, but I was diagnosed with anorexia because I was small and I restricted what I ate. It was always somewhat more complicated than that.

I can remember becoming really aware of having a body around the age of 10. It seems this is when you notice that other people are commenting on bodies and food. You notice that people make moral judgments when it comes to your health and how you look. Two more specific experiences seemed to trigger my eating disorder: I went on a five-day school trip when I was away from home for longer than I ever had been and then not long after that I transitioned to a different, larger school. In both of these novel environments, I felt different and like I didn't fit in. I didn't feel that I belonged and the stress of that led me to restrict my eating.

My physical health deteriorated quickly when I started to restrict what I ate. I was hospitalized early in my disorder for four months. But the treatment wasn't enough and I ended up in another treatment center in London (hours away from where I live). I was in and out of treatment for nearly a decade. I was really resentful at the time of the people trying to help me; I really didn't feel understood by them. Now I have regrets because so much of my life was lost and I wish I could get those years back.

After I left treatment for my eating disorder my symptoms almost morphed into something else. What I began to experience resembles obsessive-compulsive disorder (OCD) and I have to work all the time to tame my symptoms because they are really debilitating. I can feel stuck when I feel overwhelmed and I find it difficult to process anything. It feels as though there is a wall there that I just can't get past, but I don't know why. I think the narratives around mental health lead us to believe that we're responsible for our health. But it's not that simple. I understand why it may seem like it should be, but it's not.

National health care in the UK has made it possible for me to have access to treatment, but the care I received focused a lot on my physical stability and not my psychological health. My treatment has not been as holistic as it needs to be, so some of my recovery is up to me. I've been working a lot on accepting myself, but it is not a calm acceptance. My body has changed so much physically, and I still sometimes don't feel comfortable with how I look now. It's difficult to feel so much the same on the inside but to look so different on the outside.

It has helped me to try to help others. I have volunteered in different mental health spaces – at a mental health crisis line, as an eating disorder peer support person, and I talk with providers in medical facilities to try to help them understand eating disorders and mental health more. I try to advocate for more and better treatment.

If I could offer my younger self advice, I'd tell her that she's allowed to be herself – whoever that is. She should live a life that is comfortable for her. It is important to understand that we all keep growing and healing and our mental health may ebb and flow. We all have some broken parts and they don't all need to be fixed because perfection isn't the goal.

Lily's story is not that unusual. Fortunately, the majority of us will not spend a lot of our early lives in inpatient mental health treatment. However, many of us will devote a lot of mental space, time, and energy to concerns about our bodies, weight, and appearance. None of this is conducive to developing a positive body image, healthy habits, or good mental health.

I often tell my students that one of the amazing things about education is that it changes you; the more you know the more you can become a different person and see the world through different eyes. Upon reading this book, I hope you are a different person. I hope you see the ways in which you may be able to take some of the time and energy you have exerted feeling worried about your appearance and not feeling "good enough" and instead use your resources to engage in meaningful relationships and activities that enhance your life. I also hope you are motivated to share what you've learned with others. But before I offer some ideas about how you can take what you've learned and change the world (no big deal, right?), I want to reemphasize and touch on a few other topics.

Remember: Don't compare or despair

It's natural for us to compare ourselves to other people, but this tendency to compare ourselves to others, or social comparison, can be problematic. We're all unique in our own ways, and trying to be like someone else will rarely work. Changing our looks (or any of our qualities, for that matter) is harder than it appears. Most of our qualities have a strong biological component that make them difficult to change. Can we love ourselves as we are?

We can learn from the science examining social comparison. Most recently, researchers have examined how comparing ourselves to others on social media can be a negative experience for many people. One trick you can use is to focus on the emotional message in posts, not the content so much. People who see positive things ("look at how happy she looks") and think about the positive emotions shown ("it's great to see someone looking happy") have a more positive experience using social media. They actually report an improvement in their own mood. The trick is to not take it a step further and think, "He looks so happy and I'm not that happy – what's wrong with me?" Comparing is what leads to despairing, so don't go there.

Don't let body positivity become toxic

You may recall that I introduced the idea of body neutrality back in Chapter 1. Body neutrality, or aiming for self-acceptance and contentedness, may be a valuable approach for many people, especially when body positivity just doesn't feel realistic. Further, although there is evidence that body-positive messages tend to have a positive impact on most of our feelings about our bodies, the positive body image movement has its critics.

One critique has to do with body positivity being interpreted to mean that you love how you look *always*. That isn't the broad definition I've offered in this book, but it is a popular misconception. It follows that if we are supposed to love our appearances, we may spend a fair amount of time focused on our appearances. This focus can actually lead to more body anxiety – the opposite of what the body positivity movement claims to want for people! The antidote to appearance concerns is not "fixing" your appearance, but working on your mindset about these issues.

The body positivity movement emerged long before social media existed and originated alongside other important social movements including the civil rights and feminist movements. It was originally conceptualized as a fat acceptance movement and was not intended to offer comfort to those of us who think we would look better if we lost 10 pounds or wish we had a perkier derriere. The focus of the original body-positive movement was on size diversity and gaining equal treatment and rights for people living in larger bodies. Some critics believe that the current body positivity movement has moved too far away from these original goals and focuses too much on facilitating self-acceptance among relatively thin people. Re-lated research suggests that most body-positive social media accounts and posts typically feature women and white people, leaving too little attention devoted to men and ethnic, racial, and gender minorities. Further, a study conducted in 2020 found that only 43% of body-positive posts on Insta-gram included relatively larger bodies whereas nearly 70% of adults in the USA and 65% of adults in the UK are described as medically "overweight" or "obese."

I believe that body positivity is for everyone. I think that *most* people struggle with body image concerns – and the data back me up here – but I also think it is essential that we appreciate that some of us are more likely than others to experience anti-fat bias. We need to work towards equal treatment for all while being mindful of those who need the most support. We do not need to *always* feel good about *everything* about ourselves, nor do we need to put so much pressure on ourselves to be "positive" that then we feel guilty or ashamed when we can't stay positive. The last thing we want is for all of this positivity to feel obligatory and oppressive. Toxic positivity is not the end goal; being comfortable in our skin and no longer feeling held back by body image concerns is where we ultimately want to end up.

EXPERT ADVICE:

Dr. Meghan Gillen, Professor of Psychology and body image expert, The Pennsylvania State University

"We need a cultural shift away from scrutinizing, fixing, and 'working on' our bodies. Instead, think about what you love, value, respect, and appreciate about your body. Human bodies are amazing. They allow us to dance, walk, carry babies, draw, practice yoga, and recover from injuries and other physical traumas. Our bodies give us the opportunity to pursue our hobbies and pleasures."

Body image in the age of Covid-19

It turns out that a global pandemic is not great for anyone's mental health – or physical health, for that matter. A lot of the issues discussed in this book – the development of romantic relationships, coping with daily stress, vulnerability to mental health problems – were challenged by the Covid-19 pandemic, beginning in 2020. All of this has implications for our body images. As I write this book, the pandemic is not really over; however, for the most part, life has returned to "normal," or something resembling normal. People have grown tired of staying home, wearing masks, and worrying about an illness that seems nearly unavoidable. And yet, many remain emotionally fragile as a result of the pandemic years.

One recent study suggests that the pandemic has been responsible for 53.2 million cases of depression and 76.2 million cases of anxiety globally. Research further suggests an increase in eating disorder symptoms, especially in the early months of the pandemic. In the USA, inpatient treatment of eating disorders doubled during 2020 and the National Eating Disorders Association reported a 107% increase to their helpline in the early months of the pandemic. Some of my colleagues from Missouri's Center for Body Image Research and Policy (led by Dr. Virginia Ramseyer Winter) collected information from over 800 young adults in the early months of the pandemic and found that 37% of women and 44% of men indicated that they would rather contract Covid-19 than gain 25 pounds while social distancing. This last statistic suggests how deeply felt some of our body image concerns are, and how much many were suffering in the early months of the pandemic.

Perhaps a small but discernible silver lining to the body image disruption, increase in eating disorders, and soaring rates of mental health concerns in the past few years has been a parallel increase in discussion about mental health. Celebrities, influencers, educators, and possibly even your neighbors are becoming more open about discussing their own mental health problems and the importance of mental health treatment. Destigmatizing seeking treatment for any sort of health problem – mental or physical – is incredibly important if people are going to get the treatment they deserve.

Q&A:

I'm open to getting help for my body image concerns, but I can't seem to get an appointment with a therapist with this particular expertise. What should I do?

The American Psychological Association has recently reported that the demand for therapy has increased, in part, due to the pandemic. Over half of therapists indicate that they have a waiting list of potential patients. If you are having a hard time finding help, it is not your fault!

However, there may be options that you have not explored. For example, you may want to reach out to an eating disorder organization. In the USA, the Academy for Eating Disorders, in the UK, Beat Eating Disorders, and in Australia, The Butterfly Foundation are organizations that can offer referrals, resources, and support. (You don't necessarily need to live in the organization's country to utilize their services. For example, The Butterfly Foundation has an online chat feature that can be helpful at all hours of the day, no matter where you live.) EDReferral.com is a web page that includes experts in the USA and their contact information.

You should also consider therapists that offer online services. Although this may feel somewhat less personal, online options (over Zoom, for example) can be very convenient and may even be more affordable. You should also know that therapy does not always have to be a long-term investment to be helpful. In other words, if you can locate someone who is helpful to you, but they are expensive or maybe require driving farther than you'd like, it may be worth pursuing for even short-term help. There is some evidence that even one – one! – meeting with a therapist may improve people's mental health. This is especially true when people are really struggling and intervention is critical.

The bottom line: You deserve the help you desire. It is unfortunate that you may need to search harder for help than you should have to, but don't give up!

Everyday adjustments

It's possible that you don't necessarily feel like you need counseling or help from a registered dietitian, but you'd like to work on your body image and are invested in creating a world where it is easier for people to have positive body images. Maybe this book has inspired you to rethink how you perceive your body, how you take care of your body, how your relationships affect your body image, and your mental health in general. Maybe you're looking for some ways you can help to shift the cultural discourse about bodies. Here are some tips you can try, starting today:

1. Don't comment only on people's appearance

When we keep our comments focused on our appearance, we leave out conversations about more important things in our lives. Challenge yourself to ask people about their hobbies, interests, and what they are *doing*, without focusing so much on how people *look*. This may feel strange at first, because even a stranger is likely to respond positively when you tell them that you like their shirt. But you may be surprised at how positively strangers, friends, and acquaintances may respond to conversation about the weather, a movie you've seen recently, or even a new recipe you tried the other night. This isn't to say that you can't *ever* comment on others' appearance, but that you could try to shift most conversations to other topics.

2. Don't congratulate weight loss

Be careful not to assume that weight loss is always good! Often weight loss is a sign of a health problem or a disordered relationship with food. When we compliment weight loss, we reinforce the cultural value system that links weight, health, and attractiveness far more than it should. We can push back against cultural messages surrounding diet products and plans by taking care not to celebrate our own or others' weight loss. After all, our body size is not the most important thing about us!

3. Curate your social media

One of the things we all like about social media is that it is interactive, and we can help to curate our newsfeeds by liking and following certain people and topics. We can help to make mental health-focused and body-positive social media popular by choosing to engage with it and blocking content that is not helpful to us. It can be fun to keep up with popular culture, fashion, and wellness trends. But viewing a lot of that content *every day* is not conducive to positive body image as it sucks us into fads and unscientific approaches to health and happiness.

4. Enjoy food

We all need to nourish our bodies, but we should *not* adhere to trendy diets that keep us from enjoying food. It is important to develop eating habits that we can sustain over time and are good for both our physical and mental health. Eating is a form of self-care, but the pull of diet culture is strong. It can take some effort to remind ourselves that we deserve to enjoy food.

5. Develop other interests

It may seem like your appearance is a "project" that requires a lot of time and energy. But it doesn't have to. What if you invested more of that energy into other hobbies, interests, and even volunteer work?

MYTHS AND MISINFORMATION:

It's important to avoid people who don't have the same understanding of body image issues and diet culture as you do.

It's important to do what you need to do to protect your mental and physical health. Sometimes this *may* mean avoiding some people. It can be triggering to be around people who are always disparaging their bodies, dieting, or compulsively tracking what they eat or their physical activity.

On the other hand, we all need social support and our relationships are a huge piece of what makes our lives meaningful. If people that you are close to don't have the same understanding of body image issues and diet culture that you do, maybe you can help to educate them? It can be difficult to know where to start, especially because these can be very personal issues and people often have deeply held beliefs about what should or shouldn't be eaten and what is normal in terms of appearance-focused behaviors. Sometimes we can learn a great deal by teaching others, however, and we can become even more committed to a set of ideals we've shared with other people. In other words, there can be benefits not just to others but also to ourselves when we try to educate others about the issues discussed in this book.

If our culture is going to change and move away from narrow beauty ideals that are virtually unattainable without cosmetic surgery, we all need to be somewhat invested in trying to create that change.

Don't give up

Everyone experiences some form(s) of trauma. Maybe it's minor, maybe it's major, but we don't go through life unscathed. Some recent research suggests that by our teenage years, over 60% of youth in the USA experience some sort of trauma, whether it be the death of a loved one, poverty, or some sort of serious injury. I share this information to acknowledge that a lot of people experience tough stuff even before they become an adult. If this includes you, you are not alone.

Your life experiences may not leave you in a position to be able to think a lot about what you are going to eat. Clothing and cosmetics choices may not be of concern to you. Maybe right now you are too busy to even think about physical activity. If you feel like you are barely holding things together in your own life, promoting positive body image on social media is not a reasonable goal for you. Do what is possible, given the circumstances of your own life.

One of my favorite authors, Zora Neale Hurston, wrote in her book *Their Eyes Were Watching God*, "There are years that ask questions and years that answer." I think this is a beautiful quote with many possible meanings. Our lives change and some years are easier than others. We don't always have access to all the answers; sometimes we need to be patient. Sometimes we feel uncertainty and then later we gain clarity. How is this relevant to this book? Don't give up. I've offered a lot of information and advice. This isn't all meant to be implemented today. Maybe at this point you have a lot of questions. Don't worry, the answers may just come in time.

EXPERT ADVICE:

Dr. Mary Himmelstein, Assistant Professor of Psychological Sciences, Kent State University

"How we treat other bodies is often a reflection of how we feel about our own. When someone mistreats you because of the way you look remember that is a greater reflection of how they feel about themselves than about you."

Reasons for hope

Some days, it's hard not to feel like we live in a superficial world controlled by commercial interests. The statistics about people who suffer from health problems – and body dissatisfaction and disordered eating in particular – are discouraging. Many of the issues I discuss in this book are serious and worrisome, but I also deeply believe that there are reasons for hope. I am incredibly grateful that my work has put me in touch with outstanding individuals and organizations that are working to improve people's relationships with food and their bodies. I want to tell you about some of my favorite organizations here because you may find them inspiring and even want to get involved with some of their efforts.

Be Real (www.BeRealUSA.org) is a nonprofit in the USA focused on body image improvement among adolescents. Founded by Denise Hamburger, Be Real partners with psychologists, educators, dietitians, and other community members to bring evidence-based education about body image issues to school settings. Be Real has created a curriculum for students and information on how to create body-confident environments for the adults in their lives. I love their interactive approach to helping kids to reconsider what they see in the media and appreciate how amazing their bodies are.

F.E.A.S.T. (www.feast-ed.org/). F.E.A.S.T. stands for Families Empowered and Supporting Treatment for Eating Disorders and is a nonprofit dedicated to helping families and caregivers who have a loved one affected by an eating disorder. Their web page includes evidence-based guides, which offer information about diagnosis, nutrition, treatment choices, and many other topics. Videos, psychoeducational and support resources, and information about webinars are also included on their web page, which is a great place to spend time if you are interested in learning more about supporting someone with an eating disorder.

The Body Positive (https://thebodypositive.org) was created by Connie Sobczak and Elizabeth Scott, LCSW, CEDS-S over 25 years ago to train educators, student leaders, and mental health providers to use their *Be Body Positive* curriculum in the USA and countries worldwide. The Body Positive was ahead of its time in trying to spread these messages of hope and self-acceptance to people of all ages, but especially kids and teens in school settings. They offer training programs, as well as a lot of free resources on their web page and have a proven track record of offering techniques to not just help individuals but contribute also to cultural change and social justice efforts.

FEDUP Collective (https://fedupcollective.org) is an organization focused on providing services to and advocating for trans +, intersex, and gender diverse people with eating disorders. This population has been found to be at high risk of developing eating disorders yet does not often receive support and treatment that adequately addresses the intersection between gender identity and eating disorders. FEDUP's web page includes a wealth of information about eating disorders as well as providers including therapists and registered dietitians that they have vetted. They even have information about support groups that take place both online and in person.

ANAD (Anorexia Nervosa and Associated Disorders; ANAD.org) is a nonprofit organization in the USA that provides free support to people struggling with an eating disorder. They offer recovery mentors, support groups (e.g., for adults, teens, and parents), and a helpline. ANAD's web page contains a ton of information including guides for how to seek treatment and support for eating disorders and a directory for eating disorder treatment providers. They also offer a lot of volunteer opportunities for people interested in *helping others* who are struggling with an eating disorder.

STRIPED (www.hsph.harvard.edu/striped), which stands for *The Strategic Training Initiative for the Prevention of Eating Disorders*, was founded at the Harvard T. H. Chan School of Public Health and Boston's Children's Hospital in 2009. STRIPED provides training to professionals interested in eating disorders prevention, but I came to learn about their advocacy work first. For example, STRIPED director Bryn Austin has been a part of their team working towards legislation that would protect youth from non-prescription diet pills and supplements that are currently poorly regulated and potentially unsafe for developing bodies (and minds!). Their web page contains resources and information addressing beauty ideals, body image, eating disorders, colorism, weight stigma, supplement use, and the importance of advocacy about all of these issues.

The Centre for Appearance Research (CAR; www.uwe.ac.uk/car) at the University of the West of England, Bristol, is the world's largest research group focused on appearance and body image issues. However,

CAR is not just a research center but a hub of activity and innovation concerning body image. CAR's members produce *The Appearance Matters* podcast, and their web page includes videos and other resources. They've even developed a board game for children to teach them about a variety of appearance-related issues.

You'll notice that most of these organizations were developed relatively recently, and I seem to hear about other, similar organizations and opportunities for support and treatment all the time. I really do feel that there are reasons for hope.

Journal: How Will YOU Change the World?

At the beginning of this book, I asked you to reflect on your own body image goals. I hope reading *Adultish* has offered you opportunities to reevaluate your thoughts, attitudes, habits, and goals when it comes to your body and your health in general. Now it's time to set some new goals, but these goals are less about you and more about other people in your life. How can you help *others* to improve their body image? Can you alter your interactions with others in some ways that may be helpful to them (for example, shutting down fat talk)? Can you provide resources to someone who is struggling? Can you unfollow social media accounts that are not body positive and support those that are? How will you change the world in even one, very small way?

Be the change

Cultural change can be slow, but it's possible. It can be easy to forget that people have not always valued the trends and fashions that we appreciate today. When I was young, my mom used to make me and my sisters dresses from floral print fabrics, whilst boys often dressed in little sailor suits. Looking back, I'd say that the matching dresses went on for a bit too long. And I'm not referring to a historical period 100 years ago; this was just a few decades ago. I suspect that you and your friends wear casual clothes nearly always. You probably wear shorts when the weather is warm, but this was unimaginable a couple of generations ago (as women were expected to wear skirts/dresses and men to wear long pants/trousers).

My point is that norms and trends in terms of what our culture suggests we do to make our bodies look attractive *can* change. Even across one generation social change is possible.

We don't have to accept the maladaptive messages about the importance of our appearance, the ways we should modify our appearance, or the resources we should use towards "fixing" ourselves. We are not broken. When we reject certain trends, others may feel empowered to do so as well. If consumers don't buy certain products, companies will stop producing them. If we stop following certain influencers on Instagram, they may become less popular and less powerful.

We all have a role to play in creating a healthier culture. We can work to improve our own positive body images and we can become part of a movement where more and more boys, men, girls, women, trans and nonbinary people do as well. We can do our part to create a world where it is normal for people to feel good about themselves and appreciate others for their own unique qualities.

MY STORY: Abby Violet, 24 years old, she/her, USA

It's surprising, but I feel great about my body now. I didn't expect to get to this place, where I feel joyful about my relationship with my body.

Growing up, I can't remember a time when I wasn't thinking about my body or what I was eating. I thought I was the only one consumed by this self-consciousness and it was so isolating. I was always waiting for my life to start – when I lost weight. The longer I was a fat person the more defeated I felt.

I was restricting what I ate by the time I was in kindergarten. In first grade, I was bullied by kids because of my weight and I went to talk to a school counselor about this. Instead of talking to (or punishing!) the bullies, she devised a prize system to help me lose weight. I was a six-year-old trying to lose weight to appease the people around me. In hindsight, it makes sense that I developed an eating disorder by the time I was 10.

In middle school, I started to suspect that my relationship with food and my body wasn't exactly healthy. When I asked for someone to talk with, I was sent to medical providers and a dietitian. I can't even count how many doctors have prescribed weight loss as an antidote to all of my problems across the years. I now understand that what I needed was a therapist, not a diet plan.

It wasn't until I was in college taking an abnormal psychology course that I had an epiphany of sorts. My instructor explained eating disorders in a way that I hadn't heard them explained before. I realized that I had an eating disorder. Being able to name what I was experiencing helped direct me to treatment and an entirely different phase of my life.

In just the first session with a therapist, I felt like I had found this missing puzzle piece. I felt better almost immediately. And then I realized that I had a lot of work ahead of me. But within a few months my life was changing rapidly for the better.

Now, I don't worry about food anymore! I don't worry about what I'm eating. I can enjoy food and I also feel in tune with my body. I even have a candy drawer now, and I just eat candy when I feel like it. I don't restrict myself and I don't binge; candy is just another food.

I'm getting married soon and I am so excited to walk down that aisle. I had always pictured myself as a thin bride walking down the aisle and now, I picture my own body; I picture myself as I am doing things in my future. My body doesn't need to change for the wedding because I accept and love myself as I am. And I love my dress! It is really the princess dress I always wanted and I'm so thrilled not to feel like I need to hide myself – literally or metaphorically.

If I could offer my younger self advice, I'd tell her that she deserves to be exactly who she is. You don't need to conform or change who you are. Lean into the joy in your life. I'd also tell her that you never know when something you say can impact someone else's whole life. Most of us struggle with accepting ourselves in this culture we live in, but we can all be a part of changing the culture.

SUMMING UP #BETHECHANGE:

- By exhibiting positive body image you have the power to start to change how other people think about *their* bodies.
- Current attractiveness ideals and the cultural focus on our appearance can make it difficult to feel good about how we look, but small shifts in our thoughts and behaviors can promote change.
- Thinking about issues that are more important than how you look and are meaningful to you can help you become a well-rounded, confident person. By choosing to foster your positive body image you set an example for those around you and help to lead society closer to understanding the importance of self-acceptance.

FIND OUT MORE:

- Rachel Sellers and Mimi Cole's *A Body Image Workbook for Every Body* (2021) has information and exercises that can help you to explore and improve your body image.
- The Academy for Eating Disorders (www.aedweb.org), Beat Eating Disorders (www.beateatingdisorders.org.uk), and The Butterfly Foundation (https://butterfly.org.au) are organizations that can offer referrals, resources, and support for anyone struggling with body image and eating concerns.
- For references supporting this chapter's content and more information about body image and activism, see the companion website for this book: www.theBodyImageBookforLife.com.

THE EXPERTS

Here's a bit more information about the experts that provided insight, advice, and comments for this book.

Annie Aimé, PhD, psychologist and professor at the Université du Québec en Outaouais, Québec, Canada: www.uqac.ca/abeh/index.php/annie-aime-ph-d/.

Kristin August, PhD, Professor of Psychology and Health Sciences, Director of the Graduate Program in Prevention Sciences, Rutgers University, USA: https://kristinaugust.camden.rutgers.edu.

S. Bryn Austin, PhD, Professor of Social and Behavioral Sciences at Harvard Chan School of Public Health, Professor of Pediatrics at Harvard Medical School, and founder of the Strategic Training Initiative for the Prevention of Eating Disorders (STRIPE), and of the Sexual Orientation, Gender Identity and Expression Health Equity Research Collaborative, USA: www.hsph.harvard.edu/sydney-austin/.

Betsy Brenner, PhD, LMSW, author of *The Longest Match: Rallying to Defeat an Eating Disorder in Midlife*, USA: https://betsybrenner.com.

Blair Burnette, PhD, clinical psychologist, Assistant Professor at Michigan State University, creator of intuitive eating interventions, USA: https://psychology.msu.edu/directory/blair-burnette.html.

Julia Dawn, @lovejuliadawn, body-positive advocate, TikTok influencer, USA.

Kelly Devos, writer of young adult books including *Fat Girl on a Plane* and *Eat Your Heart Out*, USA: www.kellydevos.com.

Julia Elliott, award-winning hair stylist, California, USA.

John G. Fernandez, MD, FACS, reconstructive cosmetic surgeon, Director of Lymphedema Program, Trinity Health, USA: www.trinityhealthma.org/provider/john-fernandez-md.

Rachael Flatt, PhD, clinical psychologist, Olympic figure skater, USA: www.teamusa.org/us-figure-skating/athletes/rachael-flatt.

Meghan Gillen, PhD, body image expert, Professor of Psychology, The Pennsylvania State University, Abington, USA: www.abington.psu.edu/meghan-gillen-ph-d

Oona Hanson, MA, MA, parent coach, health advocate, family mentor with Equip eating disorders treatment, runs Parenting Without Diet Culture, USA: www.oonahanson.com/.

Leigh Ann Healey, influencer and self-confidence advocate, USA: www.instagram.com/leighannhealey/?hl = en.

Mary Himmelstein, PhD, Assistant Professor of Psychological Sciences, Kent State University, USA: www.kent.edu/psychology/mary-himmelstein.

Kristina Holqvist Gattario, PhD, Associate Professor of Psychology and body image scientist, Sweden: www.gu.se/en/about/find-staff/kristinagattario.

Susanne Johnson, MSN, family nurse practitioner, with focus on harm reduction, weight inclusive, and comprehensive primary care, Boulder Care, Faculty Lecturer at The University of Pennsylvania School of Nursing, USA: https://info.primarycare.hms.harvard.edu/intro-to-weight-bias.

Lexie and Lindsay Kite, PhDs, twins and co-authors of *More Than a Body: Your Body Is an Instrument, Not an Ornament.* Co-directors of the nonprofit Beauty Redefined, USA: www.morethanabody.org/about-us/.

Cheri Levinson, PhD, Associate Professor, Department of Psychological and Brain Sciences, University of Louisville, director of Eating Anxiety Treatment Lab, licensed psychologist and clinical supervisor at the Louisville Center for Eating Disorders, USA: https://louisville.edu/psychology/levinson.

Lisa Lewis, MS, author of *The Sleep-Deprived Teen*, journalist, public speaker, USA: www.lisallewis.com.

Katie Loth, PhD, MPH, RD, Assistant Professor, Department of Family Medicine and Community Health, University of Minnesota, USA: https://med.umn .edu/bio/katie-loth.

Yaffi Lvova, RDN, founder of Baby Bloom Nutrition, Toddler Test Kitchen, and Nap Time Nutrition, USA: https://babybloomnutrition.com/.

Julie Lythcott-Haims, MFA, JD, author of *How to Raise an Adult, Real American*, and *Your Turn: How to Be an Adult*, speaker, activist, USA: www.julielythcotthaims.com.

Traci Mann, PhD, Psychology Professor, founder of The Mann Lab, University of Minnesota, author of *Secrets from the Eating Lab: The Science of Weight Loss, the Myth of Willpower, and Why You Should Never Diet Again*, USA: https://cla.umn.edu/about/directory/profile/mann.

Katy Milkman, PhD, Wharton Professor, host of Charles Schwab's podcast *Choiceology*, co-founder and co-director of Behavior Change for Good Initiative, author of bestselling book *How to Change: The Science of Getting from Where You Are to Where You Want to Be*, USA: www.katymilkman.com.

Niva Piran, PhD, clinical psychologist, school consultant, Professor Emerita at University of Toronto, Fellow of the American and Canadian Psychological Associations and Academy of Eating Disorders, author of *Journeys of Embodiment at the Intersection of Body and Culture: The Developmental Theory of Embodiment*, Canada: www.uqac.ca/abeh/index.php/niva-piran/.

Sam Previte, registered dietitian, certified intuitive eating counselor, certified personal trainer, founder of Find Food Freedom, co-host of *What the Actual Fork* podcast, USA: https://find-foodfreedom.com/.

Elyse Resch, nutrition therapist, co-creator of Intuitive Eating, author of *Intuitive Eating: A Revolutionary Anti-Diet Approach* and *The Intuitive Eating Journal*, USA: https://elyseresch.com/EResch/.

Diane Rosenbaum, PhD, Assistant Professor of Clinical Psychology, Psychological and Social Sciences Department, The Pennsylvania State University, Abington, USA: www.abington.psu.edu/person/diane-rosenbaum.

Deborah Sepinwall, PhD, therapist and co-founder of Providence Psychological Services, Rhode Island, USA: http://providencepsychology.com/clinical-staff/deborah-r-sepinwall-phd/.

Gemma Sharp, PhD, Senior Research Fellow and Clinical Psychologist, leader of the Body Image Research Group at Monash University, Australia: https://research.monash.edu/en/persons/gemma-sharp.

Amanda Sobhy, professional squash player, USA #1 and World #4, USA: www.amandasobhy.com.

Virginia Sole-Smith, journalist and author of *Fat Talk: Parenting in the Age of Diet Culture* and *The Eating Instinct*, host, *Burnt Toast Podcast* and the *Burnt Toast Newsletter* (Substack), USA: https://virginiasolesmith.com/.

Alli Spotts-De Lazzer, licensed marriage and family therapist, licensed professional clinical counselor, certified eating disorders specialist, writer for *Psychology Today*, author of *MeaningFULL: 23 Life-Changing Stories of Conquering Dieting, Weight, and Body Image Issues*, USA: https://therapyhelps.us/.

Lenox Tillman, former model and contestant on America's *Next Top Model*, USA: https://antm.fandom.com/wiki/Lenox_Tillman.

Jenna Werner, registered dietitian, founder of Happy Strong Healthy online nutrition coaching, co-host of *What the Actual Fork* podcast, USA: www.happystronghealthyrd.com/.

Nichole Wood-Barcalow, PhD, licensed psychologist and founder of Wood-Barcalow Psychological Services LLC, co-author of *The Positive Body Image Workbook*, USA: www.drwoodbarcalow.com/.

Katy Zanville, MS, registered dietitian nutritionist, certified intuitive eating counselor, co-host of *Butter + Jam* podcast, USA: www.katyzanville.com/.

ACKNOWLEDGMENTS

I feel so fortunate to have had the opportunity to turn *The Body Image Book for Girls* and *The Body Image Book for Boys* into a series, with the addition of *Adultish: The Body Image Book for Life*. I am grateful to many people at Cambridge University Press for supporting my vision, being generous with resources to bring these books to fruition, and being so incredibly fun to work with. Sarah Marsh has had unwavering confidence in these books and I'm certain that without her, this series would not exist today. I am always happy to see an email from her in my inbox, whether it be correspondence about a book cover design or catching up on whichever one of our children is currently home from school sick. Lori Handelman is all a writer could want in an editor; meticulous, smart, and thoughtful. Olivia Herrick, our amazing illustrator and cover designer, helped to bring this book to life. I know that many people will benefit from this book because she made it beautiful. Zoe Naylor provided a fabulous text design (across many iterations) and artistic vision for the entire book.

No one would know about these books without the many amazing people involved in marketing who have lined up interviews, sent books to the right people, and convinced thousands to look at my books. Danny Bean, Megan Beatie, Chloe Bradley, and Chris Burrows are among those who have supported these efforts; I am eternally grateful for their validation and hard work on my behalf.

I am indebted to my colleagues and friends who have indulged my never-ending desire to discuss the issues I've written about in this book, especially Kristin August, Laurie Bernstein, Meghan Gillen, Oona Hanson, Jamie Dunaev Price, Jennifer Rappaport, Amy Sepinwall, Karen Shore, Alli Spotts-De Lazzer, Lorie Sousa, and Michelle Williams. Thank you to the many people including researchers, clinicians, health advocates, and journalists who provided expert quotes for this book. Connecting with them and so many other like-minded individuals as I've worked on these books has been energizing and I so appreciate their willingness to contribute their insights to this book.

I am thankful for my graduate and undergraduate students and research assistants who have been an invaluable source of help and encouragement offering everything from personal insights to editing suggestions, including Stacey Alston, Lily Beck, Sofia Bonsignore, Erika Frick, Nicole Holmes, Lauren Judit, Dua Malik, Hemali Patel, Simran Pillarisetty, Alexis Richeson, Ivelise Rodriguez-Ruiz, Swetha Samuel, Lycett Thiel, and Kennedy Tran.

As with my past books, I've done my best to let the audience I'm writing for shape what I include. I am indebted to all the people who read chapters and offered feedback at different stages of the process of writing this book and those who allowed me to interview them, including Nana Amponsah, Victoria Barbieri, Josie Binder, Sabrina Caputo, Caroline Casper, Jamie Chan, Rita Ciccone, Allison Cooper, Naomi Devlin, Ally Duvall, Omar Ferreira, Stephanie Gilford, Froukje de Graaf, Grace Hanna, Sajel Jani, Autumn Johnson, Cara Lisette, Abby Rose Morris, Romany Murray, Jalik Navarro, Megha Patel, Priya Patel, Isabella Schilling, Eva Thomas, Emilyann Thompson, Sophie Vale, Hannah Webb, Sydney Williams, Jaqlyn Yourell, Isabel Zarrow, and Tamara Zawistowski.

Finally, I am grateful to my family, especially my husband, Dan, and my kids who, unbelievably, will be (nearly) adults by the time this book is published. Charlie and Grace have inspired this book perhaps more than anyone else.

INDEX